Praising God beside the Sea

Praising God beside the Sea

An Intertextual Study of Revelation 15 and Exodus 15

HaYoung Son

Foreword by Gerald L. Stevens

WIPF & STOCK · Eugene, Oregon

PRAISING GOD BESIDE THE SEA
An Intertextual Study of Revelation 15 and Exodus 15

Copyright © 2017 HaYoung Son. All rights reserved. Except for brief quotations in critical publications or reviews, no part of this book may be reproduced in any manner without prior written permission from the publisher. Write: Permissions, Wipf and Stock Publishers, 199 W. 8th Ave., Suite 3, Eugene, OR 97401.

Wipf & Stock
An Imprint of Wipf and Stock Publishers
199 W. 8th Ave., Suite 3
Eugene, OR 97401

www.wipfandstock.com

PAPERBACK ISBN: 978-1-5326-1291-6
HARDCOVER ISBN: 978-1-5326-1293-0
EBOOK ISBN: 978-1-5326-1292-3

Manufactured in the U.S.A.   MARCH 9, 2017

*To my grandmother PilHyun Sim
and my parents, MyoungSan Son and HwaJa Lee,
who love me and teach me how to live in the faith via their lives
and to people
who have supported me with their prayers, wisdom, love, and finances
from South Korea and in the U.S.A.*

Contents

List of Illustrations | *ix*
Foreword by Gerald L. Stevens | *xi*
Preface | *xv*
List of Abbreviations | *xviii*
Introduction | *xxi*

1   Old Testament Sources in Revelation 15:3–4 | 1

    The Scenery Background of the Song(s)
    The Designation of the Song(s)
    The Content of the Song(s)
    The Context of the Song(s)

2   Purpose of the Exodus Theme in Revelation 15 | 17

    The Exodus Theme in the Old Testament
    The Exodus Theme in the Intertestamental Literature
    The Exodus Theme in the New Testament
    The Exodus as an Eschatological Model
    The Exodus as a Paradigm for Salvation

3   Use of the Exodus Theme in Revelation 15 | 59

    The Exodus Theme in the Book of Revelation
    The Exodus Theme in Revelation 15–16
    John's Interweaving the Exodus Theme with His Eschatological Vision

Contents

4 Conclusion | 93

    Summary and Conclusion
    Contribution and Suggestions for Further Studies

Epilogue | *103*

Bibliography | *107*

List of Illustrations

FIGURES

Figure 1   Research Design | xxiv
Figure 2   Outline of the First Chapter | 1
Figure 3   Plot of Revelation 13:1—15:4 | 8
Figure 4   Same Contents with Different Lyrics of the Songs in Revelation 15 and Exodus 15 | 13
Figure 5   Outline of the Second Chapter | 17
Figure 6   Eschatological Models and the Expected Leaders | 55
Figure 7   Outline of the Third Chapter | 59
Figure 8   John's Interweaving Skills in the Designation of the Song in Revelation 15 | 92
Figure 9   John's Inverweaving between the Exodus Theme and His Eschatological Vision | 97

TABLES

Table 1   Psalm 86:8–10 and Revelation 15:3b–4 | 2
Table 2   Thematic Parallel in the Contents of the Songs in Revelation 15 and Exodus 15 | 12–13

List of Illustrations

Table 3	Structural Parallel in the Context of Revelation 15 and Exodus	15
Table 4	Similarities of Plagues in Revelation 16 and Exodus	15
Table 5	Exodus 17–18 and 1 Samuel 7–8	21
Table 6	Psalm 77, Exodus 15, and Exodus 34	25
Table 7	Five Elements of the Exodus Theme in Psalms 78, 105, 106, 114, and 136	26
Table 8	Contrast between Egyptians and Israelites in Wisdom 16–19	36
Table 9	Exodus 9:23–25 and Revelation 8:7	64
Table 10	Revelation 11:19 Comparing with Exodus 9:23 and 19:16	68
Table 11	Parallel between the Trumpet Judgments and the Bowl Judgments	69
Table 12	The Background of the Bowl Judgments	85

Foreword

BY GERALD L. STEVENS

WHILE THE BARRAGE OF John's fantastical images can be somewhat daunting, even baffling, to a reader uninitiated into traditions of ancient Jewish apocalyptic literature, readers of the Apocalypse still seem to be able to penetrate that bizarre surface level at least to perceive, however superficially, that *some* story is being presented. This fairly universal impression of readers of Revelation over the centuries even to today is part of what feeds the typical "end-time" scenarios that propagate so effortlessly and endlessly on Internet websites as the essence of Revelation's "story." What always has been needed is a methodology that more dependably can ground deciphering the essence of the composition's complex interaction of plot(s) and characters.

Narrative methodology has been appropriated by scholars of the Apocalypse to this end. This methodology has been harnessed to show how Revelation's plot(s) and characters work together to tell a story. Uncovering the "story world" of plot and character in Revelation reveals how this perennially compelling piece of literature delivers its dramatic and engaging impact. Reading the Apocalypse as narrative, we come to appreciate more deeply what John accomplished for his original audience and what he achieved in the history of literature. Even entire dramatic productions can be built around John's powerful narrative world. Not only do we have the insights gained through John W. Bowman's approach summarized in his several publications (1955, 1962), we also have the more recent dramatic production outlined effectively by Sylvie T. Raquel (2010).[1] Recent stud-

---

1. Bowman, *The Drama of the Book of Revelation*; "Revelation," *IDB*, 4:58–71; Raquel,

ies on the Apocalypse focused on its narrative aspects include Resseguie's *Revelation Unsealed* (1998), Barr's *Tales of the End* (1998), Lee's investigation into *The Narrative Asides in the Book of Revelation* (2002), and Helms's *An Apocalypse for the Church and for the World* (2006), to mention only a few. So, narrative study of the Apocalypse has been productive and has helped readers better to grasp the visceral response John intended with his dynamically evolving kaleidoscope of images he ingeniously compiled to move the story along.

While eminently worthwhile and making decided contributions to our understanding of Revelation as story, these narrative approaches cannot address fully other pertinent questions that can be raised from within the text itself. Most particularly, these internal questions include the interrelationships of the intertexts suffused throughout the narrative in Revelation. These intertexts in their own way significantly impact and direct how to read the story. One famous part of Revelation's intertext phenomenon is Rev 15. In this chapter we encounter the "Song of Moses." This reference commonly and rightfully is seen as evocative of Exod 15. This Exod 15 intertext immediately and intuitively suggests itself as an important heuristic device by the author built into the narrative elements comprising this altogether too short a chapter.[2] Narrative methodology naturally does not address legitimate questions to be asked of the text by such intertexts for understanding what the author was doing in achieving the impact he desired on his original audience.

So we as readers have some innate sense of the presence of intertexts that also help us grasp the interpretive significance of how Revelation develops the intersecting trajectories of its story. What is astonishing, though, about John's achievement regarding his intertexts is that he has been able to convince scripturally-literate readers that he has used in a profuse manner numerous passages from the ancient Scriptures—without ever actually making one direct quote! Thus, John's writing style leaves us in the more murky waters of allusion and echoes (or whatever term you want to paste onto the admittedly nebulous concept). In this ambiguity, we are trying to "hear" these subtle nuances that we are convinced are present but hard pressed to identify specifically. Identifying which intertext John has brought

---

"Revelation as Drama: A Staging of the Apocalypse," 156–74.

2. The chapter divisions in Revelation actually are quite poorly done and significantly negatively impact how one reads the developing story. What we have learned in narrative analysis of Revelation is that one pretty much has to ignore a good number of the chapter divisions to follow Revelation's narrative flow properly.

onto the reader's or listener's horizon of understanding impacts rather tellingly how the story is "heard." The field of intertextuality holds promise to contribute toward resolving these questions. Resolving such questions rewards the reader by more sharply defining at a richer level of reading the narrative plot and its development. While the field of intertextuality has yielded an abundance of studies in the scholarly guild on a wide-ranging number of texts and topics, one of the more fruitful biblical texts, then, for such study is the Apocalypse.

What HaYoung Son has accomplished in her innovative study is an intelligent and insightful combination of both narrative and intertextual methodologies to secure a more firm foundation for what we think we intuitively "know" about John's strange pattern of profuse allusions sans quotations. Why would any writer do this? Such an approach to intertexts actually seems to be counterintuitive to being clear about the nature of the composition. Son not only methodically teases out a convincing answer to this question of allusion from the available primary evidence that feeds into the apocalyptic genre, she then works with one of the decidedly "known" allusions in Revelation, the "Song of Moses" in Rev 15, to ground this allusion not only in its background scriptural context but also as a statement crucial to John's high Christology. In this way, Son sets the stage for showing how this Christology directly addresses the needs of John's original audience.

HaYoung Son's research now has been brought to a broader readership in this new monograph that distills and condenses her work in a fine way. Converting dissertations to monographs is no easy task, as anyone knows who has made this journey. Further, when one realizes that English never was Ms. Son's native language, but that she still came to the United States from Korea to pursue more education, then her accomplishments in her rich and rewarding dissertation study resulting in this impressive publication is all the more praiseworthy. I enthusiastically commend this study to you as worth your time. I am persuaded you will profit to engage this excellent study of "the Song of Moses and of the Lamb."

Preface

THIS MONOGRAPH IS A revised version of my doctoral dissertation.[1] Being able to publish my study in the U.S.A. is an incredible honor and encouragement. I never dreamed of this happening. In the oral defense of my dissertation, the guidance committee suggested that I publish my dissertation as a monograph. I accepted this suggestion as merely a compliment, so just smiled and said "Thank you" and forgot the suggestion. However, after my oral defense, I heard the suggestion twice more from the guidance committee chairperson. I asked him, "Are you serious?" He responded that he most certainly was serious. A book proposal to Wipf & Stock resulted in an offer to publish. Of course, I was delighted.

This research gradually developed from Dr. Roy E. Ciampa's class "The Old Testament in the New" and Dr. Sean McDonough's guidance in my directed study "Exodus in the Book of Revelation" at Gordon-Conwell Theological Seminary during my ThM degree program as well as Dr. Archie W. England and Dr. Charlie Ray's class "Biblical Intertextuality" and their guidance in my directed study "Advanced Biblical Intertextuality" at New Orleans Baptist Theological Seminary during my PhD degree program. Learning from these wonderful professors and developing my interest in biblical intertextuality was a blessing from heaven. Research for a paper on biblical intertextuality during my ThM degree program, "The Exodus Theme in the Book of Revelation: Especially on the Song of Moses and the Song of the Lamb (15:2–4)," provided keen insight in theological reflection on the nature

1. HaYoung Son, "The Background of Exodus 15 in Revelation 15: Focusing on the Song of Moses and the Song of the Lamb" (PhD diss., New Orleans Baptist Theological Seminary, 2015).

of God's grace. The Old Testament context made the New Testament context clearer, and the intertextuality revealed an amplified message on God's enduring love and his sincere grace from the Old Testament to the New Testament. Further research into this topic became possible through a doctoral dissertation. Investigation during the dissertation writing process continued to deepen the appreciation for the depth of John's theological reflection.

Without prayer and the help of others, I would not have been able to finish my doctoral studies and could not publish this book. First, I would like to express my deep appreciation to my New Testament professors at New Orleans Baptist Theological Seminary: Dr. Charles A. Ray Jr., Dr. Gerald L. Stevens, Dr. Bill Warren, and Dr. Craig Price. Dr. Ray was "the Alpha and Omega" of my PhD degree program. He was my faculty advisor, the first reader of my dissertation as an expert on biblical intertextuality, and my best mentor. I am so grateful for his encouragement, advice, and help that have been given to me always beyond my expectations. Dr. Stevens has been an immeasurable blessing for my academic training, especially for my dissertation and this publication. As the second reader of my dissertation and an expert on Revelation, his elaborate and sincere guidance upgraded my dissertation and gave me courage to present a portion of my dissertation in an academic society and to publish this book. I am grateful to Dr. Warren, who gave me opportunities to work at the H. Milton Haggard Center for New Testament Textual Studies. He always encouraged me and considered my financial needs. "Thank you" is not enough for him. Dr. Price's joyful and humble attitude toward God and people is also a wonderful lesson to learn and follow, along with his academic diligent effort. His advice and help for my first teaching class in the U.S. was the best.

Having Dr. Archie W. England, an expert in biblical intertextuality and the Old Testament apocalypse, as the third reader of my dissertation was such an honor to me and God's abundant blessing. In my directed study with him, he assumed our relation—professor and student—in the opposite way and asked me diverse questions as if he was my student to make me prepare for the class more and learn more through the class. Although I was challenged like a professor with an overly intelligent student, some portions of my dissertation were prepared in this directed study. Mrs. Pam Cole also should be mentioned here. She is my sincere and wise friend. Her prayers and concerns always followed me during my journey in New Orleans. She is an expert in academic writing. Her comments on my dissertation and this monograph deserve to be praised.

Preface

I also owe a lot to faithful friends who have prayed for me and supported me financially during my doctoral studies. Although I cannot mention all of them here, I absolutely remember what they have done for me and the Lord. Special thanks to church members who continued to support me spiritually and financially from South Korea, Boston, and New Orleans; family members (my faithful mother, whom I respect and love; my loving father, who can fight against the whole world for me; my energetic sister, two aunts, and relatives); and NT professors who have taught me (Drs. Chang Hee Kang, Hae Kyung Chang, Ju Hur, Dana M. Harris, Robert W. Yarbrough, David W. Pao, Roy E. Ciampa, Eckhard J. Schnabel, Sean McDonough, Aida B. Spencer, Catherine C. Kroeger, David L. Mathewson, Jimmy W. Dukes).

I appreciate Wipf & Stock for giving me this precious opportunity, and many thanks are due to the staff at Wipf & Stock who were in charge of the contract, edition, design, and marketing for this book. God bless them and the publisher.

Finally, Lord, all praise to you! Although this humble monograph is not a masterpiece, it is a token of my love for you and a starting point of my further journey for your kingdom. Thank you for being with me every moment and for being my Savior, my Lord, my friend, and my love.

List of Abbreviations

AB	Anchor Bible
AnBib	Analecta biblica
AUSS	*Andrews University Seminary Studies*
BECNT	Baker Exegetical Commentary on the New Testament
BFCT	Beiträge zur Förderung christlicher Theologie
Bib	*Biblica*
BR	*Biblical Research*
BSac	*Bibliotheca sacra*
BT	*The Bible Translator*
CBQ	*Catholic Biblical Quarterly*
CGTC	Cambridge Greek Testament Commentary
CNTUOT	*Commentary on the New Testament Use of the Old Testament*
ConBOT	Coniectandea Biblica Old Testament Series
CTJ	*Calvin Theological Journal*
CTQ	*Concordia Theological Quarterly*
CTR	*Criswell Theological Review*
EstBib	*Estudios bíblicos*
EvQ	*Evangelical Quarterly*
ExpTim	*Expository Times*
HvTSt	*Hervormde teologiese studies*
IBS	Irish Biblical Studies
ICC	International Critical Commentary
Int	*Interpretation*
JATS	*Journal of the Adventist Theological Society*
JBL	*Journal of Biblical Literature*

List of Abbreviations

JETS	*Journal of the Evangelical Theological Society*
JR	*Journal of Religion*
JSNT	*Journal for the Study of the New Testament*
JSNTSup	Journal for the Study of the New Testament Supplement Series
JSOT	*Journal for the Study of the Old Testament*
JTS	*Journal of Theological Studies*
JTSA	*Journal of Theology for Southern Africa*
NCB	New Century Bible
Neot	*Neotestamentica*
NICNT	New International Biblical Commentary on the New Testament
NIGTC	New International Greek Testament Commentary
NovT	*Novum Testamentum*
NRTh	*La nouvelle revue théologique*
NTC	New Testament Commentary
NTS	New Testament Studies
OTL	Old Testament Library
Presb	*Presbyterion*
PRSt	*Perspectives in Religious Studies*
ResQ	*Restoration Quarterly*
RevExp	*Review and Expositor*
RevQ	*Revue de Qumran*
RivB	*Rivista biblica italiana*
RTR	*Reformed Theological Review*
SBL	Society of Biblical Literature
SBLSP	*Society of Biblical Literature Seminar Papers*
SBLSymS	Society of Biblical Literature Symposium Series
ScEccl	*Sciences ecclésiastiques*
SwJT	*Southwestern Journal of Theology*
TBT	*The Bible Today*
TJ	*Trinity Journal*
TS	Theological Studies
TynBul	*Tyndale Bulletin*
WBC	Word Biblical Commentary
WTJ	*Westminster Theological Journal*
WW	Word and World
ZNW	Zeitschrift für die neutestamentliche Wissenschaft und die Kunde der älteren Kirche

Introduction

THE PROBLEM, ITS SETTING, AND RESEARCH DESIGN

THE BOOK OF REVELATION contains many examples of praise or worship scenes. Among those, Rev 15 supplies an interesting scene in which the victorious multitude, having triumphed over the beast, appears and sings "the song of Moses, the servant of God, and the song of the Lamb" (τὴν ᾠδὴν Μωϋσέως τοῦ δούλου τοῦ θεοῦ καὶ τὴν ᾠδὴν τοῦ ἀρνίου) near the sea of glass mixed with fire. Despite the explicit designation, "the song of Moses, the servant of God," the Old Testament (hereafter OT) passages that are identified explicitly as the song of Moses (Exod 15:1–18; Deut 32:1–43; and Ps 90) have been doubted as the OT sources of Rev 15:3b–4, due to no visible linguistic links between these OT passages and Rev 15:3b–4. Consequently, other OT passages that show linguistic parallels with Rev 15:3b–4 have been suggested as the OT sources (e.g., Ps 86:8–10).

To define the OT source in a specific New Testament (hereafter NT) passage and the OT source's degree, one would examine the linguistic parallel between the OT and NT passages first. However, considering the genre of Revelation and the apocalyptic literary device at that time (alluding to the content of the source text but rereading and paraphrasing the text), the examination of the OT source of a passage of Revelation cannot be limited to or weigh too much on a linguistic parallel. Therefore, diverse approaches or analyses are required to define the OT source of a passage in Revelation.

Introduction

Through diverse analyses, this research will argue that Exod 15 needs more attention as the OT source of Rev 15:3b–4. The research question, "What is the function of Exodus 15 in the song of Moses and the song of the Lamb in Rev 15?" invites three sub-questions: (1) What are OT sources in Rev 15? (2) Why does the author use the Exodus theme in Rev 15? (3) How does the author use the Exodus theme in Rev 15? Each sub-question will be answered through a different approach. For the first sub-question, "What are OT sources in Rev 15?" this project employs linguistic and structural analysis. First, passages scholars have considered as OT sources of Rev 15 will be examined. Then, the scenery background (characters, spatial-temporal settings, and plot), designation ("the song of Moses, the servant of God"), contents (the thematic parallel), and context (the structural parallel) of the song will be examined. To be brief, Ps 86:8–10, Deut 32:4, and other passages have been considered as the OT background of the song of Moses and the song of the Lamb in Rev 15. However, the Exodus theme should receive more consideration as the OT background of the song. In particular, Exod 14–15 not only shows similarity in the scenery background but also shows a thematic and structural parallel with the content of the song in Rev 15. Revelation 15:3–4 summarizes and paraphrases Exod 15:1–18 in the same way that other intertestamental apocalyptic literature often summarizes and paraphrases the OT sources.

For the second sub-question, "Why does the author use the Exodus theme in Rev 15?" the research will use diachronic literary analysis. In other words, the Exodus theme in the OT, in intertestamental literature, and in the NT will be examined. Through the paradigm of Exodus, the OT writers expressed their hope of future salvation from a foreign power (e.g., Nahum, Habakkuk, Jeremiah, Ezekiel, and Isaiah) or salvation at the eschaton (Isa 40–66). Some intertestamental sources expected that "a new Moses" would come as the Messiah.[1] Consequently, the writers of the NT and intertestamental literature who referred to the ultimate or eschatological salvation through Jesus Christ naturally used the Exodus theme. The author of Revelation is no exception.

For the third sub-question, "How does the author use the Exodus theme in Rev 15?" the methodology used is a synchronic literary analysis. The Exodus theme in the whole book of Revelation will be examined first.

---

1. Deuteronomy 18 provides some background of the expectation of "a prophet like Moses" who will lead the new Exodus (v. 18; cf. v. 15). Some intertestamental sources such as 1 Macc 14:41, *T. Levi* 8:14–16, Philo *Special Laws* 1.11, 4QTest, 1QS 9:11 show the expectation that "a new Moses" would come as the Messiah.

Introduction

Then the research will narrow the range to the Exodus theme in Rev 15–16 (seven bowls vision), then to Rev 15, and finally to the dual designations of the song. In short, the thematic components of Exodus are interwoven fully throughout the whole book of Revelation and in the vision of the seven bowls (Rev 15–16). In the two verses of Rev 15:3–4 (the song of Moses and the song of the Lamb) and even in the dual titles of the song, John skillfully integrates the old context into his new context. The dual titles show that the first ("the song of Moses, the servant of God") plays a role of background for the second ("the song of the Lamb") and show their theological, thematic, and typological relationships—the Exodus through Moses and the new Exodus through Jesus the Lamb.

As each of the sub-questions serves the research question, each of the answers to the sub-questions will serve the thesis: by interweaving the Exodus theme (especially the Red Sea event and the Israelites' praise after the event) with his eschatological vision, the author of Revelation offers a glimpse of the readers' ultimate victory in their present time (even though they are oppressed under the "beast") and at the eschaton. This expectation would have promoted endurance of the readers.

INTRODUCTION

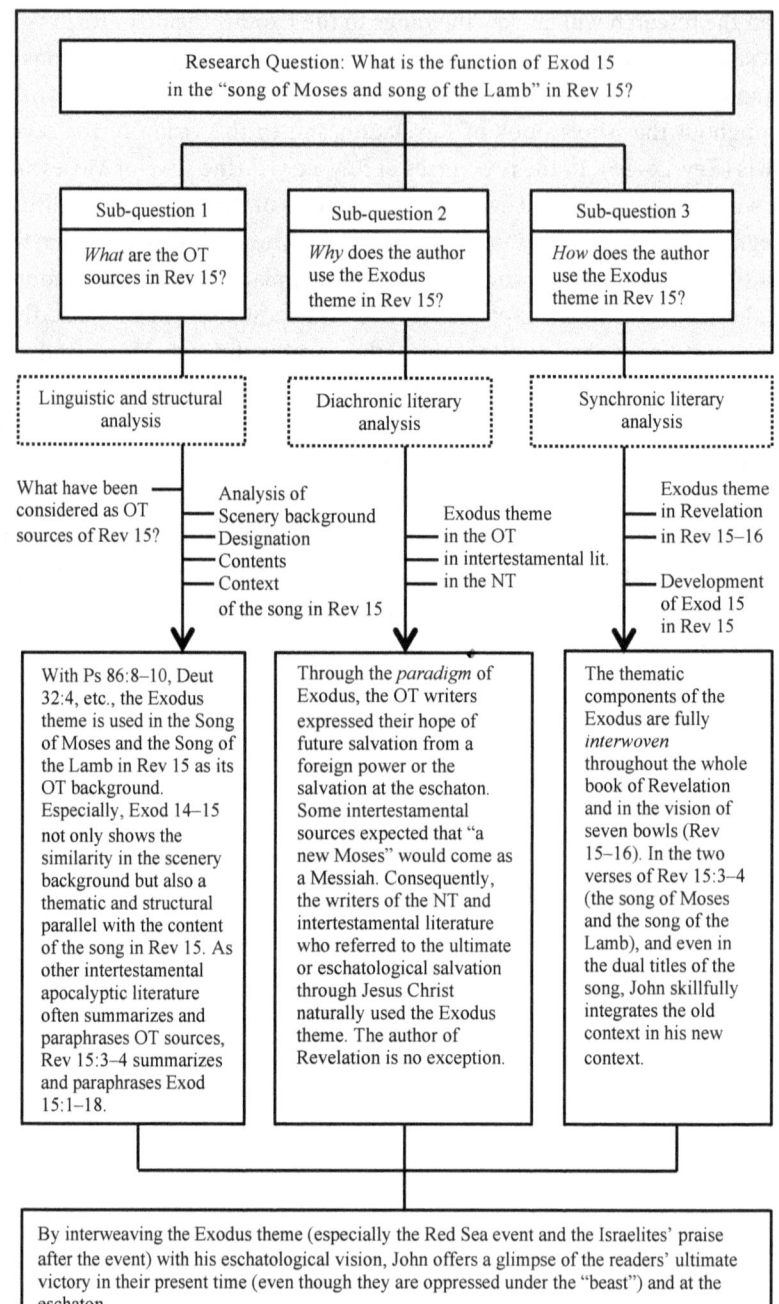

Figure 1. Research Design

Introduction

LITERARY REVIEW[2]

This research is located in the intersection of two areas: biblical intertextuality and the Exodus theme. The discussion of intertextuality can be divided into three parts: secular intertextuality,[3] biblical intertextuality,[4]

---

2. All references of Literary Review in the dissertation will remain in the bibliography of this monograph to supply the information of references. In this monograph, short citations are used in keeping with contemporary publishing guidelines. Sometimes, however, full titles will be mentioned because through the full citation of a title, readers may be able to get the big picture or the essential theme of a reference quickly and clearly.

3. For a general understanding of secular intertextuality, see Allen, *Intertextuality*, and Langford, *Defending Hope*, 9–13. The term *intertextuality* was coined in the 1960s by the Bulgarian-French literary theorist Julia Kristeva. Although her conception of intertextual theory was grounded in Saussurrean semiology, Kristeva made a shift from Saussurrean structuralism to poststructuralism. Kristeva was influenced heavily by two scholars: the French poststructuralist Roland Barthes and the Russian postformalist Mikhail Bakhtin. The following expression is the crux of Kristeva's understanding of intertextuality: "Any text is constructed as a mosaic of quotations; any text is the absorption and transformation of another" (Kristeva, *Desire in Language*, 66; cf. Kristeva, *Semeiotike*, 146). Since Kristeva introduced the concept of intertextuality, the term has been taken up by theorists of various persuasions (e.g., formalists, semioticians, structuralists, reader-response theorists, poststructuralists, deconstructionists) and developed and applied in various ways. Some continued to follow Kristeva in defining intertextuality in terms of relations between texts (e.g., Gerald Price, Laurent Jenny, Gérard Genette), but many later developments of intertextual theory tended to be more reader-oriented than Kristeva (e.g., Jonathan Culler). As outstanding successors of Kristeva, two scholars can be mentioned: Jacques Derrida and Michael Riffaterre. See the works of Kristeva, Bakhtin, Barthes, Culler, Derrida, and Riffaterre in the bibliography. See also the works of Todorov, Newsom, Gillmayr-Bucher, and Friedman.

4. Even before the term *intertextuality* was coined, the sources that the NT writers used (particularly the OT in the NT) have been researched by biblical scholars. Charles H. Dodd introduced an intertextual paradigm to the world of biblical studies in 1952 (Dodd, *According to the Scripture: The Sub-Structure of New Testament Theology*), and in few decades, Richard Hays applied secular intertextual theory to biblical intertextual study (Hays, *Echoes of Scripture in the Letters of Paul* published in 1989). Hays formulated seven tests to evaluate for the presence of echoes: availability, volume, recurrence, thematic coherence, historical plausibility, history of interpretation, and satisfaction (ibid., 29–32). Although biblical scholars do not agree universally upon his criteria of examining intertextuality, he is the first scholar who tried to standardize the criteria for examination of intertextuality in biblical society. Since Dodd, diverse scholars have suggested various views regarding the use of OT in the NT, and some scholars attempted to categorize the various approaches as four (Bock, "Part 1: Evangelicals and the Use of the Old Testament in the New" and "Part 2" published in 1985), as three (Kaiser, Bock, and Enns, *Three Views on the New Testament Use of the Old Testament* published in 2008), and as seven (Vlach, "New Testament Use of the Old Testament," 3–12, presented in 2011). For other important resources on biblical intertextuality, see the works of Walter C.

INTRODUCTION

and intertextuality in the book of Revelation.[5] The discussion of the Exodus theme can be divided into three parts: the Exodus theme in biblical literature,[6] the Exodus theme in extrabiblical literature,[7] and the Exodus

---

Kaiser Jr., D. A. Carson, Richard Hays, Steve Moyise, Stanley E. Porter, and G. K. Beale.

5. In 1988, G. K. Beale evaluated the field's research history: "In comparison with the rest of the NT, the use of the OT in the Apocalypse of John has not been given a proportionate amount of attention" (Beale, "Revelation," 318). According to his analysis, the works that have been dedicated to the topic (until 1988) are "merely three books . . . and six significant articles" (ibid.; cf. the works of Schlatter, Jenkins, Beale, Vanhoye, Lancellottie, Trudinger, Gangemi, Marconcini, Goulder). Some more books or commentaries include important discussions of this subject, though they are not wholly dedicated to the subject (e.g., the works of Swete, Charles, Vos, Caird, Waal, Ford, and Beasley-Murray; cf. Beale also added two articles of Cambier and Lohse with limited value). As Beale mentioned, research on this subject was sparse until the 1980s. Though more research on this subject was done in the 1990s, real growth in the field happened in the twenty-first century. When one examines recent and representative scholarship concerning the use of the OT in Revelation, some scholars stand out, such as G. K. Beale, Jan Fekkes III, Steve Moyise, and David Mathewson. See their works in the bibliography. See also the works of David E. Aune, Richard J. Baukham, Jon Paulien, Andreas J. Köstenberger, Ferrell Jenkins, and others (e.g., Rist, Dumbrell, Altink, Linton, Shea, Jauhiainen, Quek, Vogelgesang).

6. If one wants a glimpse of the Exodus theme in the OT and the NT, several works can be recommended: Iersel and Weiler, *Exodus—A Lasting Paradigm*; Casey, "Exodus Typology" (chs. 1–3; cf. his essay, "The Exodus Theme"); Dennison, "The Exodus: Historical Narrative, Prophetic Hope, Gospel Fulfillment"; Fox, *Reverberations of the Exodus in Scripture*. See also the works of Isbell, Dempsey, Malan, and Clifford in the bibliography. Especially for the Exodus theme in the OT, see Ninow, *Indicators of Typology within the Old Testament*. Some other works examined the Exodus theme in a specific book or a passage of the OT: e.g., Judges (Martin), 1 Samuel (Runions), 1 Kings (Frisch), Ezra-Nehemiah (Williams), Psalms (Estes, Stevenson), Isaiah (Zenger, Ceresko, Anderson, Tsan), Ezekiel (DeLapp), Hosea (McKenzie), and Jonah (Hunter). For the Exodus theme in the NT, see Piper, "Unchanging Promises"; Fisher, "New and Greater Exodus." Some works investigated the use of a specific passage of Exodus in the NT (e.g., the works of Barclay and Wilcox). Some other works examined the Exodus theme in a specific book or a passage of the NT: e.g., Gospels (Kline, Patterson and Travers), Matthew (Viviano), Mark (Sloan, Ortlund, Watts, Janzen), Luke-Acts (Mann, Fuller, Schiffner, Davis, Pao), John (Willoughby, Valletta, Hylen, Maronde, Smith, Mowvley, Hanson), Romans (Keesmaat, Piper), Corinthians (Howard, Hwang, Kooten, Webb, Belleville), Ephesians (Starling, Lincoln), Colossians (Beetham), Galatians (Morales), Hebrews (Steyn, Groenewald, Gheorghita), 1 Peter (Deterding). The Exodus theme in the OT and the NT (excluding Revelation) will be examined in detail in the second chapter.

7. For a general understanding of the meaning of Exodus in Jewish history, Lapide's essay "Exodus in the Jewish Tradition" would be helpful. However, his examination does not cover Jewish writings such as the Apocrypha and Pseudepigrapha. Casey examined typological and non-typological uses of the Exodus tradition in the Apocrypha, Pseudepigrapha, the Qumran Scrolls, and Rabbinic Literature (Casey, "Exodus Typology," 41–55). See also the works of Bergren and Engstrom. The Exodus theme in intertextual literature will

theme in the book of Revelation.⁸ Literary review of these areas was dealt with in my dissertation fully but not in this monograph.

IMPORTANCE OF THE STUDY

Scholars who study intertextuality in Revelation agree that Psalms, Isaiah, Ezekiel, and Daniel yield more than half the references, although they disagree with the most influential OT book in Revelation. Beale focused on the influence of Daniel in Revelation;⁹ Fekkes focused on the influence of Isaiah in Revelation.¹⁰ Comparatively, the influence of Exodus in Revelation has not received much attention. Recently, the study of the Exodus theme in Revelation has increased.¹¹ Generally, however, the research focused on several "thematic components" of the Exodus tradition: deliverance, judg-

---

be examined in the second chapter. Some works are devoted to the Exodus as a paradigm in contemporary movements such as liberation theology, Black theology, and feminist theology (e.g., the works of Dussel, Young, and Bergant). Some other works evaluated the effects of the Exodus paradigm on politics, the mutual effects of the Exodus theme on the history of liberation, and theological reflection (e.g., the works of Baum, Tracy, and Croatto).

8. The Exodus theme in the book of Revelation will be examined in the third chapter.

9. Cf. Beale, "The Danielic Background for Revelation 13-18 and 17:9," 163-70; "The Influence of Daniel upon the Structure and Theology of John's Apocalypse," 415-21; "A Reconsideration of the Text of Daniel in the Apocalypse," 539-43; *The Use of Daniel in Jewish Apocalyptic Literature and in the Revelation of St. John*. Beale argued that the most influential OT book in Revelation is Daniel. However, Moyise disagreed with Beale's evaluation of Daniel in Revelation and argued Ezekiel instead of Daniel. See Moyise, "The Old Testament in Revelation," 117-27 and other his works (e.g., "The Old Testament in the New: A Reply to Greg Beale," 54-58). Some works concerning Ezekiel in Revelation are the works of Lust, Vanhoye, Vogelgesang, Ruiz, Bandy, and Kowalski. Also some works about New Jerusalem motif and "God and Magog" in Revelation are related to Ezekiel (e.g., the works of Schellenberg, Deutsch, Eller, Gundry, Bøe, and Moskala).

10. Cf. Fekkes, *Isaiah and Prophetic Traditions in the Book of Revelation*; "Isaiah and the Book of Revelation," 125-43; "'His Bride Has Prepared Herself': Revelation 19-21 and Isaian Nuptial Imagery," 269-87. See also Mathewson, "Isaiah in Revelation" and the works of Ruiten, Willis, Dixon, Aus, Gangemi, and Marconcini in bibliography.

11. For example, Hre Kio, "Exodus as a Symbol of Liberation"; "The Exodus Symbol of Liberation in the Apocalypse," 120-35; Casey, "Exodus Typology," 135-219; "The Exodus Theme," 34-43; Sanborn, "The New Exodus in the Risen Lamb," 18-24; Mathewson, "New Exodus as a Background for 'The Sea Was No More' in Revelation 21:1C," 243-58; Gallus, "The Exodus Motif in Revelation 15-16," 21-43; Richard, "Plagues in the Bible," 45-54; Wold, "Revelation 16 and the Eschatological Use of Exodus Plague," 249-66; Shea, "Literary and Theological Parallel between Revelation 14-15 and Exodus 19-24," 164-79; Dochhorn, "Und die Erde tat ihren Mund auf: Ein Exodus-motiv in Apc 12,16," 140-42.

ment, covenant, presence of the liberator, and inheritance. However, this research focuses on the influence of specific OT passages (namely Exod 15) on Rev 15 (esp. vv. 3–4) rather than the thematic components of the Exodus tradition in Rev 15.

Some commentaries mention the influence of Exod 15 in Rev 15. However, they do not explain the connection fully. First, some commentaries mention Exod 15 because of the designation of the song in Rev 15:3–4 along with Deut 32 and Ps 90. Second, some commentaries mention Exod 15 because of the similarities of scenery background between Exod 14–15 and Rev 15 (the victors praise God with a song by the sea). Third, some commentaries mention Exod 15:11 as the verse to which Rev 15:3b (or Rev 15:4) alludes.[12] In these three cases, however, due to no visible linguistic links between these passages and Rev 15:3b–4, other passages have been suggested as the OT source.

This research contributes to this area of study in three ways. First, this research will expand the brief references in commentaries to a more detailed explanation using diverse analytical tools and will confirm the role of Exod 15 in Rev 15. Second, the analysis of the content of the song will support the thematic parallel between Exod 15 and Rev 15:3b–4. As other intertestamental apocalyptic literature often summarizes and paraphrases OT sources, Rev 15:3–4 summarizes and paraphrases Exod 15:1–18. To be more specific, Rev 15:3b summarizes and paraphrases Exod 15:4–7, Rev 15:4a does the same to Exod 15:14–16, and Rev 15:4b to Exod 15:11. No one has argued this perspective fully yet. Third, the researcher will examine the intertextuality between Rev 15 and Exod 15 from various angles. Commentaries mention the relation between Exod 15 and Rev 15 briefly by pointing out one element among the designation of the song ("the song of Moses"), the similarities of scenery background, or a general allusion to the contents. However, this research will develop each analysis and will synthesize the analyses. In addition, by examining *how* and *why* Exod 15 is used in Rev 15, this research will determine the OT background of Rev 15 (especially vv. 3b–4) that is essential to understanding the meaning of the passage appropriately.

---

12. Beale thought Rev 15:3b alludes to Exod 15:11; Mounce thought Rev 15:4 alludes to Exod 15:11. Beale, *Revelation*, 794; Mounce, *Revelation*, 285.

1

Old Testament Sources in Revelation 15:3-4

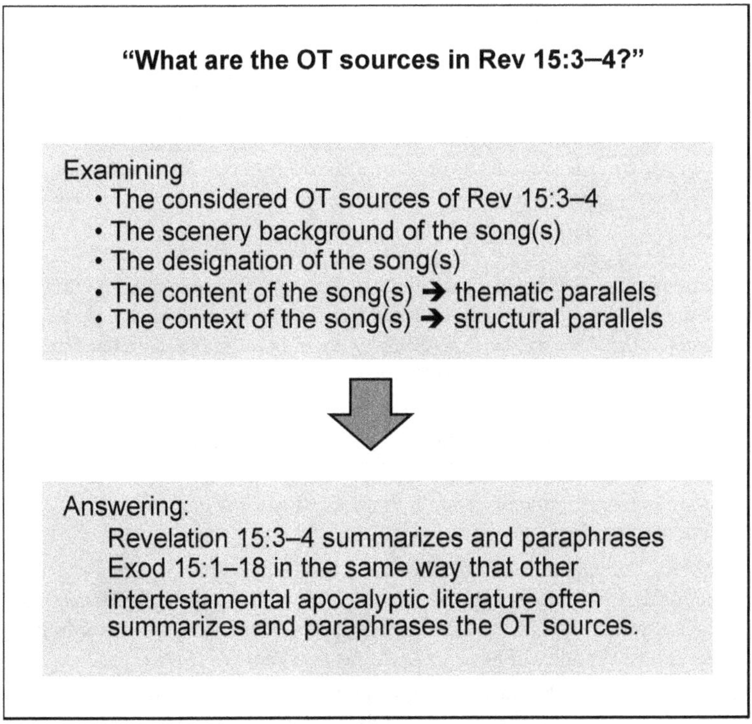

"What are the OT sources in Rev 15:3–4?"

Examining
- The considered OT sources of Rev 15:3–4
- The scenery background of the song(s)
- The designation of the song(s)
- The content of the song(s) ➔ thematic parallels
- The context of the song(s) ➔ structural parallels

Answering:
Revelation 15:3–4 summarizes and paraphrases Exod 15:1–18 in the same way that other intertestamental apocalyptic literature often summarizes and paraphrases the OT sources.

Figure 2. Outline of the First Chapter

Praising God beside the Sea

Revelation 15:3b–4 consists of a song called "the song of Moses, the servant of God, and the song of the Lamb" (τὴν ᾠδὴν Μωϋσέως τοῦ δούλου τοῦ θεοῦ καὶ τὴν ᾠδὴν τοῦ ἀρνίου, Rev 15:3a). Because of the designation, "the song of Moses," the following three passages have been suggested as the source: Exod 15:1–18,[1] Deut 32:1–43,[2] and Ps 90.[3] However, due to no visible linguistic links between these passages and Rev 15:3b–4, other passages also have been suggested as the source: for example, Exod 34:10; Ps 86:8–10; 98:2; 111:2; 139:14; 145:17; Isa 2:2; Jer 10:7; 11:20 LXX; Amos 3:13; 4:13 LXX; 5:8; Mal 1:11.[4]

Among these possibilities, Ps 86:8–10 shows "the closest linguistic parallel with Rev 15:3–4."[5] The following table will help illustrate these parallels.[6]

Ps 86:8–10	Rev 15:3b–4
οὐκ ἔστιν ὅμοιός σοι ἐν θεοῖς κύριε καὶ οὐκ ἔστιν κατὰ τὰ ἔργα σου 9 πάντα τὰ ἔθνη ὅσα ἐποίησας ἥξουσιν καὶ προσκυνήσουσιν ἐνώπιόν σου κύριε **καὶ δοξάσουσιν τὸ ὄνομά σου** 10 ὅτι μέγας εἶ σὺ καὶ ποιῶν θαυμάσια σὺ εἶ ὁ θεὸς μόνος ὁ μέγας (LXX 85:8–10)	μεγάλα καὶ θαυμαστὰ τὰ ἔργα σου, κύριε ὁ θεὸς ὁ παντοκράτωρ· δίκαιαι καὶ ἀληθιναὶ αἱ ὁδοί σου, ὁ βασιλεὺς τῶν ἐθνῶν 4 τίς οὐ μὴ φοβηθῇ, κύριε, **καὶ δοξάσει τὸ ὄνομά σου**; ὅτι μόνος ὅσιος, ὅτι πάντα τὰ ἔθνη ἥξουσιν καὶ προσκυνήσουσιν ἐνώπιόν σου, ὅτι τὰ δικαιώματά σου ἐφανερώθησαν.

Table 1. Psalm 86:8–10 and Revelation 15:3b–4

1. Exodus 15:1a, "Then Moses and the Israelites sang this song to the LORD," points out that the following content can be considered as the song of Moses. Generally, the translations of the Bible will be from NRSV without mentioning the reference. If other translations are used, the reference will be mentioned right after the translation in parentheses or in a footnote.

2. Deuteronomy 31:19, 22, 30 and 32:44 point out that Deut 32:1–43 is a song written by Moses.

3. See the superscription of Ps 90, "A prayer of Moses, the man of God" (תְּפִלָּה לְמֹשֶׁה אִישׁ־הָאֱלֹהִים).

4. Moyise, "Singing the Song of Moses and the Lamb," 350–53; Kistemaker, *Revelation*, 429; Beale and McDonough, "Revelation," 1133–34; Mounce, *Revelation*, 285–87. Cf. Aune suggested Isa 12:1–5, "another reworking of the song of Moses from Exod 15:1–18," as the OT source of Rev 15:3–4. Aune, *Revelation 6–16*, 863.

5. Moyise, "Singing the Song of Moses and the Lamb," 350. Moyise argued, "The verbatim agreement between John's Greek and the LXX of Psalm 86 runs to 16 or 17 words." Moyise, "The Psalms in the Book of Revelation," 235.

6. By adding some more observations, the researcher modified Steve Moyise's original table that was published by *AUSS* in 2004. Moyise, "Singing the Song of Moses and the Lamb," 351.

The remainder of Rev 15:3b–4, not covered by the verbal allusions to Ps 86:8–10, is covered by Deut 32:4 and Ps 145:17 (δίκαιαι... ἀληθιναὶ αἱ ὁδοί ... ὅσιος), by Amos 3:13; 4:13; 5:8 (κύριε ὁ θεὸς ὁ παντοκράτωρ),⁷ by Ps 98:2 and Jer 11:20 (τὰ δικαιώματά σου ἐφανερώθησαν), and so on.⁸ Therefore, Rev 15:3b–4 can be understood as a "pastiche of stereotypical hymnic phrases gathered primarily from the Psalms," a "collection," an "amalgam," or a "cento of quotations from many parts of the Old Testament."⁹ To evaluate the primary source used in the song of Moses and the song of the Lamb, the researcher will examine the background of the song(s) (Rev 15:2), the designation of the song(s) (Rev 15:3a), the content of the song(s) (Rev 15:3b–4), and the context of the song(s) in Rev 15.¹⁰

THE SCENERY BACKGROUND OF THE SONG(S)

In this section, literary analysis (narrative criticism) will be used for analyzing and comparing narrative elements (i.e., characters, temporal-spatial setting, and plot). First, the question "Can narrative criticism be applied to Revelation?" will be answered.

Use of Narrative Criticism

Narrative criticism is a critical method for analyzing biblical narratives.[11] In the NT, narrative criticism generally is applied to the Gospels and Acts. However, narrative criticism also has been applied to the Pauline and General Epistles and Revelation. Norman R. Petersen justified the method's application to the Epistles by saying, "Epistles may also be studied in terms of the stories that lie behind the letters."[12] Borrowing John J. Collins's

---

7. Cf. Rev 4:8; 11:17; 16:7; 19:6; 21:22; cf. other passages of Amos (5:14, 15, 16, 27) and other OT passages (Hos 12:6; Nah 3:5; Zech 10:13).

8. Cf. "μεγάλα καὶ θαυμαστὰ τὰ ἔργα σου" in Tobit(S) 12:22 (τὰ ἔργα τὰ μεγάλα καὶ θαυμαστὰ τοῦ θεοῦ); Ps 111:2 (μεγάλα τὰ ἔργα κυρίου); Ps 139:14 (θαυμάσια τὰ ἔργα σου, LXX 138:14).

9. Aune, *Revelation 6–16*, 874; Moyise, "Singing the Song of Moses and the Lamb," 353; Caird, *Revelation*, 198.

10. Until discussing whether the song of Moses and the song of the Lamb are two songs or one song in the third chapter, the expression of "the song(s)" will be used.

11. Powell, *What Is Narrative Criticism?*, 23.

12. Powell, "Narrative Criticism," 240; cf. Powell, *What Is Narrative Criticism?*, 113; For the application of narrative criticism to Pauline/General epistles, see also Petersen,

definition of apocalypse ("a genre of revelatory literature with a narrative framework"),[13] Mel Gnatkowski justified narrative criticism's application to Revelation as follows: "Revelation is an apocalyptic narrative. As such, Revelation has narrative features that interpreters can isolate and analyze in order to study its narrative structure, thereby offering the modern interpreter a clearer understanding of its meaning and message."[14]

Scholarly works that apply narrative criticism to Revelation include David L. Barr's article, in which Barr examined the use of symbolism in Revelation and the plot structure of that book.[15] Ronald Herms stated, "The particular brand of literary-narrative criticism, which David Barr applies to Revelation, is what he terms 'narratology'—the investigation into how the Apocalypse functions as a story."[16] Some other scholarly works published in the 1980s and the 1990s are the following: Michael Anthony Harris, "The Literary Function of Hymns in the Apocalypse of John" (1989); Michael Payne, "Voice, Metaphor, and Narrative in the Book of Revelation" (1990); and James L. Resseguie, *Revelation Unsealed: A Narrative Critical Approach to John's Apocalypse* (1998). Many references show their specific interest among diverse narrative elements (e.g., the implied reader, the point of view, the plot, implicit commentary such as symbolism, etc.) in the book of Revelation, but Resseguie's book applies narrative criticism to the whole book of Revelation by analyzing all narrative elements in Revelation: point of view and rhetoric (ch. 1), setting (ch. 2), character (ch. 3), and plot and structure (ch. 4).[17] During the same year, Barr published another book, *Tales of the End: A Narrative Commentary on the Book of Revelation* (1998).

Rediscovering Paul: Philemon and the Sociology of Paul's Narrative World; Lucas's dissertation, "The Use of Narrative Criticism and Discourse Analysis in Studying the Social Backdrop of the Epistles to Titus in Relation to the Challenge to 'Do Good' on the Island of Crete"; Boring's essay, "Narrative Dynamics in First Peter," 7–40.

13. Collins, "Introduction: Towards the Morphology of a Genre," 9. Gnatkowski mentioned this definition was defined by "the Apocalypse Group of the Society of Biblical Literature's Genre Project," although Collins's article did not mention the project group. Gnatkowski, "The Implied Reader in the Book of Revelation," 1–2.

14. Gnatkowski, "The Implied Reader in the Book of Revelation," 2.

15. Barr, "The Apocalypse as a Symbolic Transformation of the World," 39–50. In this section, scholarly works that apply narrative criticism to Revelation will be mentioned by chronological order.

16. Herms, *An Apocalypse for the Church and for the World*, 29.

17. Cf. Resseguie's book has an introduction explaining "a narrative critical approach" and its elements, and the fifth chapter dealing with the "theological significance of Revelation."

Like Resseguie's book, Barr's book also covers all narrative elements in Revelation.

During the twenty-first century, more scholarly works that apply narrative criticism to Revelation appeared: Robert William Klund, "The Plot of Revelation 4–22" (2002); Dal Lee, *The Narrative Asides in the Book of Revelation* (2002); Ronald Herms, *An Apocalypse for the Church and for the World: The Narrative Function of Universal Language in the Book of Revelation* (2006); Diana Jill Kirby, "Repetition in the Book of Revelation" (2009); Alexander R. Gonzales, "The Point of View of the Book of Revelation: A Literary Study" (2012). Especially in Kirby's dissertation, repetition—a characteristic narrative pattern—in Revelation is emphasized.[18]

Narrative Analysis of Revelation 15:2–4

Revelation 15 and 16 are considered as a unit for a vision of seven bowls of judgment, and Rev 15 functions as the introduction of the seven bowl judgment. In Rev 15, diverse characters appear. The first character is John, who is referred to in the narrative by the first person singular pronoun. As a narrator and a character, John illustrates what he saw and what he heard.[19] The second character is the gathering of seven angels. They are described as those who have seven plagues that are the last (15:1), who came out of the temple (of the tent of witness in heaven that was opened), and who were robed in pure bright linen, with golden sashes across their chests (vv. 5–6).

---

18. Concerning the understanding of repetition as a characteristic narrative pattern, see Powell, *What Is Narrative Criticism?*, 32; Resseguie, *Revelation Unsealed*, 12–13. Kirby argued, "Repetition is a pervasive narrative technique in the Book of Revelation. Much of what has been written about repetition has been in support of studies of literary structure, composition history, and the debate over recapitulation. This dissertation extends earlier work with repetition by considering the implications of John's use of repetition as a narrative device in support of his rhetorical goals." Kirby, "Repetition in the Book of Revelation," Abstract.

19. In Rev 15, John saw (1) a sea of glass mixed with fire; (2) the conqueror; (3) the temple of the tent of witness in heaven that was opened; (4) the seven angels who came out of the temple; (5) one of four living creatures who gave the seven angels golden bowls. Revelation 15 and 16 are summarized as "another portent in heaven, greater and amazing: seven angels with seven plagues, which are the last" (15:1). In Rev 15, John heard the conquerors singing. Cf. in Rev 16, John heard a loud voice from the temple telling the seven angels, "Go and pour out on the earth the seven bowls of the wrath of God" (ὑπάγετε καὶ ἐκχέετε τὰς ἑπτὰ φιάλας τοῦ θυμοῦ τοῦ θεοῦ εἰς τὴν γῆν, 16:1); what the angel of the waters said (16:5–6); what the altar responded (16:7), a loud voice that came out of the temple, from the throne, saying "It is done!" (γέγονεν, 16:17).

Praising God beside the Sea

The third character is one of four living creatures who gave the seven angels golden bowls full of the wrath of God (v. 7). The fourth character is the group of saints. They are described as those who had conquered the beast and its image and the number of its name, who stood beside the sea of glass with harps of God in their hands, and who sang the song of Moses and the song of the Lamb (vv. 2–4). They are one group of the conqueror groups that are mentioned in John's vision (cf. Rev 6:9–11; 7:9–14; 12:11; 20:4) and function as the model of the reader.

The temporal setting of Rev 15 and 16 is (1) while John was on the island of Patmos (Rev 1:9), (2) while John received his revelation in the Spirit "on the LORD's Day" (1:10), and (3) while he saw the seven bowl judgment vision. The spatial setting of Rev 15 and 16 can be divided roughly into heaven and earth. The earth is illustrated as the place on which the seven bowls of the wrath of God were poured (Rev 16).[20] Heaven is illustrated as the place where the conquerors sang the song of Moses and the song of the Lamb and the seven angels received the seven bowls from one of the four creatures. Especially in 15:2–4, the place where the song is sung by the conquerors is illustrated as "by/on the sea of glass" (ἐπὶ τὴν θάλασσαν τὴν ὑαλίνην; 15:2c) in heaven,[21] and the sea is "a sea of glass mingled with

---

20. On the earth, these places are mentioned: the sea that became like the blood of a corpse because of the second bowl and in which every living thing died (16:3); the rivers and the springs of water that became blood because of the third bowl (v. 4); the throne of the beast on which the fifth bowl was poured (v. 10); the great river Euphrates, of which water was dried up (v. 12); Harmagedon, where three foul spirits assembled the kings of the whole world (vv. 13–16); the great city (Babylon), cities of the nations, every island, and every mountain that are mentioned as places destroyed by the wrath of God (vv. 19–20).

21. The proposition ἐπί in Rev 15:2 was translated to three options: (1) "by/beside" (Ford, Caird, Farrer, Beasley-Murray, Mounce); (2) "on/upon" (Beckwith, Beale, Charles); (3) "near" (Aune). See Ford, *Revelation*, 252; Caird, *Revelation*, 196; Farrer, *Revelation*, 171; Beasley-Murray, *Revelation*, 235; Mounce, *Revelation*, 283; Beckwith, *Apocalypse*, 674; Beale, *Revelation*, 791; Charles, *Revelation*, 2:34; Aune, *Revelation 6–16*, 850.

Considering "the pavement before the throne" or "the picture of the solid surface of the sea," the translation "on" for ἐπί in Rev 15:2 is acceptable. See Beckwith, *Apocalypse*, 674; Beale, *Revelation*, 791; cf. Mounce, *Revelation*, 285. However, among three times in which phrase ἵστημι ἐπί with the accusative is used by John, once ἐπί means "on" (14:1) and twice "at/by" (3:20; 7:1). In addition, the parallel between the saints who stand by the sea and the angels who stand by the altar (8:3) also should be considered. See further Farrer's explanation: "Just as the spiritual meaning of the altar was set forth in 8:3–5 (on the background of 6:9–11) by relation to the saints and their prayers, so the sea or laver is interpreted here by relation to the saints and their purification. The 'sea' was to sanctify the priests, and here the saints are a priestly choir, ministering in heaven, and standing at, or by, the 'sea' which cleanses them—'by', not 'on.' . . . The saints stand by the laver here, as the angel stood by the

fire" (θάλασσαν ὑαλίνην μεμιγμένην πυρὶ, 15:2a). The temple of the tent of witness also appears as a heavenly place, out of which the seven angels came with the seven plagues (15:6) and which was filled with smoke from the glory of God and from his power, and into which no one could enter until the seven plagues of the seven angels were ended (15:8).

Revelation 15:2-4 portrays a victorious scene. In the scene, the saints who sing the song of Moses and the song of the Lamb are main characters, and they are "those who had conquered the beast and its image and the number of its name" (τοὺς νικῶντας ἐκ τοῦ θηρίου καὶ ἐκ τῆς εἰκόνος αὐτοῦ καὶ ἐκ τοῦ ἀριθμοῦ τοῦ ὀνόματος, 15:2). Their conflict (i.e., their battle against the beast and its image and the number of its name) is resolved in their victory. Then, after being victorious in battle, they are praising God—his great and marvelous deeds, glory, and holiness. The passage mentions that they had conquered three things: the beast, its image, and the number of its name. In Rev 13, a beast came out of the sea (vv. 1-10), and another came out of the earth (vv. 11-18). Between the two beasts in Rev 13, "the beast" in Rev 15:2 seems to be the first one; "its image" means the first beast's image that the second beast forced people to make and gave breath to (vv. 14-15); and "the number of its name" means the mark—that is, 666 (or 616)[22]—that the second beast forced people to receive on their right hands or foreheads (vv. 16-17). Consequently, these three are in reference to one, the beast. Viewed in this light, Aune's translation sounds appropriate: "those who were victorious over the beast, *that is,* over its image and over the number of its name."[23]

---

altar in 8:3, to offer the incense of their prayers." Farrer, *Revelation,* 171.

If ἐπί in Rev 15:2 is translated to "by/beside," the parallel in the spatial setting between Exod 15 and Rev 15 would be clearer. However, even scholars, who translated ἐπί in Rev 15:2 to "on/upon," agreed that the scenery background of Rev 15 including the spatial setting evokes the Red Sea event: e.g., Charles, *Revelation,* 2:34; Beale, *Revelation,* 791; cf. Mounce, *Revelation,* 285. Therefore, whether ἐπί in Rev 15:2 is translated to "on/upon" or "by/beside," the spatial setting in Rev 15 is understood as recalling the Red Sea event.

22. About the number, see Beale, *Revelation,* 718-28; Bauckham, *The Climax of Prophecy,* 384-407.

23. Aune, *Revelation 6-16,* 871, italics added.

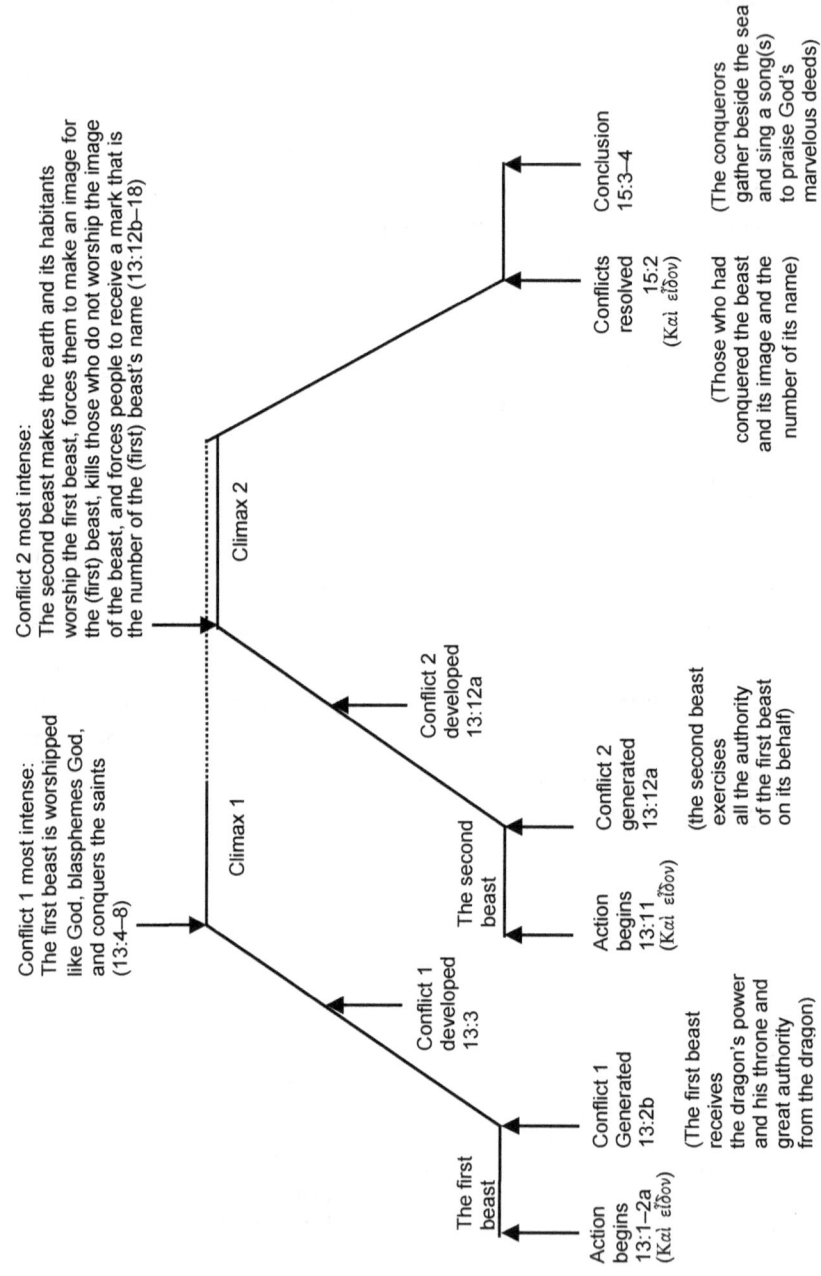

Figure 3. Plot of Revelation 13:1—15:4

Comparing Narrative Elements between Revelation 15 and Exodus 15

In Exod 15:1–18, one of the passages considered as the song of Moses, two characters appear: Moses and the Israelites (including Miriam). Exodus 14 supplies the background of what they praise. The Israelites had escaped from Egypt and were led by God—by the pillar of cloud and the pillar of fire—in the wilderness. When they arrived at Pi-hahiroth, between Migdol and the sea, they camped by the sea. The Egyptians (all Pharaoh's horses and chariots, his chariot drivers and his army) pursued the Israelites and arrived at the sea where the Israelites stayed. At that time, God drove the sea back by a strong east wind all night and turned the sea into dry land and divided the sea, so that the Israelites went into the sea on dry ground; and then, when the Egyptians went into the sea, God brought back the waters of the sea upon them. Moses and the Israelites were saved from the Egyptians who opposed God and God's people. Moses and the Israelites were victorious in the battle with their oppressors. After their victory, they sang a song that praises not what they did but what God did for them.

Concerning the main characters in Rev 15:2–4 and Exod 15:1–18, some common features are observed: "Moses and the Israelites" in Exod 15 and the saints who had conquered the beast in Rev 15 are multitudes who belong to God; they had been suffering on account of the oppressor who stood against God, but they are saved from the oppressor (or they conquer the oppressor); they sing a song after their redemption, and the songs of both groups exalt God and praise his miraculous deeds with instruments.[24]

Regarding the spatial setting of the victorious singing scenes, Rev 15 and Exod 15 are the same, near the sea. The sea in Rev 15 is described as "a sea of glass mingled with fire" (ὡς θάλασσαν ὑαλίνην μεμιγμένην πυρὶ, 15:2a) and as "the sea of glass" (τὴν θάλασσαν τὴν ὑαλίνην, 15:2b). This expression shows some links with Rev 4:6 ("a sea of glass, like crystal" before the throne, ὡς θάλασσα ὑαλίνη ὁμοία κρυστάλλῳ)[25] or Ezek 1:22 ("the likeness of a firmament, shining like crystal," ὡσεὶ στερέωμα ὡς ὅρασις κρυστάλλου) or Gen 1:6–7.[26] However, Exod 15:8 ("the deeps congealed in the heart of the sea") gives the strongest clue for the "sea of glass." *Mekilta*

---

24. In Exod 15, Miriam takes a tambourine; in Rev 15, the saints take harps.

25. Cf. *T. Levi* 2:7a and *2 En.* 3:3 for a sea in heaven.

26. Cf. Beale, *John's Use*, 64; *Revelation*, 327–28, 789–92; Osborne, *Revelation*, 562; Beale and McDonough, "Revelation," 1133. See also Beasley-Murray's argument: "As this sea was seen in heaven, the fire would be heavenly fire, perhaps associated with the throne vision; cf. Ezek 1:4, 13, 27." Beasley-Murray, *Revelation*, 253.

de Rabbi Ismael, Beshallah 5.15 (on Exod 14:16–21) and *'Abot de Rabbi Nathan* 30a state that "one of the miracles at the Red Sea episode was that the sea became congealed and appeared like glass vessels."[27] Furthermore, *'Abot de Rabbi Nathan* adds that "fire was present in the midst of the glass" (cf. Exod 15:8; Rev 15:2).[28] *Midrash* Psalms 136:7 also says that, based on Exod 15:8, the sea appeared as a "crystallized . . . kind of glass."[29] Therefore, the description of the sea in Rev 15 also shows some links with the Red Sea episode in Exod 14–15.[30]

In addition, concerning plot, these two victorious scenes appear after their conflict has been resolved. Before these scenes, the conflict is generated and developed by the oppressors' advantageous situations (e.g., they exercise their power to cause suffering for God's people and to stand against God). The saints look like they are almost dying or being defeated by the oppressor. However, the saints appear as the conqueror of the battle; and as the conclusion of the plot, the songs are sung by the conquerors.

In sum, these analyses on the scenery background of the songs in Rev 15 and Exod 15 show obvious similarities in the main characters, the spatial setting, and the plot. Especially in the spatial setting, both songs in Rev 15 and Exod 15 are sung at the same location (i.e., near the sea, to be more exact, beside the sea), and the illustrations of the sea also show their correlation.

THE DESIGNATION OF THE SONG(S)

The first part of the designation of the song(s), "the song of Moses," may be a clue to its source.[31] As already mentioned, Exod 15 is one of three OT passages that can be considered as the song of Moses (cf. Deut 32; Ps 90). Furthermore, in Rev 15:3a, "the song of Moses" (τὴν ᾠδὴν Μωϋσέως) is

---

27. Beale and McDonough, "Revelation," 1133; cf. Beale, *Revelation*, 791–92; cf. Mc-Namara, *New Testament and Palestinian Targum to the Pentateuch*, 203–4.

28. Beale, *Revelation*, 792.

29. Ibid.

30. See Caird's argument: "By a slight shift of the kaleidoscope the ocean of blood through which the martyrs have passed in the great vintage now becomes a heavenly Red Sea, poised after the passage of the true Israel to engulf Israel's persecutors." Caird, *Revelation*, 196–97.

31. Here, only the first part of the designation, "the song of Moses," will be dealt with as a clue of the source. The latter part of the designation, "The song of the Lamb," and the combined full designation, "The song of Moses and the song of the Lamb," will be dealt with later (in ch. 3).

followed by "the servant of God" (τοῦ δούλου τοῦ θεοῦ), an appositional phrase describing Moses. His designation as the servant of God can be found easily in the OT and other literature.[32] However, Moses' designation and the song of Moses are mentioned together only in Exod 14–15 and even in the same order (the designation of Moses as God's servant preceding the content of Moses' song) as Rev 15:3 does.[33]

> Exod 14:31—15:1. Israel saw the great work which the LORD did against the Egyptians. So the people feared the LORD and believed in the LORD and in <u>his servant Moses</u>. Then Moses and the Israelites sang this song to the LORD: "<u>I will sing to the LORD, for he has triumphed gloriously; horse and rider he has thrown into the sea</u>."

> Rev 15:3. And they sing the song of <u>Moses, the servant of God</u>, and the song of the Lamb: "<u>Great and amazing are your deeds, LORD God the Almighty! Just and true are your ways, King of the nations!</u>"

THE CONTENT OF THE SONG(S)

Even though no explicit linguistic parallel is between the song of Moses in Exod 15 and the song of Moses (and the song of the Lamb) in Rev 15, they have thematic parallels. They praise God's great and marvelous deeds, God's omnipotence, God's just and true ways and his righteous acts, his glory and holiness, and his worthiness to be praised. For example, in Rev 15:3, the saints sing, "Great and marvelous are your deeds, LORD God Almighty" (μεγάλα καὶ θαυμαστὰ τὰ ἔργα σου, κύριε ὁ θεὸς ὁ παντοκράτωρ); in Exodus, Israel saw "the great work that the LORD did against the Egyptians" (14:31), and Exod 15:4–7 concretely portrays the great work of God.

> Pharaoh's chariots and his army he cast into the sea; his picked officers were sunk in the Red Sea. The floods covered them; they went down into the depths like a stone. Your right hand, O LORD, glorious in power—your right hand, O LORD, shattered the enemy. In the greatness of your majesty you overthrew your adversaries; you sent out your fury, it consumed them like stubble. (Exod 15:4–7)

---

32. For instance, Exod 14:31; Num 12:7; Deut 34:5; Josh 1:1, 15; 8:31; 9:24; 14:7; 1 Kgs 8:53; 2 Kgs 18:12; 21:8; 1 Chr 6:49; 2 Chr 24:9; Neh 1:8; Ps 105:26; Dan 9:11; Mal 4:4 [MT 3:22]; Bar 1:20; Jos. *Ant.* 5.39; 1 Clem. 4:17; 51:5, 8.

33. Cf. Beale, *Revelation*, 792.

In Rev 15:4a, the saints sing "who will not fear you, O LORD" (τίς οὐ μὴ φοβηθῇ, κύριε), and in Exod 15:14a, Moses and the Israelites sing, "The peoples heard, they trembled." Exodus 15:14b–15 depict this point by citing examples: "Pangs seized the inhabitants of Philistia. Then the chiefs of Edom were dismayed; trembling seized the leaders of Moab; all the inhabitants of Canaan melted away." In other words, all nations or everybody is described as "the inhabitants of Philistia," "the chiefs of Edom," "the leaders of Moab," "all the inhabitants of Canaan"; and to fear is illustrated diversely in the expressions of "pangs seized," "be dismayed," "trembling seized," and "melt away." That all nations or everybody fears God is expressed briefly with a rhetorical question in Rev 15:4a and is expressed in a detailed illustration in Exod 15:14–15. In Rev 15:4b, the saints sing, "Who will not . . . bring glory to your name? For you alone are holy" (τίς οὐ μὴ . . . δοξάσει τὸ ὄνομά σου; ὅτι μόνος ὅσιος); and in Exod 15:11, Moses and the Israelites praise, "Who is like you, O LORD, among the gods? Who is like you, majestic in holiness, awesome in splendor, doing wonders?"[34] Both praise God's uniqueness in his holiness and glory.

Rev 15	Exod 15	Theme
"**Great** and **marvelous** are your <u>deeds</u>, LORD God **Almighty**" (15:3)	Cf. "The **great** <u>work</u> that the LORD <u>did</u> against the Egyptians" (14:31) (illustrating *God's great and marvelous deeds*) "Pharaoh's chariots and his army he cast into the sea; his picked officers were sunk in the Red Sea. The floods covered them; they went down into the depths like a stone. Your right hand, O LORD, glorious in power—your right hand, O LORD, shattered the enemy. In the greatness of your majesty you overthrew your adversaries; you sent out your fury, it consumed them like stubble. At the blast of your nostrils the waters piled up, the floods stood up in a heap; the deeps congealed in the heart of the sea." (15:4–8)	God's great/ marvelous deeds Key expressions: Great/marvelous Work/deeds/did

---

34. Mounce thought that Rev 15:4 echoes Exod 15:11. Mounce, *Revelation*, 285.

Old Testament Sources in Revelation 15:3-4

Rev 15	Exod 15	Theme
"Who will not **fear** you, O LORD" (15:4a)	"The people heard, they **trembled**; pangs seized the inhabitants of Philistia. Then the chiefs of Edom were **dismayed**; **trembling** seized the leaders of Moab; all the inhabitants of Canaan **melted away**. **Terror and dread fell upon** them; by the might of your arm, they became still as a stone until your people, O LORD, passed by, until the people whom you acquired passed by." (15:14-16)	Human fear of God Key expressions: Human beings Fear
"Who will not ... bring **glory** to your name? For you alone are **holy**" (15:4b)	"Who among the gods is like you, O LORD? Who is like you—majestic in **holiness**, awesome in **glory**, working wonders?" (15:11)	God's uniqueness in glory and holiness Key expressions: Alone/unique Holy, glory

Table 2. Thematic Parallel in the Contents of the Songs in Rev 15 and Exod 15

In short, the song in Exod 15 and the song in Rev 15 praise God's salvific actions and God himself—God's great and marvelous deeds, human fear of God, and God's uniqueness in glory and holiness—rather than their own actions. On this point, the two songs in Exod 15 and in Rev 15 sing the same things with somewhat different lyrics: short expressions like a proclamation (Revelation) and longer, more detailed and more concrete expressions like an illustration or explanation (Exodus).

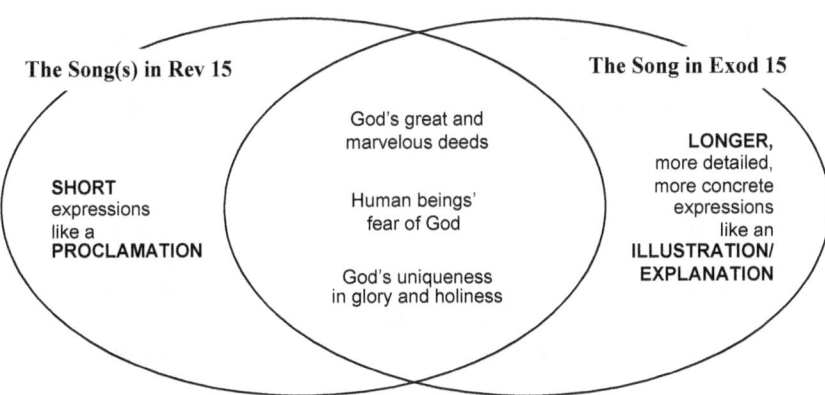

Figure 4. Same Contents with Different Lyrics of the Songs in Rev 15 and Exod 15

Concerning this characteristic, Stephen Hre Kio's argument is significant. He showed other apocalyptic books that do not quote their OT sources directly and literally but paraphrase the sources: for example, Dan 9:2, 11–13 (Ezek 4:12; 31:6; cf. 17:23); 2 Esd 3:19 (Exod 19:16); 2 Esd 7:42 (Isa 60:19); 2 Esd 1:12–21 (Exod 14:29 in v. 13; Exod 13:21 in v. 14; Exod 16:13 in v. 15; Num 14:2–3 in v. 18; Ps 78:25 in v. 19; Num 20:11 in v. 20).[35] Especially 2 Esd 10:20–22 summarizes and paraphrases 2 Kgs 25:8–21.[36] This example shows a very similar pattern with Rev 15:3–4 that summarizes and paraphrases Exod 15:1–18. He argued the following:

> It is probable that many apocalyptic writings do not quote literally from their sources. *Not quoting literally from their sources* may be due to their practice of rereading their sources with great freedom. Thus, that the book of Revelation does *not* quote directly from the OT is not an exception. The author simply follows a widely used apocalyptic literary device. Most probably the Apocalyptists felt free to transform the ideas and concepts from their sources, and molded them in the literary form of their writings.[37]

In other words, Revelation's indirect quotation (alluding to the content of the source text but rereading the text and paraphrasing it in their apocalyptic writings) is an "apocalyptic literary device" at that time. This point supports Exod 15:1–18 as the source of Rev 15:3–4 based on the thematic parallels in the contents of the two songs, although Exod 15:1–18 does not show a vivid linguistic parallel.

THE CONTEXT OF THE SONG(S)

The whole context of Rev 15 shows "a more complete and systematic use of Exodus typology than in any other part of John's book."[38] In v. 1, the plagues are mentioned (cf. Exod 7–11); in v. 2, the multitude who are redeemed from enemies and sing a song beside the sea is mentioned (cf. Exod 14); in

---

35. Hre Kio, "Exodus as a Symbol of Liberation," 208–16.

36. According to Hre Kio, "In II Esdras 10:20–22, we find that the author presents a poignant enumeration of the misfortunes that attended the destruction of Jerusalem in 587 BC. The same kind of enumeration we find in 2 Kings 25:8–21. However the wording and phraseology are entirely different. II Esdras summarizes the whole affair with passion and engagement while 2 Kings is detailed and detached, cool and objective, perhaps the mark of a true historian." Hre Kio, "Exodus as a Symbol of Liberation," 212–13.

37. Hre Kio, "Exodus as a Symbol of Liberation," 215–16; emphases are Hre Kio's.

38. Caird, *Revelation*, 197.

vv. 3–4, the content of the song of Moses is mentioned (cf. Exod 15); in v. 5, the erection of the tent of testimony is mentioned (cf. Exod 40); and in v. 8, the smoke of YHWH's presence is mentioned (cf. Exod 40).[39]

Revelation	Parallel	Exodus
15:1	The plagues	Chs. 7–11
15:2	The multitude who are redeemed from enemies and sing a song beside the sea	Ch. 14
15:3–4	The content of the song of Moses	Ch. 15
15:5	The erection of the tent of testimony	Ch. 40
15:8	The smoke of YHWH's presence	Ch. 40

Table 3. Structural Parallel in the Context of Revelation 15 and Exodus

Furthermore, the plagues—"seven angels with the seven last plagues"—that were mentioned before the song of Moses and the song of the Lamb (15:1) start after the song(s) and are illustrated as sores (Rev 16:2; cf. "boils" in Exod 9:8–12), blood in which the creatures die (Rev 16:3–4; Exod 7:17–19), darkness (Rev 16:10; Exod 10:21–23), three evil spirits that look like frogs (Rev 16:13; cf. Exod 8:1–15), flashes of lightning, rumblings, peals of thunder, and a severe earthquake (Rev 16:17–21; Exod 9:23). The bowl judgments as well as the trumpet judgments (especially the first four) recall the plagues in Exodus.[40]

Revelation	Plagues	Exodus
16:2	Sores	9:8–12
16:3–4	Blood in which the creatures die	7:17–19
16:10	Darkness	10:21–23
16:13	Three evil spirits that look like frogs	8:1–15
16:17–21	Flashes of lightning, rumblings, peals of thunder and a severe earthquake	9:23

Table 4. Similarities of Plagues in Revelation 16 and Exodus

39. Cf. Ibid.; Casey, "Exodus Typology," 190; Beasley-Murray, *Revelation*, 232–33; Stevens, *Revelation*, 451–52.

40. This point will be examined in detail in ch. 3 (see the section of "The Exodus Theme in Judgment," especially the subsection of "The Bowl Judgments").

In sum, Ps 86:8–10 shows the closest linguistic parallels with the song of Moses and the song of the Lamb (Rev 15:3b–4), and other passages also can be considered as the source (or a part of source) that shows some verbal allusions (e.g., Jer 10:7, Ps 98:1–2). However, Exod 15 shows its strongest influence in Rev 15:3b–4 according to the analysis of the background (the multitude who are redeemed sing a song to praise God the Redeemer beside the sea), the designation ("the song of Moses, the servant of God"), the content (thematic allusions), and the context (structural allusions) of the song(s).

2

Purpose of the Exodus Theme in Revelation 15

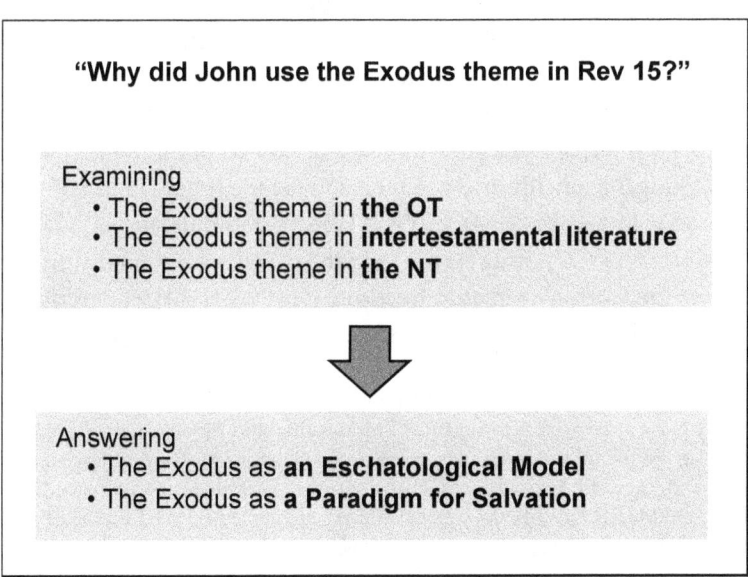

Figure 5. Outline of the Second Chapter

WHY DID JOHN USE the Exodus theme in Rev 15? In other words, what did the author want to express by implementing the Exodus theme, and why did he choose the Exodus theme among diverse tools? Before answering these questions, this research will examine briefly the Exodus theme in the

OT, intertestamental literature, and the NT. Through the examinations, this research will extract the perceptions that the people contemporary with John had regarding the end times and their expectations of the Messiah who would lead the end times and fulfill their redemption, so that this research will demonstrate how effectively John expresses the eschatological redemption and ultimate victory through the Exodus theme.

THE EXODUS THEME IN THE OLD TESTAMENT

Historical Books

The historical books in the OT are the books from Joshua to Esther. However, the book of Joshua will be excluded in this section because the historical event of the Exodus is written in the Hexateuch (Pentateuch plus Joshua).[1] When the Exodus is defined as "the collection of traditions about Israel's experiences from the time of the Egyptian captivity until its settlement in Canaan,"[2] the book of Joshua describes the last part of the Exodus, namely, the process of Israel's settlement in Canaan.[3]

As Lee Roy Martin mentioned, "the memory of the Exodus pervades the Hebrew Bible, and the book of Judges is no exception to the rule."[4] The book of Judges explicitly refers to the Exodus nine times (Judg 2:1, 12; 6:8, 9, 13; 10:11; 11:13, 16; 19:30). In YHWH's self-testimony through his angel or prophet (2:1–5; 6:7–10; 10:11–13), in the narrator's testimony (2:11–12), and even in Gideon's sarcastic question (6:13), YHWH is described repeatedly as the one who brought Israel up from Egypt.[5] By making Israel

---

1. Even in the book of Joshua, recitations of the Exodus can be observed (e.g., Josh 2:10–11; 9:9–10; 24:5–7). Cf. Merrill, "The Meaning and Significance of the Exodus Event," 14; see the following essay to compare the figure of Moses with Joshua and the literary and linguistic parallels between the crossing narratives in Exodus and Joshua: Dallaire and Morris, "Joshua and Israel's Exodus from the Desert Wilderness," 18–34; see also the following studies pointing to the allusions to the Exodus in the conquest stories under the leadership of Joshua: Fishbane, *Text and Texture*, 122–24; Zakovitch, *"And You Shall Tell Your Son . . .": The Concept of the Exodus in the Bible*, 61–67.

2. Casey, "Exodus Typology," ix.

3. According to Casey, the clusters of the Exodus tradition can be identified as four: "Events in Egypt" (including the deliverance of Israel at the Red Sea), "The Wilderness," "Sinai," and "The Conquest." Casey, "Exodus Typology," 4. The book of Joshua covers "The Conquest" tradition.

4. Martin, "'Where Are All His Wonders?,'" 87.

5. This expression is "probably the earliest and at the same time the most widely used"

recall the event of Exodus, YHWH or the narrator reminds them of God's election, deliverance, and covenant. This retrospect of divine action in their past becomes the reason why Israel should obey YHWH and why Israel can expect God's salvific action in their present or future. In other words, the Exodus tradition "serves the narrative of Judges as a witness to Yahweh's power and faithfulness that calls Israel to obedience and encourages their hope in Yahweh's present and future attentiveness."[6]

Judges 19 portrays a story of a Levite's second wife who is raped and murdered in Gibeah. When the Levite came back to his house, he cut up his concubine with a knife into twelve pieces, limb by limb, and sent the pieces into all areas of Israel. The people responded, "Nothing like this has ever happened or been seen from the day when the sons of Israel came up from the land of Egypt to this day" (v. 30). Here, the expression "the day when the sons of Israel came up from the land of Egypt" can be understood as a historically important moment for Israel. As Martin argued, this moment can be understood as "Israel's founding moment" as a nation.[7] Genesis begins with the stories of Patriarchs and ends with Jacob's story. Before Jacob moved to Egypt, God spoke to him in visions of the night: "I am God, the God of your father; do not be afraid to go down to Egypt, for I will make you a great *nation* there" (Gen 46:3).[8] Exodus 1 depicts the changes of the times between Joseph and Moses. As God promises, the seventy persons of the house of Jacob who came to Egypt (Gen 46:26–27) increased greatly (Exod 1:7), but their multiplication resulted in Israel's slavery. The event of the Exodus not only gives Israel political freedom but also gives Israel their identity (the people of God and his worshippers), the law, and the land. Therefore, through the Exodus, Israel was born as a nation.

In the first book of Samuel, Samuel mentions the Exodus twice before and after Saul becomes the king of Israel (1 Sam 10:18; 12:6–8). Both references focus on God, the real king of Israel who brought them up from

---

of Israel's confessional formulae. Rad, *The Theology of Israel's Historical Traditions*, 1:121.

6. Martin, "'Where Are All His Wonders?,'" 88.

7. Ibid., 106. Durham's explanation also supports Martin's argument: "In the Book of Exodus God gives Israel his special name, his special deliverance, his special guidance, his special covenant, his special worship, his special mercy and his special description of himself. In the Book of Exodus, the people Israel is born; Torah is born, and with it the Bible; the theology of Presence and response to Presence is born." Durham, *Exodus*, xix.

8. Italics added. This promise can be understood as either the process of fulfillment or the ultimate fulfillment of the promise that God made with Abraham (cf. Gen 12:2).

Egypt.⁹ In the second book of Samuel, the Exodus is mentioned twice in the conversations about David's desire to build God's temple. First, God told Nathan, "I have not dwelt in a house since the day I brought up the sons of Israel from Egypt, even to this day; but I have been moving about in a tent, even in a tabernacle" (2 Sam 7:6; cf. 1 Chr 17:5). Second, David praised the Exodus-God in his response to Nathan or God: "What one nation on the earth is like your people Israel, whom God went to redeem for himself as a people and to make a name for himself, and to do a great thing for you and awesome things for your land, before your people whom you have redeemed for yourself from Egypt, from nations and their gods?" (2 Sam 7:23). Like Judges, these verses of Samuel recall the historical event of Exodus and the Exodus-God.

In addition to these verses showing historical memory of the Exodus, some scholars investigated the Exodus motif in 1 Samuel by comparing 1 Sam 7–8 (the figure of Samuel) with Exod 17–18 (Moses). Henry P. Smith pointed out,

> Throughout the chapter [1 Sam 7], Samuel reminds us of Moses. Like the great Law-giver, Samuel rebukes the people, judges them, intercedes for them. Their victory is due to his prayers, as the victory over Amalek in the Wilderness is due to the upraised hands of Moses. The parallel continues in the next chapter [1 Sam 8].¹⁰

The implications of Smith's comments were explored more deeply by J. Ernest Runions. Runions argued, "In comparing Exodus 17 and 1 Samuel 7 the parallelism suggests that the writer of the account in Samuel was actively drawing on Exodus motifs to organize his account."¹¹ Runions tabulated his observations on the similarity in structure and content.¹² The researcher added the last row to show the parallel continues in 1 Sam 8.

---

9. Cf. Merrill, "The Meaning and Significance of the Exodus Event," 14: "Samuel also used the exodus miracle as a reminder of the past in his case harking back to the day when YHWH was king and Israel had no yearning for another."

10. Smith, *Samuel*, xvii.

11. Runions, "Exodus Motifs in First Samuel 7 and 8," 130.

12. Ibid., 130–31 (used by permission of Paternoster Periodicals).

Purpose of the Exodus Theme in Revelation 15

Exod 17–18	1 Sam 7–8
1. Israel is in rebellion (17:3)	1. Israel has neglected YHWH (7:1–2)
2. Water is demanded by and poured out to the people (17:6)	2. Water is poured out (7:6a)
3. Moses judges Israel (17:7)	3. Samuel judges Israel (7:6b)
4. Israel is attacked by Amalek (17:8)	4. Israel is attacked by Philistines (7:8)
5. Moses lifts his hands in intercession (17:11–12)	5. Samuel offers sacrifice and prayer on behalf of the people (7:9)
6. The Amalekites are routed (17:13)	6. The Philistines are defeated (7:10–11)
7. Moses erects an altar, named YHWH-nissi (17:16)	7. Samuel erects a pillar, named Ebenezer (7:12)
8. Moses' status as a judge is clarified and some of his duties are delegated (ch. 18)	8. Samuel exercises prerogatives of a judge in Israel (7:15–ch. 8)

Table 5. Exodus 17–18 and 1 Samuel 7–8

The parallel may be caused by the similar situation of Israel.

> Exodus 17 and 18 are preparatory to the establishment of Israel under the constitution of the covenant (ch. 19; 20); while 1 Samuel 7 and 8 are preparatory to the re-establishment of Israel as a nation on the political basis of kingship with their narration of Israel's repentance after long neglect of Yahweh, an unexpected attack by a Philistine horde, a victory as a result of Samuel's intercession, and a brief account of Samuel's political establishment.[13]

The Exodus theme is observed also in a number of passages of Kings and Chronicles.[14] First Kings 6:1 depicts the time when Solomon began to build the temple: "In the four hundred eightieth year after the Israelites came out of the land of Egypt, in the fourth year of Solomon's reign over Israel, in the month of Ziv." In this verse, two temporal points are mentioned. One is counted from the Exodus event, and the other is counted from Solomon's reign.[15] The account of Solomon's temple (especially about

---

13. Ibid., 131.

14. For example, 1 Kgs 6:1; 8:9 (parallel with 2 Chr 5:10), 16 (parallel with 2 Chr 6:5–6), 21, 51, 53; 9:9 (parallel with 2 Chr 7:22); 2 Kgs 17:7, 36; 21:15; 1 Chr 17:21; 2 Chr 20:10.

15. Amos Frisch named these two datings as "external" (since the Exodus event) and "internal" (since Solomon's reign). Frisch, "The Exodus Motif in 1 Kings 1–14," 6.

the starting point) is recorded also in 1 Kgs 6:37–38 and 2 Chr 2:1–2.[16] In 1 Kgs 6:37–38, however, the point of reference is expressed only in terms of the year of Solomon's reign; in 2 Chr 2:1–2, the dating is not mentioned.[17] The dating to the Exodus event is mentioned only in 1 Kgs 6:1. About this use, Frisch pointed out, "The dating of 6.1 highlights the significance of the erection of the Temple, while simultaneously underscoring the importance of the Exodus as a temporal landmark."[18]

In 1 Kgs 8:16, the Exodus is mentioned also as a temporal landmark: "Since the day that I brought my people Israel out of Egypt, I have not chosen a city from any of the tribes of Israel in which to build a house, that my name might be there; but I chose David to be over my people Israel."[19] This verse is God's word that was delivered by Solomon in his prayer of thanksgiving at the dedication of the Temple. In this verse, if the election of David is "a turning point, bringing in its wake the election of Jerusalem," the Exodus is "a significant point of departure forming the basis for renewal and innovation in the spiritual life of the nation."[20]

A similar emphasis is illustrated in 1 Kgs 8:46–53 in Solomon's prayer, which shows the "Exodus experience is important not only for the Creed of the Israelites . . . , but also in the practical life of prayer" even in the later generation.[21] This prayer is offered to God after Solomon builds the Temple in order to request God's forgiveness of sins not just for Solomon himself but for the whole people of Israel. When one considers when, where, and by whom this prayer is made, this prayer shows that "the Exodus motif has

---

16. "In the fourth year [of Solomon's reign over Israel] the foundation of the house of the LORD was laid, in the month of Ziv. In the eleventh year [of Solomon's reign over Israel], in the month of Bul, which is the eighth month, the house was finished in all its parts, and according to all its specifications. He [Solomon] was seven years in building it" (1 Kgs 6:37–38); "Solomon decided to build a temple for the name of the LORD, and a royal palace for himself. Solomon conscripted seventy thousand laborers and eighty thousand stone-cutters in the hill country, with three thousand six hundred to oversee them" (2 Chr 2:1–2).

17. Concerning the omission of the dating (to the Exodus), Sara Japhet argued, "The Chronicler plays down the significance of the Exodus, especially its constitutive function in the history of Israel, and so here the relevant reference is omitted." Japhet, *I & II Chronicles*, 550.

18. Frisch, "The Exodus Motif in 1 Kings 1–14," 6.

19. Cf. parallel with 2 Chr 6:5–6.

20. Frisch, "The Exodus Motif in 1 Kings 1–14," 7–8.

21. Hre Kio, "Exodus as a Symbol of Liberation," 118.

become part of that deepest deposit of Israel's heart."[22] Solomon requests God to forgive Israel and deliver them from the enemy's land, as God delivered them from Egypt in the past. To be more accurate, Solomon mentions divine election and divine deliverance out of Egypt as the foundation of his request:

> For they are your people and your inheritance which you have brought forth from Egypt. . . . For you have separated them from all the peoples of the earth as your inheritance, as you spoke through Moses your servant, when you brought our fathers forth from Egypt. (1 Kgs 8:51–53)

In other words, this prayer is concluded focusing on the Exodus event in which Israel is elected as the people of God.[23]

As the Exodus motif forms the framework for Solomon's (Israel's) prayer to God in 1 Kgs 8, this motif also forms the framework for God's warning to Solomon (Israel) in 1 Kgs 9:6–9, which is parallel with 2 Chr 7:19–22. This warning was given to Solomon (Israel) when God appeared to Solomon after the dedication of the Temple.[24]

> But if you turn away and forsake the decrees and commands I have given you and go off to serve other gods and worship them, then I will uproot Israel from my land, which I have given them, and will reject this temple I have consecrated for my name. I will make it a byword and an object of ridicule among all peoples. And though this temple is not so imposing, all who pass by will be appalled and say, "Why has the LORD done such a thing to this land and to this temple?" People will answer, "Because they have forsaken the LORD, the God of their fathers, who brought them out of Egypt, and have embraced other gods, worshipping and serving them—this is why he brought all this disaster on them." (2 Chr 7:19–22)

The possibility of Israel's being plucked up from the land is caused by their disobedience to God's statutes and his commandments that were given to them in the process of the Exodus. Thus, one could say that "the ultimate foundation for the warning of the people rests on the Exodus motif."[25]

---

22. Ibid.
23. Cf. DeVries, *1 Kings*, 126.
24. Pointing out the shift to second person plural in 7:19, Raymond B. Dillard understood this warning is given to Israel, although the previous passage that shows God's promise (7:12–18) is given to Solomon. Dillard, *2 Chronicles*, 59.
25. Hre Kio, "Exodus as a Symbol of Liberation," 120.

Psalms

Among Poetry books, finding passages that refer to the Exodus in Job, Proverbs, Ecclesiastes, and Song of Songs is hard; but finding those passages in Psalms is not difficult. At least sixteen psalms, in whole or in part, explicitly show the Exodus theme.[26] Out of 150, sixteen is not a large portion. "Nonetheless, it is clear that the Exodus is by far the most common historical event referred to in the psalms."[27]

Clark Hyde divided the sixteen into two groups: (1) "brief mentions of the Exodus in the Psalms" (e.g., Pss 44, 66, 68, 74, 77, 80, 81, 95, 99, 103, 135); (2) "major treatments of the Exodus in the Psalms" (e.g., Pss 78, 105, 106, 114, 136).[28] The passages of the first group generally note one element of the Exodus in a part of a Psalm: for example, the plagues that afflicted Egypt (135:8–9), the redemption at the Red Sea (66:1–6; 74:12–14), or the wandering and/or murmuring in the wilderness (81:5–10; 95:8–11).[29] In the case of Ps 77, some explicit expressions of the Exodus theme can be observed: for example, v. 19, "Your [God's] way was through the sea, your path, through the mighty waters," reminds readers of the Red Sea event; v. 20, "You [God] led your people like a flock by the hand of Moses and Aaron," summarizes the whole Exodus event. The other verses that do not show the explicit Exodus theme also allude to the song of Moses in Exod 15.[30]

---

26. Pss 44, 66, 68, 74, 77, 78, 80, 81, 95, 99, 103, 105, 106, 114, 135, and 136.

27. Hyde, "The Remembrance of the Exodus in the Psalms," 405; cf. Haglund, *Historical Motifs in the Psalms*, 102–3. Haglund argued that the Exodus, along with its associated events, "is the most common historical motif in the Book of Psalms" (102).

28. Hyde, "The Remembrance of the Exodus in the Psalms," 404–14.

29. Cf. Casey, "Exodus Typology," 39; Westermann, *The Praise of God in the Psalms*, 141.

30. Cf. Stevenson, "Communal Imagery and Individual Lament," 220–25; Harman, "The Exodus and the Sinai Covenant in the Book of Psalms," 23.

Purpose of the Exodus Theme in Revelation 15

Ps 77	Exod 15	Exod 34
Has God forgotten to be gracious? Has he in anger shut up his compassion? (v. 9)		The LORD, the LORD, a God merciful and gracious, slow to anger, and abounding in steadfast love and faithfulness. (v. 6)
And I say, "It is my grief that the right hand of the Most High has changed." (v. 10)	Your right hand, O LORD, glorious in power—your right hand, O LORD, shattered the enemy. (v. 6) You stretched out your right hand, the earth swallowed them. (v. 12)	
Your way, O God, is holy. What god is so great as our God? You are the God who works wonders. (vv. 13–14a)	Who is like you, O LORD, among the gods? Who is like you, majestic in holiness, awesome in splendor, doing wonders? (v. 11)	
You have displayed your might among the peoples. With your strong arm you redeemed your people (vv. 14b–15a)	In your steadfast love you led the people whom you redeemed; you guide them by your strength to your holy abode. The people heard, they trembled (vv. 13–14a; cf. 14b–16)	
You led your people like a flock ... (v. 20)	In your steadfast love you led the people ... (v. 13)	

Table 6. Psalm 77, Exodus 15, and Exodus 34

In short, the psalmist sang an individual lament (vv. 1–10) and then changed the mood by saying, "I will call to mind the deeds of the LORD; I will remember your wonders of old" (v. 11). By alluding to the song of Moses in Exod 15 and also explicitly mentioning the Exodus theme (vv. 19–20), the psalmist "expresses the paradox of Israel's faith—that one looks to the past to find hope for the future."[31]

The passages of the second group include many elements of the Exodus in a large portion of a Psalm. The elements included in the Psalms of the second group and tabulated below were based on the five elements constituting the Exodus theme argued by Julien Harvey.[32]

---

31. Ibid., 229.

32. Hyde, "The Remembrance of the Exodus in the Psalms," 404–5; quoted and

	Ps 78	Ps 105	Ps 106	Ps 114	Ps 136
Israel's departure from Egypt (including plagues)	vv. 43–52	vv. 24–38			vv. 10–12
The wondrous crossing of the Sea	vv. 13, 53		vv. 7–12 (cf. v. 22)	v. 3	vv. 13–15
Wandering and murmuring in the wilderness	vv. 14–42	vv. 38–42	vv. 13–46	v. 8	v. 16
The theophany at Sinai				(v. 7, alluding to Exod 19:18)	
The entry into the Promised Land	vv. 54–55	v. 44			vv. 17–22
Other allusions	v. 12			v. 7 (alluding to Exod 15:14–16)	vv. 23–24

Table 7. Five Elements of the Exodus Theme in Pss 78, 105, 106, 114, and 136

As Table 7 shows, the greatest number of elements of the Exodus theme are in Pss 78 and 136. Especially Ps 78 is evaluated as "the longest extended treatment of the Exodus in the Psalter."[33] As Richard J. Clifford analyzed, the structure of Ps 78 shows one introduction (vv. 1–11) and "two recitals each followed by a sequel in which divine merciful response is depicted."[34]

---

translated from Harvey, "La typologie de l'exode dan les Psaumes," 383–86. For Ps 78:54–55, see Leander Keck et al., *The New Interpreter's Bible*, 4:992; Clifford, "In Zion and David a New Beginning," 135; Tate, *Psalms 51–100*, 293. For Ps 114:7, see Allen, *Psalms 101–150*, 142.

33. Hyde, "The Remembrance of the Exodus in the Psalms," 407.
34. Clifford, "In Zion and David a New Beginning," 129; cf. Tate, *Psalms 51–100*, 287.

Purpose of the Exodus Theme in Revelation 15

Introduction (vv. 1–11)

First Recital:	Second Recital:
Wilderness Events (vv. 12–32)	From Egypt and Canaan (vv. 40–64)
gracious act (vv. 12–16)	gracious act (vv. 40–55)
rebellion (vv. 17–20)	rebellion (vv. 56–58)
divine anger & punishment (vv. 21–32)	divine anger & punishment (vv. 59–64)
Sequel (vv. 33–39)	Sequel (vv. 65–72)

The first recital starts with v. 12: "In the sight of their ancestors he worked marvels in the land of Egypt, in the fields of Zoan." This verse is paralleled with v. 43 in the second recital: "When he displayed his signs in Egypt, and his miracles in the fields of Zoan." The first recital depicts the Red Sea event (v. 13), God's guidance with the pillars of cloud and fire during day and night (v. 14), God's supply of water from the rock (v. 15), and the Israelites' murmuring in the wilderness (vv. 17–20). About the Israelites' rebellion, divine anger and punishment are illustrated (vv. 21–32); but that divine grace is given also to them is emphasized by mentioning God's supply with manna and quails in the wilderness as the answer to Israel's murmuring (vv. 23–29). The second recital depicts plagues inflicted on Egypt (vv. 44–51; cf. rivers turning to blood, swarms of flies, frogs, grasshoppers, sleet, hail, lightning, and the death of the firstborn of Egypt),[35] shortly summarizes divine "guidance and care of the Israelites in their wandering" (vv. 52–53),[36] and notes entry into the land (vv. 54–55). The usages of the Exodus theme in Psalms are historical rather than typological because "the chief emphasis of the psalmists is on the celebration, rather than anticipation, of the salvation of God" that God performed in Israel's history.[37]

Major Prophetic Books

If references to the Exodus tradition in historical books and psalms are historical, the characteristic of references to the Exodus tradition in Isaiah is its typological uses. When one divides the book of Isaiah into three sections (chs. 1–39; 40–55; 56–66),[38] the occurrences of Exodus typology in

---

35. See Campbell, "Psalm 78," 69; cf. Tate, *Psalms 51–100*, 292.
36. Tate, *Psalms 51–100*, 293.
37. Casey, "Exodus Typology," 40.
38. Cf. Childs, *Introduction to the Old Testament*, 311–38; Muilenburg, "Isaiah 40–66," 381–419; Westermann, *Isaiah 40–66*, 3–30, 295–308; Whybray, *Isaiah 40–66*, 20;

the first section are rare. The passages that show the typology in the first section are "regarded generally to be additions of material related originally to Deutero-Isaiah."[39] For instance, two passages are considered as the references to the Exodus in the first section: Isa 10:24–27 and 11:10–16.[40]

In the second section (Isa 40–55), the historical setting of the prophecies is the Babylonian Exile. While his prophetic predecessors mentioned the memory of the Exodus,[41] the author applies the meaning of the Exodus in an eschatological dimension. In other words, his prior prophets used the reference to the Exodus historically; but the author uses the reference to the Exodus typologically and eschatologically. Arguing that "in the development of Second Isaiah's eschatological message, one of the dominant themes is that of the new exodus," Bernhard W. Anderson suggested ten key passages in which the new Exodus theme appears.[42]

1. 40:3–5   The highway in the wilderness
2. 41:17–20   The transformation of the wilderness
3. 42:14–16   YHWH leads his people in a way they know not
4. 43:1–3   Passing through the waters and the fire
5. 43:14–21   A way in the wilderness
6. 48:20–21   The exodus from Babylon
7. 49:8–12   The new entry into the Promise Land
8. 51:9–10   The new victory at the sea
9. 52:11–12   The new exodus
10. 55:12–13   Israel shall go out in joy and peace

Knight, *The New Israel*, xi–xvii.

39. Casey, "Exodus Typology," 37.

40. These passages depict God's promised punishment on Assyria as he did to Egypt and God's promised return of the remnant of Israel from captivity in Assyria as Israel was delivered from captivity in Egypt. As another instance of Exodus reference in the first section, Isa 35 can be mentioned. Like 11:16 ("a highway from Assyria"), "a highway" is cited also in this chapter. The way is headed to Zion; only the redeemed will walk the way, and the ransomed of the LORD will return through the way (vv. 9–10). With their return, nature is changed marvelously and universally. These elements "convey an appreciation of the Exodus as a typology of salvation" and "bear all the marks of a genuine writing of Second Isaiah." Casey, "Exodus Typology," 38; Smart, *History and Theology in Second Isaiah*, 292–94; cf. Kaiser, *Isaiah 13–39*, 362.

41. For example, Hos 2:14–15; 11:1; 12:9, 13; 13:4–5; Amos 2:9–10; 3:1–2; 9:7; Mic 6:4; Jer 2:6–7; 7:22, 25; 11:4, 7; 23:7–8; 31:32; 32:20–22; 34:13–14; Ezek 20:5–10.

42. Anderson, "Exodus Typology in Second Isaiah," 181–82; cf. Watts, *Isaiah 34–66*, 81.

The second section of Isaiah can be said to be paved with the new Exodus theme. Based on his historical understanding of the Exodus in the past, the prophet extracts his eschatology in the framework of new Exodus. He compares the Babylonian captivity to Israel's Egyptian bondage (cf. Isa 48). The (old) Exodus can be a guarantee—or hope—that the new Exodus will happen again. But the new Exodus is not just the repetition of the old Exodus. The old Exodus is the basis for the new (cf. Isa 43:16–19; 52:4), but the former things that happened in the old Exodus are not sufficient to describe fully the new things that will happen in the new Exodus (cf. Isa 43:16–21). Anderson expressed the marvelous transformation from the old Exodus to the new as "the shift of music into a new key as it crescendoes to a climax."[43] The old and new show continuity but also show discontinuity in depth. The new Exodus is "a renewal that surpasses the old."[44]

The references to the Exodus in the third section (Isa 56–66) are less than the references in the second section (Isa 40–55) and not typological. Especially Isa 63:9–14 illustrates the old Exodus—the departure from Egypt, crossing of the Red Sea, and divine guidance in the wilderness.[45]

The Exodus motif in Jeremiah is applied to Israel's captivity in Babylon. As other OT books frequently show, the Exodus formula that illustrates YHWH as Exodus-God, "I brought you up out of the land of Egypt," appears often in Jeremiah (e.g., 2:6; 7:22; 11:4; 32:21; 34:13; cf. 16:14; 23:7). In contexts in which the formula is cited, other elements of the Exodus story (wilderness wandering, Sinai, conquest) also appear.[46]

In Jeremiah, the wilderness is illustrated as the location of Israel's disobedience and God's punishment (8:14; 9:15; 23:15; cf. 8:17).[47] This "dis-

---

43. Anderson, "Exodus Typology in Second Isaiah," 190. See his further explanation: "It is erroneous to assume that the new exodus is the same as old, as though the endtime were a return to primeval time.... In the new exodus, historical conditions will be marvelously transformed.... [Second Isaiah] transposes the whole sacred story into a higher key as he announces the good tidings of salvation. The new exodus will be a radically new event" (190–91).

44. Ninow, *Indicators of Typology*, 194.

45. Cf. Muilenburg, "Isaiah 40–66," 733–35.

46. Casey, "Exodus Typology," 12. Casey argued, "In these lengthened contexts the formula becomes the key to the identity of both Yahweh and Israel/Judah. Israel/Judah is identified as the disobedient and rebellious people, and the reminiscences of the whole story of the Exodus provide a history of their disobedience (22:21; 32:30)" (12).

47. The first three verses (8:14; 9:15; 23:15) mention "poisoned water." According to Num 5, "water of bitterness" was used to test an unfaithful wife. In addition, according to Exod 32:20, water polluted with the remains of the golden calf was drunk by the

obedience" is unfaithfulness to the covenant. In other words, the Exodus theme (especially the wilderness image) in Jeremiah is based on the marital analogy between YHWH and Israel. Therefore, Israel's disobedience or unfaithfulness to the covenant or commands of YHWH corresponds to Israel's apostasy or adultery (cf. 3:20; 31:32). In Jer 2:2, however, the LORD says, "I remember the devotions of your [Israel's] youth, your love as a bride, how you followed me in the wilderness, in a land not sown." Here, the wilderness is illustrated as the location of early marriage life between God and Israel, where Israel shows her devotion, love, and obedience. "The divine memory was of pure love, before the religious and political perversions of love had arisen in later times to spoil the continuing relationship."[48] Therefore, the LORD requests Israel to come back to the wilderness and to recover her pure love. This understanding of the wilderness is well illustrated in Hosea, too.

Comparing the book of Exodus with the book of Ezekiel, Nevada L. DeLapp argued that in both books, three types of characters exist: a protagonist (knowledge revealer), a mediate character, and knowledge receivers.[49] According to him, the protagonist or knowledge revealer in Exodus and Ezekiel is YHWH;[50] the mediate characters are Moses (in Exodus) and Ezekiel (in Ezekiel); the knowledge receivers are Pharaoh and Israel (in Exodus) and Israel (in Ezekiel). DeLapp concluded that Ezekiel corresponds to "a New Moses" and the people of Israel play a double role of "their rebellious ancestors" and "a New Pharaoh/Egypt."[51]

Israelites, who were accused of apostasy of the idol. Apostasy is illustrated sometimes as adultery. In this context, the poisoned water seems to be a proper punishment for Israel, who was unfaithful to YHWH's covenant.

48. Craigie et al., *Jeremiah 1–25*, 24.

49. DeLapp, "Ezekiel as Moses," 53.

50. For example, Ezek 20:42, 44: "You [Israel] shall know that I am the LORD, when I bring you into the land of Israel, the country that I swore to give to your ancestors. . . . And you shall know that I am the LORD, when I deal with you for my name's sake, not according to your evil ways, or corrupt deeds, O house of Israel, says the LORD God." See DeLapp's argument: "All of YHWH's actions are calculated to make YHWH known to Israel and the nations. In the end, YHWH will cause all to know that YHWH is God. . . . Both [the books of Exodus and of Ezekiel] are concerned with God's self-revelation in deeds of mercy and judgment. With this in mind, one can argue that, despite the various important characters contained in the stories of both books, it is ultimately God who is the protagonist." DeLapp, "Ezekiel as Moses," 54.

51. DeLapp, "Ezekiel as Moses," 72. "When read together, Ezekiel and Exodus display a high degree of analogous material. Their intertextual relationship invites readers to view the prophet Ezekiel as a New Moses and to see the people of Israel as both a

Differently from other OT books that use familiar Exodus formula, Ezekiel views the purpose of Exodus not from Israel's side but from God's side: "I [YHWH] acted for the sake of my name, so that it should not be profaned in the sight of the nations, in whose sight I had brought them [Israel] out" (20:9, 14, 22). Ezekiel explains the reason of Exodus—focusing not on "out of Egypt" but on "into the wilderness":

> But they [Israel] rebelled against me [YHWH] and would not listen to me; not one of them cast away the detestable things their eyes feasted on, nor did they forsake the idols of Egypt. Then I thought I would pour out my wrath upon them and spend my anger against them in the midst of the land of Egypt.... I will bring you into the wilderness of the peoples, and there I will enter into judgment with you face to face. As I entered into judgment with your ancestors in the wilderness of the land of Egypt, so I will enter into judgment with you, says the LORD God. (Ezek 20:7–8, 35–36)

This unique point is argued by only Ezekiel, that God brought Israel out of Egypt and into the wilderness to judge Israel, who disobeyed and committed apostasy in Egypt. As God did so to the Israelites' ancestors, he would bring the Israelites contemporary with Ezekiel into the wilderness to judge them because they did not forsake the idols of the nations, and he would wash out of them the detestable things and idolatry. The wilderness is the location of judgment but, at the same time, the location of restoration.

Minor Prophetic Books

Otto Piper argued that the reminiscences from Egypt provide the central themes in the book of Hosea:

> God will renew his covenant by leading his people again through the wilderness (Hos. 2:14–20). The Exodus furnishes the evidence of God's love for Israel (Hos. 11:1, 13:4–5) and out of that same love he will lead them home again (Hos. 11:11). But first they will be brought to Egypt (Hos. 11:5) and the wilderness again (Hos. 12:9). For their salvation God will raise a prophet as he had raised Moses (Hos. 12:13).[52]

---

recapitulation of their rebellious ancestors and as a New Pharaoh/Egypt" (72).

52. Piper, "Unchanging Promises," 3–4. In Hosea, "Egypt" means sometimes Egypt itself from which Israel came out (e.g., 2:15; 12:9, 13; 13:4–5) and sometimes a parallel of Assyria (e.g., 7:11; 9:3, 6; 11:5, 11; 12:1). In 7:11, both Egypt and Assyria are mentioned

In Hos 2, the wilderness is illustrated as the location where YHWH and Israel, his bride, had their honeymoon (cf. Jer 2). There, YHWH gave her his covenant, and she responded with obedience. However, now when she loses her pure love toward her husband, YHWH wants to renew his covenant by leading her again to the honeymoon place, that is, the wilderness.[53]

This marriage imagery is changed to the father-son imagery in Hos 11: "When Israel was a child, I loved him, and out of Egypt I called my son" (11:1). However, because of their disobedience and idolatry (11:2), Assyria would become their king (11:5). Despite Israel's continual disobedience (11:6–7), God did not give them up (11:8) and promised his compassion and love (11:8–9). God commanded Israel to return to him and maintain love with justice and wait for him always (12:6). YHWH said, "I am the LORD your [Israel's] God ever since the land of Egypt" (12:9a; cf. 13:4a) and promised he would bring them back into the poverty of the wilderness: "I will make you live in tents again, as in the days of the appointed festival" (12:9b). God expected that "they may learn again to depend upon him and not upon themselves or their affluence"[54] and that they may know no God but YHWH, and besides him is no savior (13:4b). Like Hos 2, in Hos 11–13 the wilderness is depicted as the location to which Israel should come back for restoration and the location in which Israel showed their obedience to and dependence on YHWH in the past (cf. Jer 2:2). However, their return to the wilderness is not the final step of their salvation because God promises their return home again (cf. 11:11; 12:13).

The book of Amos has five references to the Exodus tradition (2:10; 3:1; 4:10; 5:25; 9:7). These verses are understood generally as non-typological interpretations; only 4:10a ("the manner of Egypt") is uncertain as to whether the phrase "was intended to be a typological reference to the Egyptian plagues."[55] In Amos, election is one of most important events in Exodus tradition: "You only have I known of all the families of the earth" (3:2a). In addition, the special relationship between YHWH and Israel appears even in YHWH's judgment proclamation. According to Amos 4:6–11, YHWH punished them through drought, blight, mildew, locusts, and pestilence (after the manner of Egypt); and the reason for his punishment was not

---

together, but "both are noted as contemporary political powers only." Casey, "Exodus Typology," 9.

53. McKenzie, "Exodus Typology in Hosea," 100–101.
54. Ibid., 101.
55. Casey, "Exodus Typology," 7–8.

Purpose of the Exodus Theme in Revelation 15

just for discipline but for restoration of the relationship—in order to make them return to him (cf. 4:6b, 8b, 9b, 10b, 11b). Francis I. Anderson and David L. Freedman rightly pointed out that "Amos saw disasters as calls to repentance (4:6–11)."[56] Like Jeremiah (cf. 2:2) and Hosea (cf. 2:16), Amos also showed his understanding of the wilderness time of Israel as a time of faithfulness in Israel's life: "In 5:25 an oblique reference to the Wilderness tradition appears, showing that Amos regarded that era in Israel's life as a time of faithfulness."[57]

In the book of Micah, the Exodus tradition can be observed in two passages.[58]

> For I [YHWH] brought you [Israel] up from the land of Egypt, and redeemed you from the house of slavery; and I sent before you Moses, Aaron, and Miriam. O my people, remember now what King Balak of Moab devised, what Balaam son of Beor answered him, and what happened from Shittim to Gilgal, that you may know the saving acts of the LORD. (6:4–5)

> As in the days when you came out of the land of Egypt, show us marvelous things. (7:15)

In 6:4–5, Micah delivered what YHWH said to him. Here, the Exodus tradition illustrates the historical events that happened in Israel's history. "This is followed by the typological application of the same acts in 7:15."[59] This link between these two passages means that the historical Exodus events become the basis of the new Exodus expectation. Furthermore, this expectation is not limited to Israel's return from the Babylonian exile but also is "expanded into an eschatological future."[60] The new Exodus expectation is applied also to the new "messianic ruler and shepherd [who] will renew and reestablish the Davidic monarchy."[61]

---

56. Anderson and Freedman, *Amos*, 435.

57. Casey, "Exodus Typology," 7.

58. Ninow argued that the Exodus tradition can be observed even in Mic 4:9–10. Ninow, *Indicators of Typology*, 220–24.

59. Casey, "Exodus Typology," 11.

60. Ninow, *Indicators of Typology*, 228.

61. Ibid. In addition, for the Exodus tradition in Zechariah (esp. 10:6–12), see Ninow, *Indicators of Typology*, 228–37; for Exodus motifs in Jonah 2, see Hunter, "Jonah from the Whale: Exodus Motifs in Jonah 2," 142–58.

THE EXODUS THEME IN THE INTERTESTAMENTAL LITERATURE

In this section, the Exodus theme in the intertestamental literature will be examined. This literature includes the Apocrypha and Pseudepigrapha of the OT.

Apocrypha[62]

As was true with the OT, some passages of Apocrypha use the Exodus tradition to identify YHWH as the God of Israel who brought Israel out of Egypt (for example, Bar 2:11 and 2 Esd 1:7a). Even the expressions of these passages are similar to the OT expressions.

> And now, O LORD God of Israel, who brought your people out of the land of Egypt with a mighty hand and with signs and wonders and with great power and outstretched arm, and made yourself a name that continues to this day. (Bar 2:11)
>
> Was it not I who brought them out of the land of Egypt, out of the house of bondage? (2 Esd 1:7a)

Two other passages, 2 Esd 1:10–14a and 2:1a, also describe God's deliverance of Israel from Egypt; but these passages end up with an emphasis on Israel's disobedience, contrasting with God's wondrous salvific acts and faithful guidance.[63] Some passages also point out Israel's disobedient and ungrateful attitude during the Exodus events and add that Israel still does so "to this day" (e.g., 2 Esd 1:16, 14:28–30, and Bar 1:19–22).

As the Exodus tradition is mentioned in Solomon's prayer (1 Kgs 8:46–53), the Exodus tradition is mentioned also in prayers in the Apocrypha: for example, in the prayer of the high priest Simon (3 Macc 2:6–8) and the prayer of Eleazar (3 Macc 6:4). Both passages recall the Exodus events,

---

62. All citations of the Apocrypha are from NRSV.

63. "For their sake I have overthrown many kings; I struck down Pharaoh with his servants and all his army. . . . But speak to them and say, Thus says the LORD: Surely it was I who brought you through the sea, and made safe highways for you where there was no road; I gave you Moses as leader and Aaron as priest; I provided light for you from a pillar of fire, and did great wonders among you. Yet you have forgotten me, says the LORD" (2 Esd 1:10–14); "Thus says the LORD: I brought this people out of bondage, and I gave them commandments through my servants the prophets; but they would not listen to them, and made my counsels void" (2 Esd 2:1).

Purpose of the Exodus Theme in Revelation 15

especially the Red Sea deliverance. In Judas's saying before the battle at Emmaus (1 Macc 4:9–11), the Red Sea deliverance is mentioned also; and the Red Sea event became the basis of their request for delivery in the present time ("crush this army before us today").

The Exodus tradition also is used typologically in some passages of the Apocrypha (e.g., 2 Esd 14; 15:10–11; Sir 36:1–17). As Samuel was parallel with Moses (cf. 1 Sam 7–8; Exod 17–18), Ezra the prophet is parallel with Moses in 2 Esd 14: "God speaks to Ezra from a bush (v. 1); the visions received by Ezra are compared to God's revelations of secrets to Moses (vv. 3–8); Ezra leaves the people for a forty day period to receive God's written revelation (vv. 23–25)."[64] In 2 Esd 15:10–11, an oracle was given to Ezra from God (cf. 15:1), and in the oracle the term "Egypt" is used to describe the foreign power from which Israel should be brought out.[65] The political power of that time is mentioned as Persia in the beginning of the book (2 Esd 1:3). Therefore, this use of "Egypt" in 2 Esd 15 is typological.

The Wisdom of Solomon shows extensive use of the Exodus. As Metzger pointed out, this book belongs to "that genre of ancient literature known as sapiential or 'wisdom' literature" and "carries the personification of Wisdom to its highest point in the Apocrypha."[66] In ch. 10, the work of wisdom from Adam to Moses is described. Wisdom is illustrated as a personage who led the Israelites out of Egypt, including the Red Sea deliverance (10:15–21). In ch. 11, wisdom led the Israelites through the desert. In the following chapters until ch. 15, Israel's wilderness idolatry is described. From ch. 16 to ch. 19, Israel is contrasted with Egypt. As the beginning of the book (chs. 1–9) compares the righteous man with the unrighteous man, the latter chapters of the book (in particular chs. 16–19) compare Israel (the righteous nation) with Egypt (the unrighteous nation).

---

64. Casey, "Exodus Typology," 43.

65. "See, my people are being led like a flock to the slaughter; I will not allow them to live any longer in the land of Egypt, but I will bring them out with a mighty hand and with an uplifted arm, and will strike Egypt with plagues, as before, and will destroy all its land" (2 Esd 15:10–11).

66. Metzger, *An Introduction to the Apocrypha*, 65, 67.

Egyptians	Israelites
"Therefore those people were deservedly punished through such creatures, and were tormented by a multitude of animals." (16:1)	"Instead of this punishment you showed kindness to your people, and you prepared quails to eat, a delicacy to satisfy the desire of appetite." (16:2)
"For they were killed by the bites of locusts and flies, and no healing was found for them, because they deserved to be punished by such things." (16:9)	"But your children were not conquered even by the fangs of venomous serpents, for your mercy came to their help and healed them." (16:10)
"For the ungodly, refusing to know you, were flogged by the strength of your arm, pursued by unusual rain and hail and relentless storms, and utterly consumed by fire." (16:16)	"Instead of these things you gave your people food of angels, and without their toil you supplied them from heaven with bread ready to eat, providing every pleasure and suited to every taste." (16:20)
"For when lawless people supposed that they held the holy nation in their power, they themselves lay as captives of darkness and prisoners of long night, shut in under their roofs, exiles from eternal providence." (17:2)	"Therefore you provided a flaming pillar of fire as a guide for your people's unknown journey, and a harmless sun for their glorious wandering." (18:3)
"When their firstborn were destroyed, they acknowledged your people to be God's child." (18:13b)	"The experience of death touched also the righteous, and a plague came upon the multitude in the desert, but the wrath did not long continue." (18:20)
The punishment of the Egyptians (19:13–17)	God's guidance and protection for his people (19:6–12)

Table 8. Contrast between Egyptians and Israelites in Wisdom 16–19

Pseudepigrapha[67]

In the Pseudepigrapha, the Exodus tradition is not easily found, though three references can be mentioned here. The whole passage of 3 *En.* 1:4–9 deals with the final judgment, and v. 4 depicts Sinai, where the law was

---

67. All citations of the Pseudepigrapha are from Charles, *Pseudepigrapha*.

given, as the place of future judgment.[68] In 2 *Bar.* 29:8, the expectation of manna that "shall again descend from on high" in the consummation of time is described.[69] *Sibyline Oracles* 5:256–59 shows the expectation of a Joshua-figure "who shall one day cause the sun to stand still" in the consummation of time.[70] The three references all describe the final judgment time or the consummation of time ("i.e., the Messianic age") and show specific expectations on those times (e.g., place, event, and figure), alluding to the Exodus event.[71]

THE EXODUS THEME IN THE NEW TESTAMENT[72]

Gospels and Acts

As the title of Dennison's article "The Exodus: Historical Narrative, Prophetic Hope, Gospel Fulfillment" shows, the Exodus is one of the most important OT patterns in the NT, and the NT authors see that pattern fulfilled in Jesus Christ.[73] Although the Exodus theme is less clear in the Gospels and Acts compared to the OT, "the typology of the Exodus was fundamental for the Evangelists."[74] Mark will be considered before Matthew because Matthew is dependent on Mark as a source, so one can expect Mark's use of the Exodus theme to reappear in Matthew. Luke will be combined with Acts; therefore, John will be examined before Luke.

---

68. Charles, *Pseudepigrapha*, 188. Cf. "And the eternal God will tread upon the earth, (even) on Mount Sinai, [And appear from His camp] And appear in the strength of His might from the heaven of heavens" (3 *En.* 1:4).

69. "And it shall come to pass at that self-same time that the treasury of manna shall again descend from on high, and they will eat of it in those years, because these are they who have come to the consummation of time" (2 *Bar.* 29:8). Similarly, in *Sib. Or.* 7:149, "manna is [described as] the food of the members of the Messianic kingdom." Charles, *Pseudepigrapha*, 498.

70. "Then there shall come from the sky a certain exalted man, whose hands they nailed upon the fruitful tree, the noblest of the Hebrews, who shall one day cause the sun to stand still, when he cries with fair speech and pure lips" (*Sib. Or.* 5:256–59).

71. Charles, *Pseudepigrapha*, 498.

72. The Exodus theme in Revelation will not be examined here but will be considered in ch. 3.

73. Cf. Nixon, *The Exodus in the New Testament*, 11.

74. Sahlin, "The New Exodus of Salvation according to St. Paul," 83.

The Gospel of Mark

The Exodus typology can be found in some selected passages of Mark (e.g., 1:1–13; 3:13–19; 6:30–44; 7:31–37; 8:1–10; 9:2–8; 14:12–26).[75] However, one should not miss the point that the whole gospel holds "an Exodus-based scheme, in terms of its structure and the ordering of the narratives."[76] This point will be argued after examining the Exodus theme in some passages.

William L. Lane called Mark 1:1–13 the "prologue to the gospel" and argued, "The motif of the wilderness dominates the prologue."[77] The whole gospel focuses on the fulfillment of OT prophecy, and especially 1:2–3 points out the fulfillment of Isaiah's (and Malachi's) prophecy, "particularly the eschatological prophecy of a second exodus in the wilderness."[78] Robert A. Guelich also supported this point:

> The "wilderness" motif expresses the eschatological hope of the Exodus typology found in Hos 2:14; 12:9 (cf. Micah 7:14–15) and especially in Isaiah (e.g., 40:3–4; 41:18–19; 43:19–20; 48:20–21; 51:9–11). The "wilderness" represented the place where God would once again act to deliver the people. . . . The evangelist's failure to locate the Baptist's ministry more specifically in either the

---

75. Cf. Casey, "Exodus Typology," 59–71.

76. Ibid., 59.

77. Lane, *The Gospel according to Mark*, 39; cf. Mauser, *Christ in the Wilderness*, 77–102; Seitz, "Praeparatio Evangelica in the Markan Prologue," 201.

78. Casey, "Exodus Typology," 59. Mark mentioned 1:2 as Isaiah's prophecy, but actually the verse is Malachi's prophecy (cf. Mal 3:1) and at the same time recalls Exod 23:20.

ἰδοὺ ἀποστέλλω τὸν ἄγγελόν μου πρὸ προσώπου σου, ὃς κατασκευάσει τὴν ὁδόν σου (Mark 1:2)

ἰδοὺ ἐγὼ ἐξαποστέλλω τὸν ἄγγελόν μου καὶ ἐπιβλέψεται ὁδὸν πρὸ προσώπου μου (Mal 3:1, LXX)

ἰδοὺ ἐγὼ ἀποστέλλω τὸν ἄγγελόν μου πρὸ προσώπου σου (Exod 23:20, LXX)

The messenger of God (τὸν ἄγγελόν μου) in Exod 23:20 is an angel sent before Israel (πρὸ προσώπου σου) to guide Israel into the land; the messenger of God (τὸν ἄγγελόν μου) in Mal 3:1 is Elijah (cf. Mal 4:5), sent before YHWH (πρὸ προσώπου σου) to prepare the way for the YHWH's coming; and the messenger of God (τὸν ἄγγελόν μου) in Mark 2:1 is John the Baptist, sent before Jesus (πρὸ προσώπου σου) to prepare the way for Jesus' coming (cf. Mark 1:7–8). The combination of these verses shows that Jesus identifies with Israel (cf. Exod 23:20 vs. Mark 1:2) and also with God (cf. Mal 4:5 vs. Mark 1:2). Mark 1:3 also applies YHWH (τοῦ θεοῦ ἡμῶν) in Isa 40:3 to Jesus (αὐτοῦ). The quotation of Isa 40:3 "may be a pointer to the idea of the new Exodus." Nixon, *The Exodus in the New Testament*, 13. Cf. Guelich, *Mark 1–8:26*, 11–12, 26.

Purpose of the Exodus Theme in Revelation 15

"wilderness of Judea" (Matt 3:1) or "around the Jordan" (Luke 3:3; cf. John 1:28) suggests that the "wilderness" had more theological than geographical importance for him.[79]

Mark 3:13–19 depicts Jesus appointing the Twelve. Unlike Matthew and Luke, Mark emphasized the place where Jesus chose the Twelve: the mountain (τὸ ὄρος). The mountain is a place of divine revelation in the OT, especially in the Exodus narratives, as well as in the remainder of Mark's Gospel (cf. 6:46; 9:12; 13:3).[80] When one considers the Twelve "represent in a new form the people of the twelve tribes, Israel,"[81] the Twelve's calling by the LORD at the mountain "to be with him" (cf. Mark 3:14) recalls Exod 24.[82]

Mark 6:30–44 portrays the miracle of feeding the five thousand in the wilderness. Before the miracle happened, Jesus' compassion on the crowd is mentioned in 6:34: "because they were like sheep without a shepherd" (ὅτι ἦσαν ὡς πρόβατα μὴ ἔχοντα ποιμένα). This expression recalls the shepherd-leader in Moses' prayer (Num 27:16–17): "so that the congregation of the LORD may not be like sheep without a shepherd" (καὶ οὐκ ἔσται ἡ συναγωγὴ κυρίου ὡσεὶ πρόβατα οἷς οὐκ ἔστιν ποιμήν, LXX 27:17).[83] This prayer would be fulfilled first in Joshua but ultimately in Jesus. "Undoubtedly, Mark considers Jesus' activity to be the 'eschatological fulfillment of the second exodus,' as he leads the people of Israel like a shepherd in the wilderness, providing rest and food for them there."[84]

Mark 7:31–37 depicts Jesus' healing of a deaf and mute man with saying "*Ephphatha*," which is recorded only in Mark. In this episode, μογιλάλον is used to describe the man's impaired ability in speech. This word is used

---

79. Guelich, *Mark 1–8:26*, 18.

80. Guelich argued that the location of the mountain has "more theological than geographical significance for Mark," and "against its OT context 'the mountain' represents a place of divine revelation, a place near to God. . . . More precisely, the events here represent a Sinai typology with Exod 19:3–6." Guelich, *Mark 1–8:26*, 156. Cf. Schweizer, *The Good News according to Mark*, 81; Lane, *Mark*, 132. Concerning the relation to Exod 19:3–6, see Nineham, *The Gospel of St. Mark*, 115.

81. Lane, *Mark*, 133; cf. Cranfield, *Mark*, 127; Schweizer, *Mark*, 81.

82. Casey argued that this passage evokes Exod 19 as the "counterpoint to the reality of Israel's election in Exodus, where Yahweh promises to be with them." Casey, "Exodus Typology," 62.

83. Guelich, *Mark 1–8:26*, 340; cf. 1 Kgs 22:18; Ezek 34:5.

84. Casey, "Exodus Typology," 64. Guelich argued that the miracle of feeding five thousand people is placed "under the motif of Jesus as the good shepherd, the promised eschatological shepherd" in Ezek 34:23 (cf. Jer 23:4; *Pss. Sol.* 17:40). Guelich, *Mark 1–8:26*, 340–41.

only here in the NT but is used once in the OT (LXX), Isa 35:6.⁸⁵ Isaiah 35 is filled with Exodus typology,⁸⁶ and Isa 35:6a (the prophecy that the lame will leap like a deer and the mute tongue shout for joy) is included in "a rehearsal of the marvelous events in nature that accompany the second exodus deliverance of Yahweh."⁸⁷ According to the exegetical tradition of the rabbis (e.g., *Genesis Rabba* 95; *Midrash Tehillin* 146:8), the prophecy was expected to be fulfilled in the Days of the Messiah.⁸⁸ The fulfillment of the prophecy (of the second exodus) in Jesus is emphasized by Mark in this passage, especially in the doxological conclusion of the story (v. 37), which "affirms again this significance of the miracle as a sign of the promised eschatological salvation of God."⁸⁹

Mark 9:2–8 depicts Jesus' transfiguration episode. The Exodus theme in the episode, especially the allusion to Exod 24:12–18, is argued by some scholars.⁹⁰ Four bases for Mark's alluding to Exod 24 can be summarized as follows. First, both Mark 9:2–8 and Exod 24:12–18 describe the vision of unveiling God's/Jesus' glory. Second, the locus of these events is the same: the mountain (cf. Mark 9:2, ὄρος ὑψηλὸν; Exod 24:12, 13, 15, 16, 17, 18, τὸ ὄρος τὸ Σινα). Third, the temporal reference is similar. The two verses immediately preceding Jesus' transfiguration episode (i.e., Mark 8:38 and 9:1) refer to the parousia;⁹¹ and between these two verses and the transfiguration episode, the precise temporal reference appears: "after six days" (μετὰ ἡμέρας ἕξ, 9:2). Mentioning a specific temporal point is unusual in Mark, and this temporal reference recalls Exod 24:16 (ἓξ ἡμέρας . . . τῇ ἡμέρᾳ τῇ ἑβδόμῃ . . .).⁹² Fourth, Mark 9:7 mentions that a cloud overshadowed the

---

85. Lane, *Mark*, 266; cf. Guelich, *Mark 1–8:26*, 394.

86. Cf. Casey, "Exodus Typology," 37: "The most extensive use of Exodus typology in Isaiah 1 through 39 occurs in chapter thirty-five. The chapter is clearly a version of Deutero-Isaiah's prophecy. The subject of the chapter is the return of the ransomed to Zion (v. 10), a return accompanied by all the marvelous changes in nature that Deutero-Isaiah includes in his description of the 'way' through the wilderness."

87. Casey, "Exodus Typology," 65–66.

88. Lane, *Mark*, 266.

89. Casey, "Exodus Typology," 66.

90. Lane, *Mark*, 317; Evans, *Mark 8:27–16:20*, 34; Mauser, *Christ in the Wilderness*, 110–19.

91. Lane explained the relation between the reference to parousia (Mark 8:31 and 9:1) and the transfiguration episode as follows: "The unveiling of Jesus' glory in the presence of the three disciples corresponds to the assurance that *some will see*." Lane, *Mark*, 317. Italics are Lane's.

92. Lane, *Mark*, 317. "The glory of the LORD settled on Mount Sinai, and the cloud

disciples and a voice came from the cloud. In the OT, the cloud is mentioned frequently as the symbol of God's presence and protection (e.g., Exod 16:10; 19:9; 24:15–16; 33:1); but only in Exod 24:15–16, the correlation of the cloud and the voice appears.[93]

Mark 14:12–26 portrays Jesus' Last Supper. This scene echoes Exod 24:6–11, when the leaders of the Israelites saw God and ate and drank (ὤφθησαν . . . τοῦ θεοῦ καὶ ἔφαγον καὶ ἔπιον).[94] Especially Jesus declared wine "my blood of the covenant" (τὸ αἷμά μου τῆς διαθήκης, Mark 14:24) as the sealing of the new covenant. This reference echoes Moses' words "the blood of the covenant" (τὸ αἷμά μου τῆς διαθήκης) in Exod 24:8, "where Yahweh seals His covenant with the people whom He has just brought out of Egypt."[95] Through these allusions, Casey affirmed, "The sacrifice and seal of the new exodus covenant is now Jesus, whose sacrifice is presently effective but also anticipatory."[96]

The following sentence, "everything in Mark's Gospel can be explained from Exodus," may be considered as too exaggerated; but, as examined above, "the framework within which the material was arranged was based upon a typological use of Exodus."[97] In addition, the Exodus typology hardly can be described as "a complete innovation on the part of the earliest witnesses and Gospel tellers"; but "in all probability it goes back to Jesus himself."[98]

---

covered it *for six days; on the seventh day* he called to Moses out of the cloud" (Exod 24:16, italics added). Cf. Lane argued, "Elsewhere precise notes of time are found only in the passion narrative" in Mark 14–16 (e.g., 14:1, 12, 17; 15:1, 25, 33, 34, 42; 16:2) (317).

93. Lane, *Mark*, 320. Cf. Evans argued the "typological connection" of the transfiguration episode in Mark 9:2–8 to Exod 24 and 33–34 and summarized six parallels between them: "(1) the reference to 'six days' (Mark 9:2; Exod 24:16), (2) the cloud that covers the mountain (Mark 9:7; Exod 24:16), (3) God's voice from the cloud (Mark 9:7; Exod 24:16), (4) three companions (Mark 9:2; Exod 24:1, 9), (5) a transformed appearance (Mark 9:3; Exod 34:30), and (6) the reaction of fear (Mark 9:6; Exod 34:30)." Evans, *Mark 8:27–16:20*, 34.

94. The leaders of the Israelites were Moses, Aaron, Nadab, Abihu, and the seventy elders of Israel (cf. Exod 24:9).

95. Nixon, *The Exodus in the New Testament*, 19; cf. Evans, *Mark 8:27–16:20*, 393.

96. Casey, "Exodus Typology," 70. See also Watts's understanding of the theological use of the passage: "On the more immediate level, Jesus' use of Exod 24 continues Mark's ecclesiological argument that the people of God find their vocational identity as his kingdom of priests in loyalty to Jesus, his messianic Son. . . . Soteriologically and eschatologically, Exod 24 indicates that Jesus' death constitutes both the new Passover and the atoning/purifying sacrifice of Exod 24. . . . At a deeper level it also speaks of God himself. At this new-covenant meal reconstituted Israel, like Israel of old, sees something of the face of God, who in Jesus lays down his life for his enemies." Watts, "Mark," 231–32.

97. Piper, "Unchanging Promises," 19.

98. Ibid.

The Gospel of Matthew

Exodus typology has been examined in some passages of Matthew (e.g., 2:13–23; 3:1–12; 3:13–17; 4:1–11; 5–7; 10:1–15; 11:2–25; 14:13–21; 15:32–39; 17:1–8; 26:26–29).[99] Nixon emphasized Matthew's use of Exodus typology especially in three stories: "St. Matthew is often thought to be the evangelist who stresses the Exodus typology most with the infancy narratives, the Sermon on the Mount and the five blocks of teaching."[100] Therefore, Matt 1–2 (infancy narratives) and Matt 3–8 will be examined briefly.

The evangelist considerably modified Mark's outline of the Gospel story. "By adding the infancy narratives, Matthew has given increased emphasis to the parallelism of the Gospel narratives with Exodus."[101] Matthew narrates the birth of Jesus by correlating it with the birth of Moses in content and order: (1) the murder of Hebrew boys by Pharaoh and Herod (Exod 1:22; Matt 2:16); (2) the escape of Moses and of Jesus with the help of their parents (Exod 2; Matt 2); (3) after the death of Pharaoh and Herod, the return of Moses and Jesus (Exod 4:19; Matt 2:20).[102] Here Pharaoh corresponds to Herod, and Moses corresponds to Jesus. In particular, Exod 4:19 is very similar to Matt 2:20 in the structure of the sentence (a command and the reason), the content, and the words used and shows well the correspondence of Jesus to Moses: "your" (Moses') life corresponds to "the child's" (Jesus') life.[103]

> Exod 4:19 (βάδιζε ἄπελθε εἰς Αἴγυπτον τεθνήκασιν γὰρ πάντες οἱ ζητοῦντές σου τὴν ψυχήν, "Go back to Egypt, for all those who were seeking *your* life are dead")
>
> Matt 2:20 (πορεύου εἰς γῆν Ἰσραήλ· τεθνήκασιν γὰρ οἱ ζητοῦντες τὴν ψυχὴν τοῦ παιδίου, "Go to the land of Israel, for those who were seeking *the child's* life are dead")

---

99. Cf. Casey, "Exodus Typology," 72–86.

100. Nixon, *The Exodus in the New Testament*, 19. Sahlin added one story to these three stories: "The ten miracles described in chapters viii–ix correspond to the ten plagues in Egypt, though antithetically; instead of judgments on the oppressors of Israel, they are acts of salvation on behalf of the new people of God." Sahlin, "The New Exodus of Salvation according to St. Paul," 82.

101. Piper, "Unchanging Promises," 19.

102. Cf. Childs, *The Book of Exodus*, 20–22, 24–26; Hagner, *Matthew 1–13*, 33–35.

103. Cf. Hagner, *Matthew 1–13*, 39.

Purpose of the Exodus Theme in Revelation 15

As Richard A. Burridge pointed out, the places in Matt 3–8 remind readers of the Exodus: the Jordan River, wildness, and a mountain.[104] In Exodus, Israel was called "my first-born son" (υἱὸς πρωτότοκός μου, 4:22), crossed over the Red Sea (14:15–31), and was tested in the desert for forty years (cf. Deut 8:2); Moses went up to Mount Sinai to receive God's words and law. In Matthew, Jesus was called "my son" (ὁ υἱός μου, 3:17), was baptized in the Jordan (3:13–17), was tested in the desert for forty days (4:1–11), and went up to the mountain (τὸ ὄρος) to give God's words about the gospel of the kingdom and a new law to the crowd (Matt 5–7).[105] In this parallel, Israel is applied to Jesus. As many of the NT writers argued, the application of Israel to Jesus is reasonable because God's words toward Israel were fulfilled in Jesus. In addition, in this parallel Moses is applied to Jesus. The correspondence of Moses to Jesus is not limited in this parallel but can be examined in the whole book.[106]

The Gospel of John

The event of Jesus' feeding the five thousand with "five barley loaves and two fish" (πέντε ἄρτους κριθίνους καὶ δύο ὀψάρια) is recorded in all four Gospels. Interestingly, John explains when the event happened: "Now the Passover, the festival of the Jews, was near" (ἦν δὲ ἐγγὺς τὸ πάσχα, ἡ ἑορτὴ τῶν Ἰουδαίων, 6:4). Israel came into Canaan, and the day after the Passover, that very day, the manna stopped (Josh 5:10–12). Therefore, the

---

104. Burridge, *Four Gospels, One Jesus?*, 71–73. Cf. Willard M. Swartley also similarly argued that the Exodus theme can be observed in the changing order of place in Mark 1–8: sea (Mark 1:16–20), mountain (3:13–19), wilderness (6:31–35). Swartley, *Israel's Scripture Traditions and the Synoptic Gospels*, 49.

105. In Luke, Jesus taught "on a level place," not on a mountain (Luke 6:17, 20–49). As Hagner argued, the mountain might be intentionally mentioned by Matthew, who wanted to express the Exodus theme: "Since Matthew emphasizes mountains in special narratives usually having to do with revelation, τὸ ὄρος, 'the mountain,' here functions as a literary device. Matthew may well have had in mind the parallel of Moses going up to Mountain Sinai to receive the law (Exod 19–20; cf. '*Abot* 1:1; *Pirqe R. El.* 46; see too Matt 23:2)." Hagner, *Matthew 1–13*, 86.

106. Dale C. Allison summarized, "The passages in which Moses' tacit presence is the strongest display an order which mirrors the Pentateuch" as follows: Matt 1–2 (Exod 1:1—2:10, infancy narrative); Matt 3:13–17 (Exod 14:10–31, crossing of water); Matt 4:1–11 (Exod 16:1—17:7, wilderness temptation); Matt 5–7 (Exod 19:1—23:33, mountain of lawgiving); Matt 11:25–30 (Exod 33:1–23, reciprocal knowledge of God); Matt 17:1–19 (Exod 34:29–35, transfiguration); Matt 28:16–20 (Deut 31:7–9; Josh 1:1–9, commissioning of successor). Allison, *The New Moses*, 268.

Jews expected that, when a new Moses (i.e., the Messiah) came, the manna would be given to Israel again, probably during the Passover dinner (cf. 2 *Bar.* 29:3, 8).[107] *Ecclesiates Ranbbah* 1:9 also portrays this expectation: "As the former redeemer caused manna to fall, so the latter redeemer will cause manna to descend."[108] The crowd seems to have this expectation, according to John 6:14 (cf. 6:30-31): "After the people saw the miraculous sign that Jesus did, they began to say, 'Surely this is the prophet who is to come into the world.'" From this point of view, the miracle of feeding the five thousand can be a sign of the Messiah and a new Exodus. So, John mentions not only the event itself but also the timing of the event by using the term "the Passover."[109] The mention of Passover—the term recalls not only a part of the Exodus event but also the expectation of reoccurring manna by the Messiah—and Jesus' feeding miracle in the wilderness, which mirrors the miracle of manna in the wilderness, evoke the Exodus.

In addition, Jesus declares himself as the true manna in this discourse. He told the crowd who eagerly followed him after the feeding miracle, "I am the bread that came down from heaven" (ἐγώ εἰμι ὁ ἄρτος ὁ καταβὰς ἐκ τοῦ οὐρανοῦ, 6:41; cf. 6:32-35). In regard to the crowd's prior question to Jesus about the manna (6:30-31),[110] Jesus' answer alludes to the Exodus theme in addition to the recorded event of feeding the five thousand. Beasley-Murray argued,

> The statement as to the nearness of the Passover (v. 4), the identification of Jesus as the prophet who should come (cf. Deut 18:15), and the discussion on the bread from heaven within the discourse (vv. 31-33) combine to indicate that the feeding miracle

---

107. "And it shall come to pass when all is accomplished ... that the Messiah shall then begin to be revealed. And it shall come to pass at that selfsame time that the treasury of manna shall again descend from on high, and they will eat of it those years, because these are they who come to the consummation of time" (2 *Bar.* 29:3, 8). Cf. Morris, *The Gospel according to John*, 321.

108. This translation is quoted from Talbert, *Reading John*, 133.

109. Michaels argued, "The mention of Passover evokes Moses, keeping alive in the reader's mind the conclusion of the preceding discourse (5:45-47; also 5:37-40), and anticipating further controversy over Moses and the provision of manna in the desert (vv. 30-32, 49, 58)." Michaels, *The Gospel of John*, 343.

110. "Then what sign do you do, that we may see, and believe you? What work do you perform? Our fathers ate the manna in the wilderness; as it is written, 'He gave them bread from heaven to eat'" (John 6:30-31).

is understood as falling within the fulfillment of the hope of a second Exodus.[111]

Other passages—for example, John the Baptist's expression about Jesus in John 1:29[112] and the illustration of Jesus' death in John 19:33-36,[113] and Jesus' prediction about his own death in John 3:14-15 (cf. Num 21:4-9)[114]—also take readers back to the Exodus. As Smith argued, the Exodus theme in the Fourth Gospel is expressed more elaborately in the structure, outline, and detailed illustrations than the other Gospels.[115]

Luke and Acts

Scholars have observed Exodus typology in several passages in Luke (e.g., 1:13-17; 3:1-17; 3:21-22; 4:1-13; 4:16-21; 6:12-16; 9:10-17; 9:28-36; 10:1-2; 11:20; 22:14-23).[116] Comparing Matthew's outline, Luke's is more in agreement with Mark. By adding Jesus' appointment of the seventy and their mission (Luke 10:1-20), Luke emphasizes the parallelism with Exodus. The seventy disciples evoke "seventy of the elders of Israel" (ἑβδομήκοντα

---

111. Beasley-Murray, *John*, 88.

112. "The lamb of God who takes away the sin of the world" (ὁ ἀμνὸς τοῦ θεοῦ ὁ αἴρων τὴν ἁμαρτίαν τοῦ κόσμου). Beasley-Murray linked this expression in John to the slaughtered lamb in Revelation and argued that in both passage, Jesus is portrayed as "God's Passover Lamb, to bring about the new Exodus for the liberty and life of the kingdom of God." Beasley-Murray, *John*, 25.

113. "They [the soldiers] did not break his leg. . . . These things occurred so that the scripture might be fulfilled, 'None of his bones shall be broken'" (John 19:33-36). According to Exod 12:46 (cf. Num 9:12), these verses are in reference to the lamb of the Passover. Psalm 34:20, mentioning the righteous suffer ("[God] keeps all their bones; not one of them will be broken"), also can be considered as the OT source. Lindars argued that both typologies would be in the fourth evangelist's mind. Lindars, *The Gospel of John*, 590. However, if one understands the Evangelist's "marked interest in the Exodus typology," the paschal lamb typology would be the better choice as the OT source, as Beasley-Murray, Bultmann, and Barrett argued. Beasley-Murray, *John*, 355; Bultmann, *The Gospel of John*, 676-77. See also Barrett's conclusion: "It may be that John's source referred to the Psalm but that he, with his paschal interests, preferred the Passover reference." Barrett, *The Gospel according to St. John*, 558.

114. "And just as Moses lifted up the serpent in the wilderness, so must the Son of Man be lifted up, that whoever believes in him may have eternal life" (John 3:14-15).

115. Cf. Smith, "Exodus Typology in the Fourth Gospel," 329-42.

116. Cf. Casey, "Exodus Typology," 86-99.

τῆς γερουσίας Ισραηλ, Exod 24:1, 9; cf. Num 11:24–25) and/or the seventy of Jacob's original offspring in Egypt (Exod 1:5; cf. Gen 46:27).[117]

The Gospel of Luke does not have an Exodus-based structure. As Casey argued, "Luke's interests are broader than what could be directed by an Exodus pattern, and the paucity of Exodus motifs in his special section (9:51—19:27) confirms this."[118] However, through his interest that OT prophecy is fulfilled in Jesus, "Luke comes to draw on the Exodus tradition."[119] Piper summarized Luke's use of Exodus typology as follows:

> Luke points to the parallelism between the people to whom Jesus comes, with the Israelites in the wilderness rather than to that between Jesus and the Israelites. Jesus appears more in the role of the Lord, who guided and assisted his people in those days, and he is described as their leader and helper rather than as their representative. Thus Luke's Gospel is a real prelude to Acts. The Gospel story points forward to the things to come rather than backwards to Israel's Exodus.[120]

Like the Gospel of Luke, Acts implicitly expresses the Exodus background.[121] The most important references with Exodus background in Acts are 3:22–23 and 7:37. In Peter's discourse (Acts 3:22) and Stephen's discourse (7:37), Jesus is described as "the prophet like Moses" who was prophesized in Deut 18:15. With the mention of divine promise about the prophet like Moses in Acts 3:22, the strong mention of punishment in Acts

---

117. Cf. Piper, "Unchanging Promises," 19. Concerning the number of people sent out (cf. Luke 10:1, 17), some manuscripts have "seventy" (ἑβδομήκοντα; e.g., P^{75} B D 0181), and some manuscripts have "seventy-two" (ἑβδομήκοντα δύο; e.g., ℵ A C L W Θ Ξ Ψ). Cf. Bruce M. Metzger, "Seventy or Seventy-Two Disciples?," 299–306; Nolland, *Luke 9:21—18:34*, 546. Referring to Metzger's observations, Nolland argued, "The numbers seventy and seventy-two are often effectively interchangeable in Jewish traditions. In particular this is the case with the traditional number of the nations of the world, which is based ultimately on the list in Gen 10, which has seventy names in the MT but seventy-two in the LXX text. Luke is fond of anticipations and almost certainly uses the number here to anticipate later mission to all the nations of the earth. . . . This is surely better in the Lukan framework than to link the number with the translator of the LXX, or with the number of members of the Jewish Sanhedrin. The seventy elders who received the Spirit to share the burden with Moses in Num 11:24–25 provide an alternative link. Here the 'seventy-two' is explicable in terms of the Spirit also falling on Eldad and Medad (v. 26)" (549).

118. Casey, "Exodus Typology," 98–99.

119. Ibid., 99.

120. Piper, "Unchanging Promises," 19–20.

121. Casey, "Exodus Typology," 114.

3:23, "it will be that everyone who does not listen to that prophet will be utterly rooted out of the people" (cf. Deut 18:19; Lev 23:29), emphasizes the promised prophet's (i.e., Jesus') importance in his existence and ministry.[122]

In an intriguing book, Pao argued, "The scriptural story which provides the hermeneutical framework for Acts is none other than the foundation story of Exodus as developed and transformed through the Isaianic corpus."[123] Beyond the explicit quotations of Isaiah in Acts, Pao expanded his investigation to include allusions and motifs or themes of the Isaianic New Exodus. Taking Isa 40:1–11 as a hermeneutical lens in the Lukan writings, he examined "the various components of the Isaianic New Exodus program that are already embedded in Isa 40:1–11 and reappear throughout the narrative of Acts" (i.e., the restoration of the people of God; universal revelation of the glory or salvation of God; the power of the word of God and the fragility of the people; the restoration of the people of God).[124] Pao focused on five passages in which programmatic use of Isaiah is used to construct Luke's narrative (Luke 4:16–30; 24:44–49; Acts 1:8; 13:46–47; and 28:25–28) and concluded as follows.

> Through an examination of individual Isaianic quotations, the wider narrative framework of Acts, and the role of Isaianic motifs in the narrative of Acts, the significance of the Isaianic New Exodus behind the story of Acts can no longer be doubted. The influence of the Isaianic vision cannot be limited to isolated quotations and allusions. The entire Isaianic New Exodus program provides the structural framework for the narrative of Acts as well as the various emphases developed within this framework. The national story of the ancient Israelite tradition provides the foundation story through which the identity of the early Christian movement can be constructed.[125]

---

122. Ibid., 114–15. Cf. Teeple, *The Mosaic Eschatological Prophet*, 86–87; Bruce, *Acts*, 86–87, 131, 142.
123. Pao, *Acts and the Isaianic New Exodus*, 5.
124. Ibid., 37.
125. Ibid., 250.

Pauline Epistles[126]

The Exodus background can be observed in Paul's Christology. First, Paul described Jesus as the "paschal lamb" (τὸ πασχα, 1 Cor 5:7; cf. Exod 12).

> Christ, our paschal lamb, has been sacrificed. Let us, therefore, celebrate the festival, not with the old leaven, the leaven of malice and evil, but with the unleavened bread of sincerity and truth. (1 Cor 5:7–8)

By mentioning "unleavened bread" (ἀζύμοις, 1 Cor 5:8; cf. Exod 12; Deut 16) in the context, Paul makes the Exodus background of the passage clearer.[127] To be more exact, this passage depicts the Passover festival, and "Christians are a new Israel redeemed through a new Passover Lamb," that is, Jesus Christ.[128] To evaluate the Exodus background of this passage, "this passage must be linked with [Paul's] treatment of the Lord's Supper in 1 Corinthians 11:23ff., where the words 'Do this in remembrance of me' [τοῦτο ποιεῖτε... εἰς τὴν ἐμὴν ἀνάμνησιν] occur, emphasizing strongly the Exodus associations of the Holy Communion" (cf. Exod 12:14).[129]

Second, Paul described Jesus as "the spiritual rock" (πνευματικῆς πέτρας) from which the spiritual drink comes out (1 Cor 10:4; cf. Exod 17; Num 20).[130] Around the verse, Paul mentioned the Israelites' baptism

---

126. The following works are used for this section: Sahlin, "The New Exodus of Salvation according to St. Paul," 81–95; Casey, "Exodus Typology," 117–24; Nixon, *The Exodus in the New Testament*, 23–24; Davies, *Paul and Rabbinic Judaism*, 104–10.

127. Gordon D. Fee argued, "The mention of 'leaven' in v. 6 naturally suggests imagery from Paul's own history as a law-abiding Jew, namely the two religious rituals of Passover. He begins with a direct allusion to the ceremonial removal of all leaven from their homes (Exod 12:15), which in turn prompts an allusion to the most important event of all, the sacrifice of the Paschal Lamb (Exod 12:6)." Fee, *The First Epistle to the Corinthians*, 216. See also Thiselton, *The First Epistle to the Corinthians*, 404–5.

128. Nixon, *The Exodus in the New Testament*, 23. Fee also argued, "As in John's Gospel, this is a direct application of the death of Christ to the slaughter of the Paschal lambs on the first day of Unleavened Bread. The slaying of the lamb is what led to the Jew's being 'unleavened.' So too with us, Paul says." Fee, *The First Epistle to the Corinthians*, 218.

129. Nixon, *The Exodus in the New Testament*, 23. See also Alan Richardson's argument: "Unquestionably the primary meaning of εἰς τὴν ἐμὴν ἀνάμνησιν is to be found in the conception of the Eucharist as the Christian passover-feast. The passover of the Jews was above all things a memorial of the deliverance of Israel from Egypt at the exodus: 'This day shall be unto you for a memorial (LXX, μνημόσυνον) and ye shall keep it a feast (ἑορτή) to Yahweh; throughout your generations ye shall keep it a feast by an ordinance for ever' (Ex. 12:14)." Richardson, *An Introduction to the Theology of the New Testament*, 370.

130. Fee argued, "That Paul now identifies the rock with Christ thus serves his double

into Moses, which was received by the Israelites by being under the cloud and by passing through the sea (πάντες εἰς τὸν Μωϋσῆν ἐβαπτίσθησαν ἐν τῇ νεφέλῃ καὶ ἐν τῇ θαλάσσῃ; 1 Cor 10:1–2; cf. Exod 13–14). He also mentions the spiritual food (πνευματικὸν βρῶμα; 1 Cor 10:3; cf. quail and manna, Exod 16) and the wilderness as the place where most of the Israelites were struck down (κατεστρώθησαν γὰρ ἐν τῇ ἐρήμῳ; 1 Cor 10:5; cf. Num 32:13). Thus, not only the expression of Jesus as "the spiritual rock" in 1 Cor 10:4 but also the whole context of the passage 1 Cor 10:1–11 supports an Exodus background.[131]

Through the two kinds of Christology discussed above, Paul showed his understanding of "the status of Christians as the result of a new Exodus, the typological counterpart of the Exodus out of Egypt,"[132] and argued that the starting-point of the new Exodus (i.e., "the counterpart of the actual departure from Egypt"[133]) is Christ's death and resurrection. This point is also obvious in Rom 6. Knox argued, "In Rom 6 it is stated in terms of the Christian revision of the *kerygma* of Judaism, in which the death and resurrection of Jesus replace the Exodus from Egypt. The proselyte through circumcision and the proselyte's bath was enabled to come out of Egypt and pass through the Red Sea into the promised land of Israel."[134]

---

aim: (1) to emphasize the typological character of Israel's experience, that it was by Christ himself that they were being nourished in the wilderness; and (2) thereby also to stress the continuity between Israel and the Corinthians, who by their idolatry are in the process of repeating Israel's madness and thus are in danger of experiencing their judgment." Fee, *The First Epistle to the Corinthians*, 449.

131. Hans Conzelmann argued, "Verses 1–10 [of 1 Cor 10] constitute a self-contained, scribal discourse on passages from the biblical exodus narratives: the cloud (Ex 13:21), the sea (Ex 14:21f), the manna (Ex 16:4, 14–18), the spring (Ex 17:6; Num 20:7–13), the apostasy (Ex 32:6)." Conzelmann, *1 Corinthians*, 165. Cf. Thiselton, *The First Epistle to the Corinthians*, 722–27. Thiselton concluded his argument on the allusions to the Exodus narrative in 1 Cor 10 by borrowing Hanson's argument: "In 1 Cor 10 we have an instance of the real presence of Christ in Israel's history of old" (726). Here, "Israel's history of old" means the Exodus event, especially the wilderness journey. Cf. Hanson, *Studies in Paul's Technique and Theology*, 100.

132. Sahlin, "The New Exodus of Salvation according to St. Paul," 87.

133. Ibid.

134. Knox, *St. Paul and the Church of the Gentiles*, 97. Sahlin extracted an idea of St Paul's understanding of Christian baptism by examining 1 Cor 10:1–2 and Rom 6:3–4 and argued, "Jesus Christ is the New Moses, effecting the New Exodus of Salvation. The actual starting-point of this work of salvation by Christ is in His death and resurrection. Thus the death and resurrection of Christ have the same meaning for the Church as the crossing of the Red Sea has for Israel. As through circumcision and proselyte baptism the Jewish proselyte is incorporated into the people of God and becomes a partaker in God's

In 2 Cor 3, Paul compared the old covenant with the new and argued that the new covenant is superior to the old because the new is not of the letter but of the Spirit and not of death but of life (v. 6). The thought that the new covenant is "inward, personally applied by the Spirit and brings justification and life"[135] recalls Jer 31:31–33. The old covenant is described as "chiseled in letters on stone tablets" (ἐν γράμμασιν ἐντετυπωμένη λίθοις), and its temporary glory is depicted as "the glory of Moses' face" (τὴν δόξαν τοῦ προσώπου αὐτοῦ [Μωϋσέως]; 2 Cor 3:7). This illustration of the old covenant evokes the Sinai covenant (Exod 34). In the later verses, Paul continually mentions the veil that covered Moses' face (2 Cor 3:13–16), and this mention of the veil confirms that the OT background of this passage is Exod 34.[136] Paul's contrast between the law and Spirit—consequently, between death and life—permeates his epistles (e.g., Rom 7:6–10; 1 Cor 1:18; 15:43). Furthermore, the Exodus background can be observed in Paul's contrast between the tabernacle (or temple) of the old covenant and Christ or the saints in whom God dwelled (for Christ, Col 1:19; for the saints, 1 Cor 3:16), and in Paul's contrast between the sacrifices of the old covenant and the sacrifice of Christ by which God and human beings are reconciled (Rom 3:25; 2 Cor 5:18–21; Col 1:19–20).

According to the previous examinations, the Exodus background in Pauline Epistles is observed generally in the letters to the Corinthians and Romans. However, Paul's Christology on "paschal lamb," his contrast between the old covenant (that is, the Sinai covenant) and the new covenant, and his thoughts of salvation (especially about baptism and the Eucharist)

---

act of salvation as recorded in the Exodus narrative, and primarily in the crossing of the Red Sea, so the Christian proselyte, receiving Christian baptism, becomes a partaker of Christ's act of salvation, His death and resurrection. As the Jewish proselyte becomes by baptism one with the Exodus generation, so the Christian through baptism becomes one with Christ in His death and resurrection. This is what St Paul says in Romans vi. 3–5." Sahlin, "The New Exodus of Salvation according to St. Paul," 91.

135. Nixon, *The Exodus in the New Testament*, 24.

136. According to Ralph P. Martin, "Taking a cue from Göttsberger, [Windrich] proposed that 3:7–18 is a Christian midrash on Exod 34:29–35, added to show the superior glory of the new administration in Christ to the old." Martin, *2 Corinthians*, 200. Paul Barnett also declared 2 Cor 3:7–18 as a "Christian midrash—an analogical commentary in the rabbinic style—based on Exod 34:29–35." Barnett, *The Second Epistle to the Corinthians*, 178–79. Although William J. Dumbrell disagreed with the midrashic character of 2 Cor 3:7–18, he agreed with the Exodus background (especially Exod 34:29–35) in the passage. Dumbrell, "Paul's Use of Exod 34 in 2 Corinthians 3," 179–94.

that is based on the Exodus typology[137] are not limited in the three letters but pervade all his letters.

Hebrews

The Exodus background is observed in the Christology of the Epistle to the Hebrews.[138] The writer compares Christ with others and emphasizes Christ's superiority to others (e.g., angels in chs. 1–2, Moses in ch. 3, Aaron and Melchizedek in ch. 5). Among them, the Exodus background underlies the comparison between Jesus and Moses (or Aaron). Although the comparison between Jesus and Aaron emphasizes Jesus' position as high priest (which is the most highly developed theme in Hebrews), the focus will be on the comparison between Jesus and Moses in this section.[139]

Hebrews 3:1 depicts the double office of Jesus, "the apostle and high priest" (τὸν ἀπόστολον καὶ ἀρχιερέα).[140] The unique Christology, "the apostle," derives from the figure of Moses in Exod 3:10 LXX (καὶ νῦν δεῦρο ἀποστείλω σε πρὸς Φαραω βασιλέα Αἰγύπτου). "Although Moses is never designated ὁ ἀπόστολος, the conception of him as one called, appointed,

---

137. After examining the Exodus background in Paul's thoughts of salvation (especially baptism and the Eucharist), Sahlin concluded, "The New Exodus of salvation determines the thought of St Paul as well as the entire Primitive Church. The New Testament can, as a whole, be regarded as a detailed fulfillment of the types of the Old Testament Exodus, God's great act of salvation for the people of His election. Baptism and the Eucharist as they appear in St Paul must be related to this typological background if we are to understand their full meaning." Sahlin, "The New Exodus of Salvation according to St. Paul," 94.

138. The Exodus background can be found even in the ecclesiology of the letter. Casey argued, "The basis of the ecclesiology of Hebrews is the pilgrimage motif. Several emphases and themes contribute to the presentation of the motif, but the fundamental analogy for the portrayal is the typological relationship between the wilderness generation of Israel and the experience of the Church. Two passages [Heb 3:7—4:11; 11:23-29] are important in the structuring of the motif of journey." Casey, "Exodus Typology," 129 (cf. 130); cf. Johnsson, "The Pilgrimage Motif in the Book of Hebrews," 239-51.

139. "The figure of Moses as the mediator of Israel's covenant and cult is of critical importance in Hebrews. The writer contrasts the Mosaic era, the Mosaic covenant, and the Mosaic cult with the new situation introduced by God through Jesus." Lane, *Hebrews 1–8*, 73.

140. Concerning the double office of Jesus in Heb 3:1, Casey argued, "The idea of an apostle christology has Mosaic origins, while the picture of Jesus' priesthood begins in Hebrews with an Aaronic basis but is developed fully only on the pattern of Melchizedek (5:1ff.)." Casey, "Exodus Typology," 126.

and sent by God stands behind the term."[141] That the writer's Christology is derived from the figure of Moses is supported also by the content of Heb 3:2–6 (the comparison between Jesus and Moses) and the content of Heb 3:7–19 (cf. expressions about the Israelites in the desert for forty years). In Heb 3:2–6, the comparison between Jesus and Moses emphasizes Jesus' superiority to Moses but also extracts the common point between Moses and Jesus, that is, their faithfulness to their calling. The faith of Moses appears again in the list of instances of faith in Heb 11.

In Heb 12:18–24, called "a magnificent piece of imaginative writing,"[142] the writer of the epistle "juxtaposes the two covenants (Sinai and Zion) and the two mediators [Moses and Jesus]."[143] Compared with the heavenly city of Zion, the Sinai mountain is touchable (ψηλαφωμένῳ; Heb 12:18). However, Sinai is described as unapproachable (Heb 12:18–21);[144] but the heavenly city of Zion is depicted as accessible (Heb 12:22–24).

> Heb 12:18 For you have not come to a touchable mountain [Sinai]
>
> Heb 12:22 On the contrary you have come to Mt. Zion[145]

The Jesus-Moses comparison appears again in Heb 13:20–21. In this passage, Jesus is called "the great shepherd of the sheep" (τὸν ποιμένα τῶν προβάτων τὸν μέγαν, Heb 13:20). Although the name of Moses is not mentioned in this passage, the background of the passage is considered to be Isa 63:11 (LXX), where Moses is portrayed as "the shepherd of the sheep" (τὸν ποιμένα τῶν προβάτων).[146] As Westcott argued, "The work of Moses was a shadow of that of Christ: the leading up of him with his people out of the sea was a shadow of Christ's ascent from the grave: the covenant with Israel a shadow of the eternal covenant."[147] Through these comparisons in Heb 12 and 13, the author consequently emphasizes the superiority of "Jesus, the

---

141. Lane, *Hebrews 1–8*, 76; cf. Jones, "The Figure of Moses," 98.

142. McKelvey, *The New Temple*, 152.

143. Jones, "The Figure of Moses," 101.

144. The command "If even an animal touches the mountain [Sinai], it shall be stoned to death" (Heb 12:20; cf. Exod 19:12–13) was given before the Sinai covenant. In addition, the mediator Moses also felt fear, saying, "I tremble with fear" (Heb 12:21; cf. Deut 9:19).

145. Cf. Jones's translation. Jones, "The Figure of Moses," 100.

146. Cf. Westcott, *Hebrews*, 448; Montefiore, *Hebrews*, 251; Bruce, *Hebrews*, 388.

147. Westcott, *Hebrews*, 448.

Purpose of the Exodus Theme in Revelation 15

mediator of a new covenant" (διαθήκης νέας μεσίτῃ Ἰησοῦ, Heb 12:24) or of "the eternal covenant" (διαθήκης αἰωνίου, Heb 13:20) established by his sacrifice.

Four passages (Heb 3:1–6; 11:23–29; 12:18–24; 13:20–21) have been examined as passages that show the Exodus background. In these passages, Jesus is compared with Moses, and Jesus' superiority to Moses (or the new covenant over the old covenant) is emphasized. As Nixon argued,

> The author sees the situation of his readers as being parallel to that of the people of the first Exodus. The cross and resurrection are the second Exodus; the forty years are running out as AD 70 approaches; the people of Israel are to bring upon themselves the curses threatened in an Exodus context in the book of Deuteronomy and they will be dispossessed of their inheritance as the heathen were; the new people of God will then be led by the new Joshua, Jesus, into their true spiritual inheritance.[148]

Based on this research into the background of use of Exodus imagery, this research will be the basis of development of an explanation for John's use of an Exodus theme in Rev 15. Briefly, the answers are two. First, Exodus is one of three eschatological models frequently used by the OT, intertestamental literature, and the NT. Second, Exodus is a paradigm for salvation that also frequently is used by the OT, intertestamental literature, and the NT. These two reasons will be dealt with in the following two sections as the conclusion of this chapter.

THE EXODUS AS AN ESCHATOLOGICAL MODEL

In the OT, intertestamental literature, and the NT, the eschaton was described chiefly on the basis of three important events in the history of Israel that shaped Israel's identity: Eden, the Exodus, and the Davidic kingdom. In other words, the final age was described as "Paradise returned, the Garden of Eden restored" (Isa 4:2; 11:6–9; 55:13; 65:25; Amos 9:13–15; *T. Levi* 18:10–14; *T. Dan.* 5:12; 2 *Bar.* 4; 2 *En.* 8; 2 Esd 7:36–44, 123), "a new Exodus" (Isa 51:9–11; 52:12), and "a renewed Davidic kingdom" (2 Sam 7:13, 16; the Royal Psalms [e.g., 2; 19; 20; 21; 72; 89:19–37; 101; 110; 132:11; 144:1–11]; Isa 9:6–7; 11:1; Jer 23:5–6; 30:8–9; 33:14–22; Amos 9:11;

---

148. Nixon, *The Exodus in the New Testament*, 27.

Zech 12:7–9; *Pss. Sol.* 17:4–10, 21; 2 Esd 12:31–32).[149] Each model has a specific leader: "the last Adam" for the Garden of Eden restored model,[150] "a prophet like Moses" (Deut 18:15, 18) for a new Exodus model, and "the son of David/Davidic king" for a renewed Davidic kingdom model. The characteristics of these three leaders would be molded into one individual who will lead the perfect, eschatological redemption described in the NT, primarily in the book of Revelation. For the authors of the NT, including Revelation, that individual is Jesus Christ.

---

149. Scott, *Jewish Backgrounds of the New Testament*, 288–90.

150. I am not sure whether Paul had the restored Edenic model in mind when he used the expression "the last Adam" in 1 Cor 15:45, "the second man" in 1 Cor 15:47, and "one man" who obeyed God in contrast to one man—Adam—who disobeyed God in Rom 5. However, a leading figure for the Garden of Eden restored model is "the last Adam" in 1 Corinthians and Romans.

Purpose of the Exodus Theme in Revelation 15

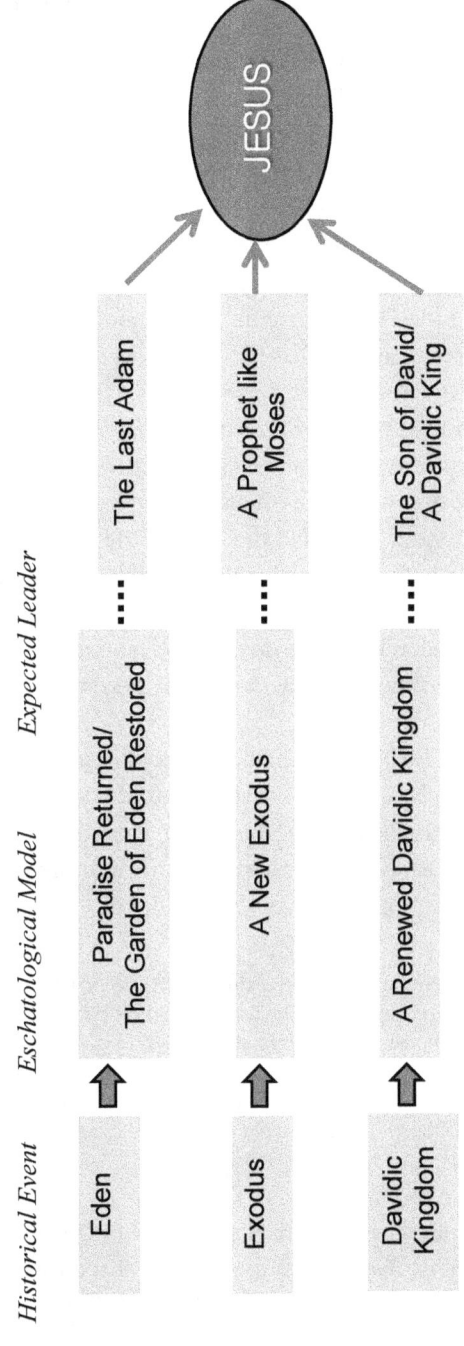

Figure 6. Eschatological Models and the Expected Leaders

THE EXODUS AS A PARADIGM FOR SALVATION

Through the Exodus, God showed his power and love by delivering his people from slavery. Before the Exodus, God told Moses, "I will take you [Israel] as my people, and I will be your God. You shall know that I am the LORD your God, who has freed you from the burdens of the Egyptians" (Exod 6:7). Then, the Exodus was mentioned as an important event in the relationship between God and Israel (e.g., Exod 29:46; Lev 19:36; 22:33; 23:43; 25:38; Num 15:41; Deut 5:15; 13:5; Ps 81:10; Ezek 20:5; Hos 12:9; 13:4).[151] In addition to the Abrahamic and Davidic promises, the Exodus is another basis for the relationship between God and Israel; the basis as to why Israel should obey God and follow his law (e.g., Lev 19:36; Deut 5:15; 13:5; Judg 6:8–10; 1 Kgs 9:6–9; cf. 1 Sam 10:18–19); and the basis as to why Israel should ask God for his continuing protection and blessing (e.g., Ps 81:10).

As Israel's history is filled with oppression from diverse countries, the Exodus is a memorable event and the basis of the Israelites' hope for God's salvation. Therefore, the OT Exodus theme seems to overlap when the OT prophets mentioned Israel's salvation from foreign powers, such as Assyria (e.g., Nahum, Habakkuk) or Babylon (e.g., Jeremiah, Ezekiel, Isaiah).[152] In other words, the event of Exodus seems to "become a paradigm" for the Israelites' salvation.[153]

Especially in the book of Isaiah, the prophet mentions the Exodus as something new (cf. Isa 43:14–21) beyond the old[154] and as relative to Israel's eschatological salvation. This Exodus is not limited to a past event or the repetition of the past event of Exodus, or only a future event that has not

---

151. With God's self-expression (ἐγώ εἰμι κύριος ὁ θεὸς ὑμῶν ὁ ἐξαγαγὼν ὑμᾶς ἐκ γῆς Αἰγύπτου), God's purpose as to why he delivered his people from oppression demonstrates well the relationship between Israel and God (e.g., "I am the LORD your God, who brought you out of the land of Egypt, to give you the land of Canaan, *to be your God*" in Lev 25:38; "I am the LORD your God, who brought you out of the land of Egypt, *to be your God*: I am the LORD your God" in Num 15:41; italics added).

152. Cf. Nah 1:15; 2:10–13; Hab 1:6–12; 2:4–14; Jer 2:1–3; 16:14; 23:7; 31:31–34; 50:1–5; Ezek 34:1–25; Isa 40:1—50:11.

153. This expression is borrowed from Iersel and Weiler, *Exodus*, xv.

154. Isaiah 43:18–19, "Forget the former things; do not dwell on the past. See I am doing a new thing," does not mean the discontinuation between the old and the new. The new Exodus would be relative to the old but, at the same time, much beyond the old one. This passage from Isaiah urges the hearer to look forward and anticipate a new redemptive action by God and not look backward only to dwell on past actions.

Purpose of the Exodus Theme in Revelation 15

started. In the viewpoint of Isaiah, namely his eschatological viewpoint, the new Exodus already has begun and is proceeding now.[155]

Deuteronomy 18 provides background for the expectation of "a prophet like Moses" who will lead the new Exodus: "I [God] will raise up for them a prophet like you [Moses] from among their brothers" (v. 18; cf. v. 15). Some intertestamental sources such as 1 Macc 14:41, *T. Levi* 8:14-16, Philo *Special Laws* 1.11, 4QTest, and 1QS 9:11 show the expectation that "a new Moses" would come as the Messiah.[156] Therefore, when they call the Messiah a new Moses, they expect the Messiah to "lead a new exodus from bondage, reestablish the covenant, bring a better revelation of God (a new law or better interpretation of the law), and, in short, serve as a new national founder."[157]

The NT writers, too, illustrate Jesus' salvation by alluding to the Exodus theme. Through the Exodus theme, Jesus corresponds to Moses (e.g., Matt 2; Exod 1-4), to Israel (e.g., Matt 5-7; Exod 4-34), to manna itself and/or Moses who caused manna to descend (e.g., John 6; Exod 16; cf. Josh 5:10-12; 2 *Bar.* 29:3, 8), to the Passover lamb (John 1:29; 19:33, 36; 1 Pet 1:19; Exod 12:5, 46), and the baptism corresponds to the event of crossing over the Red Sea (1 Cor 10:2; Exod 14).

Through the paradigm of Exodus, the OT prophets expressed their hope of future salvation from a foreign power or the salvation at the eschaton. Therefore, for the NT (and intertestamental literature) writers who refer to the ultimate or eschatological salvation through Jesus Christ, naturally they would use the Exodus theme. The author of the book of Revelation is no exception.

The contemporary expectation of the fulfillment of the promised New Exodus in the prophetic books probably would influence the NT writers to use the Exodus theme.[158] As one of three frequently used escha-

---

155. Cf. Watts, *Isaiah 34-66*, 130. Watts properly pointed out Isaiah's emphasis on the present meaning of Exodus rather than the past or future.

156. The expression of "a new Moses" is borrowed from Aage Bentzen, *King and Messiah* (London: Lutterworth, 1955), 66. For the Mosaic eschatological prophet in Judaism, see Teeple, *The Mosaic Eschatological Prophet*, 29-73. Scott briefly explained the Samaritans' interesting concept on this Messianic model: "They [Samaritans] believe that Moses did not really die but was hidden away until the appointed time. He would then reappear as Messiah." Scott, *Jewish Background of the New Testament*, 318. For Samaritans' concept on the Mosaic eschatological prophet, see also Stevens, "The Literary Background and Theological Significance of ΟΡΓΗ ΘΕΟΥ in the Pauline Epistles," 83-85.

157. Scott, *Jewish Background of the New Testament*, 318.

158. N. T. Wright confidently asserted that "most first-century Jews" thought that they were "still in exile" and "Israel's exile was still in progress." Wright, *Jesus and the*

tological models, the Exodus theme would be a good tool for the author of Revelation, who expressed the eschatological redemption by God, the ultimate victory of God and of his people, and the redeemed people's praise toward God.

Victory of God, xvii; *New Testament and the People of God*, 268–69 (cf. pp. 280–338). Thomas R. Schreiner said the same thing in a somewhat roundabout way: even though not all would admit that they were under exile, certainly "all Jews would admit that the promises of a glorious future were not yet realized." Schreiner, *Paul, Apostle of God's Glory in Christ*, 131. See also Wright's similar explanation: "Although she had come back from Babylon, the glorious message of the prophets remained unfulfilled. . . . Israel has returned to the land, but is still in the 'exile' of slavery, under the oppression of foreign overlords." Wright, *New Testament and the People of God*, 269.

3

Use of the Exodus Theme in Revelation 15

IN THIS CHAPTER, THE researcher will examine briefly the Exodus theme in the book of Revelation, and then will focus on the Exodus theme in Rev 15 (including Rev 16). Through the examinations, the researcher will try to answer the question, "How does the author use the Exodus theme in Rev 15?"

> **"How does the author use the Exodus theme in Rev 15?"**
>
> Examining
>   • The Exodus theme in **the book of Revelation**
>   - The Exodus theme in judgment
>   - The Exodus theme in redemption & inheritance
>   • The Exodus theme in **Revelation 15–16**
>
> ⬇
>
> Answering:
>   John's **interweaving** the Exodus theme with his eschatological vision
>   - In the whole book of Revelation
>   - In the Bowl Judgment vision (Rev 15–16)
>   - In the Song of Moses and the Lamb (15:3–4)
>   - In the dual titles of the song

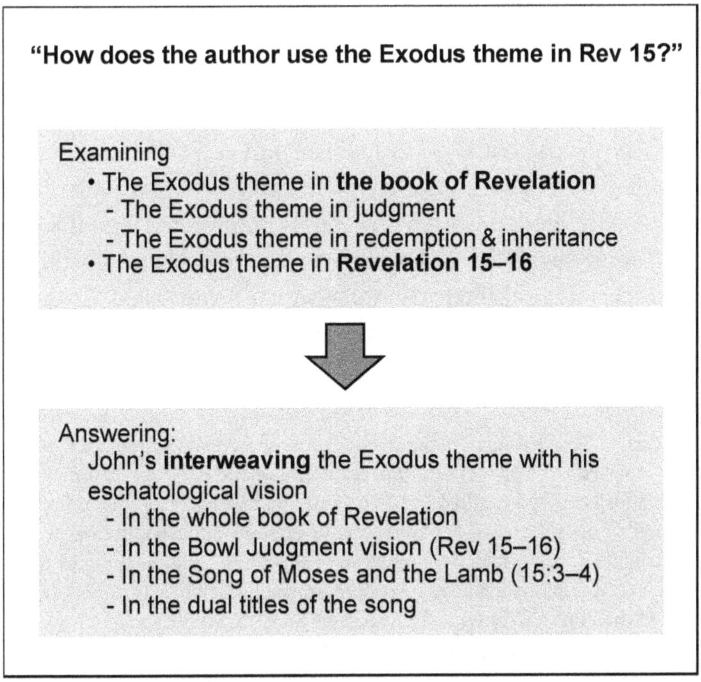

Figure 7. Outline of the Third Chapter

THE EXODUS THEME IN THE BOOK OF REVELATION

Scholars have observed diverse facets of the Exodus theme: the presentation of judgment (to the oppressors of God's people) and the presentation of redemption and eternal inheritance (to the people of God). Likewise, God is described as his people's redeemer, the judge of their oppressors, and the guarantor of their eternal inheritance.[1] This section has two subsections: (1) the Exodus theme in judgment and (2) the Exodus theme in redemption and inheritance.

The Exodus Theme in Judgment

During the Exodus, judgment toward the oppressors was depicted by plagues (Exod 7–12). Three series of seven judgments in the book of Revelation take readers back to ten Exodus plagues because of the similarity to the plagues: for example, hail (Rev 8:7; cf. Exod 9:22–26), sea that becomes blood and in which the creatures die (Rev 8:8–9; 16:3–4; cf. Exod 7:17–19); darkness (Rev 8:12; 9:2; 16:10; cf. Exod 10:21–23); locusts (Rev 9:3–11; cf. Exod 10:12–15); thunder and lightning (Rev 8:5; 10:3; 11:19; 16:18; cf. Exod 9:23); frogs (Rev 16:13; cf. Exod 8:1–15).

Beale argued that the Exodus plagues were "understood as typological of later plagues to come upon subsequent generations of humanity" not only in John's Apocalypse but also "in Judaism and early Christian literature."[2] Aune pointed out, "Though the Egyptian plagues were a recurring theme in early Jewish literature, they are rarely interpreted *eschatologically*."[3] However, Aune suggested an important piece of evidence for the Exodus plagues' eschatological interpretation—which Aune called "an important major exception"[4]—namely *Apoc. Ab.* 30.14–16.

---

1. Cf. Casey, "The Exodus Theme in the Book of Revelation," 34–43. Casey argued that John departed from the Jewish understanding of the Exodus when he proclaimed that the Exodus is a hope fulfilled in Christ and a paradigm of God's continuing activity on behalf of his people. In the midst of Revelation's apocalyptic images of cosmic evil and struggle, John's conviction concerning the continuing meaning of the Exodus is observed: God remains his people's redeemer, the judge of their oppressors, and the guarantor of their eternal inheritance. See also Casey, "Exodus Typology," 135–214.
2. Beale, *John's Use*, 197–98.
3. Aune, *Revelation 6–16*, 499; italics are Aune's.
4. Ibid.

Before the age of justice starts to grow, my judgment will come upon the heathen who have acted wickedly through the people of your seed who have been set apart from me. In those days I will bring upon all earthly creation ten plagues through evil and disease and the groaning of the bitterness of souls. Such will I bring upon the generations of those who are on it, out of anger and corruption of their creation with which they provoke me.[5]

Whether Beale and Aune agreed or disagreed that the first-century Jews viewed the Exodus plagues as eschatological, Beale and Aune agreed that John used the Exodus plagues tradition in his Apocalypse to express the eschatological plagues.

Furthermore, the seven plagues in Ps 78:43–52,[6] Ps 105:27–36,[7] and Amos 4:6–13,[8] which are helpful to understand the Jews' understanding of the Exodus plague tradition, are extremely noteworthy.[9] In Exodus, Psalms, and Revelation, the plagues mean divine judgments against the oppressors of Israel. Through divine judgments against the oppressors of Israel, Israel is delivered. Therefore, the plagues can be a kind of method for the deliverance of God's people.[10] In addition, the plagues express the wrath of God (cf. Rev 6:16–17).

Three series of judgments are in the book of Revelation: the seals, trumpets, and bowls. Among these three, two series of judgments (trumpets and bowls) will be dealt with in the following subsections because the Exodus theme is not prevalent in the seal series of judgments.

5. The translation is from Charlesworth, *Apocalyptic Literature and Testaments*, 704.

6. Rivers turned to blood (v. 44), flies (v. 45), frogs (v. 45), caterpillars and locusts (v. 46), hail and frost destroying vegetation (v. 47), hail and lightning destroy livestock (v. 48), death of firstborn (vv. 49–51).

7. Darkness (v. 28), waters become blood and fish die (v. 29), frogs (v. 30), flies and gnats (v. 31), hail and lightning destroy vines and trees (vv. 32–33), locusts destroy crops (vv. 34–35), destruction of firstborn (v. 36).

8. Famine (v. 6), drought (vv. 7–8), blight and mildew destroy crops (v. 9), locusts devour trees (v. 9), pestilence (v. 10), conquest in war (v. 10), some overthrown as were Sodom and Gomorrah (v. 11).

9. Cf. Aune, *Revelation 6–16*, 502–3.

10. In Amos, the plagues were given to the Israelites in order to make them return to God (cf. Amos 4:6, 8, 9, 10, 11). In that the object of the judgment and the object of the redemption are the same, the case of Amos is different from the cases of Exodus, Psalms, and Revelation. However, in that the plagues were given by God for his people's redemption, the case of Amos is the same as the cases of Exodus, Psalms, and Revelation. Therefore, in all cases mentioning plagues in Exodus, Psalms, Amos, and Revelation, the plagues can be said to function as a method for the deliverance of God's people.

The Trumpet Judgments

The opening of the seventh seal is immediately followed by the seven trumpet judgments.[11] As the seven seal judgments could be divided into two sets (the first four related judgments and the last three related judgments), the seven trumpet judgments also can be divided into two sets (the first four and the last three). The distinction between these two sets of trumpet judgments is caused by the difference in the objects for the judgments: "The first four trumpets affect primarily the elements (land, sea, rivers, sky) but with devastating effects on men also. The last three are directed against 'those who dwell on the earth,' i.e., the rebellious of mankind (cf. 9:4)."[12] The Exodus background usually is observed in the first four (or five) trumpet judgments.[13]

Before examining each trumpet judgment in the book of Revelation, the trumpet symbolism in the biblical and Jewish literature needs to be examined. In the OT and early Jewish literature, the trumpet was used for the following purposes:[14] (1) as a means of warning,[15] (2) to signal an attack by military forces,[16] (3) to give an alarm within a city to indicate an

---

11. As Stevens argued, "Seal 7 is not intended to be a climax and has some other literary function than portraying a judgment. This unusual nature of the content of Seal 7 gives support to the idea that the seventh in each series of Seals and Trumpets is not a judgment but rather a literary connecting device meant to 'telescope' out to the next heptad of judgments." Stevens, *Revelation*, 408.

12. Beasley-Murray, *Revelation*, 154–55. Stevens simplified this understanding with two sentences: "The first four strike the earth. The last three strike humans directly." Stevens, *Revelation*, 411.

13. Scholars' understanding about the background of the fifth trumpet judgment (locust judgment) is diverse. However, scholars generally agreed upon the Exodus background of the first four trumpet, even though the degree of their agreement with the Exodus background may be diverse. Beale argued the Exodus background for the first five trumpet judgments: "The first five trumpets are patterned after five of the plagues inflicted upon the Egyptians immediately preceding Israel's Exodus: first trumpet (Exod. 9.22–25 [seventh Exodus plague]); second and third trumpets (Exod. 7.20–25 [first Exodus plague]); fourth trumpet (Exod. 10.21–23 [ninth Exodus plague]); and fifth trumpet (Exod. 10.12–15 [eighth Exodus plague])." Beale, *John's Use*, 205; cf. 199.

14. The following content (ten purposes of the trumpet usage) is borrowed from Aune, *Revelation 6–16*, 510; cf. Beasley-Murry, *Revelation*, 153–54; Beale, *Revelation*, 468–72.

15. Num 10:1–8; Ezek 33:3–6; Hos 8:1; Joel 2:1.

16. Num 31:6; Judg 7:8–22; 2 Chr 13:12; Zeph 1:16; 2 Macc 13:25; *Pss. Sol.* 8:1; *Sib. Or.* 8.253.

imminent attack,[17] (4) to signal a retreat,[18] (5) as a cry to God for help,[19] (6) to indicate that a victory had been won,[20] (7) to signal the announcement of good news,[21] (8) as an accompaniment to religious ritual,[22] (9) as part of a theophany scene,[23] and (10) in various eschatological contexts.[24] Among these ten purposes, Casey focused on the first and the tenth for understanding the trumpet judgments in Revelation, which were used especially by the OT prophets.

> Israel's prophets pictured the trumpet's blast as the signal of God's impending judgment (Ezek 33:1; Zeph 1:15; Joel 2:1ff) and the dawning of the new age of salvation (Zech 9:14; cf. 1 Thess 4:16). John's use of the trumpet symbolism has been influenced by these prophetic conceptions, especially in his emphasis on the intention of the judgments linked with the trumpets' sounding to bring about mankind's repentance rather than destruction.[25]

These two purposes of the trumpet are observed in the NT "to designate the point at which final events begin to unfold, particularly the Parousia" (e.g., Matt 24:31; 1 Thess 4:16; 1 Cor 15:52).[26] In Revelation, however, "the trumpet is *never* used to signal the return of Christ.... The seventh trumpet in 11:15–18 does... mark the arrival of the end."[27] In Revelation, the trumpet is used as a "metaphor for a loud voice" (1:10; 4:1) and as a "structuring device for the plagues unleashed upon the sounding of each of the seven trumpets in 8:2—9:21 and 11:15–18."[28]

When one compares the first trumpet judgment (Rev 8:7) with the seventh plague of Egypt (Exod 9:23–25), one may observe the common

---

17. Jer 20:16; Hos 5:8; Amos 3:6; Zeph 1:16.
18. 2 Sam 2:28; 18:16; 20:22; 2 Kgs 9:13.
19. Num 10:9; 1 Macc 4:40.
20. Ps 47:5.
21. *Pss. Sol.* 11:1.
22. Lev 25:9; Joel 2:15; 1 Macc 3:54.
23. Exod 19:13, 16, 19; 20:18. Cf. Casey, "Exodus Typology," 160.
24. 1QM 2:16—3:11; 7:12—9:3.
25. Casey, "Exodus Typology," 160. Casey mentioned Ezek 33:1, but vv. 1–6 would be more correct. The trumpet or trumpet sound is mentioned four times, once in each verse of Ezek 33:3–6.
26. Aune, *Revelation 6–16*, 510.
27. Ibid. Italics are Aune's.
28. Ibid.

features of these. First, two elements of disaster, hail and fire (χάλαζα καὶ πῦρ), are commonly observed in the two passages. Second, as the result of hail and fire, the objects of destruction are observed: the land or the earth (γῆ), vegetation or green grass (βοτάνη; χόρτος χλωρὸς), and trees (ξύλα; δένδρον). One also may observe different features of the passages. First, in the passage of Revelation, one element is added to hail and fire, that is, blood. This addition has been explained by scholars as the influence of Joel 2:30 and *Sib. Or.* 5:377–8 (cf. Acts 2:19).[29] Second, although "all" the land and "all" the trees are struck by hail and fire in Exod 9, "a third" of the earth and "a third" of trees are burned up in Rev 8. "The limitation of the tribulation to one-third of the land is above all due to the influence of Ezek. 5:2, 12 (cf. Zech. 13:8–9)."[30] These changes, namely the addition (blood) and the limitation (one-third), mark "the modification of the Egyptian plague tradition by an already established eschatological combination."[31]

Exod 9:23–25	Rev 8:7
And the LORD gave . . . <u>hail, and fire</u> ran upon the land. And the LORD rained <u>hail</u> upon all the land. . . . And there was <u>hail</u> and <u>flaming fire mingled with the hail</u>. . . . And the <u>hail</u> struck in **all the land**. . . . And the <u>hail</u> struck **all the vegetation** in the field, and the <u>hail</u> shattered **all the trees** in the field.	The first angle blew his trumpet, and there came <u>hail and fire</u>, mixed with <u>blood</u>, and they were hurled to the earth; and **a third of the earth** was burned up, and **a third of the trees** were burned up, and **all green grass** was burned up.
καὶ κύριος ἔδωκεν . . . <u>χάλαζαν</u> καὶ διέτρεχεν τὸ <u>πῦρ</u> ἐπὶ τῆς γῆς καὶ ἔβρεξεν κύριος χάλαζαν ἐπὶ πᾶσαν γῆν . . . ἦν δὲ ἡ <u>χάλαζα</u> καὶ <u>τὸ πῦρ φλογίζον ἐν τῇ χαλάζῃ</u> . . . ἐπάταξεν δὲ ἡ <u>χάλαζα</u> ἐν **πάσῃ γῇ** . . . καὶ **πᾶσαν βοτάνην** τὴν ἐν τῷ πεδίῳ ἐπάταξεν ἡ <u>χάλαζα</u> καὶ **πάντα τὰ ξύλα** τὰ ἐν τοῖς πεδίοις συνέτριψεν ἡ <u>χάλαζα</u> (LXX)	Καὶ ὁ πρῶτος ἐσάλπισεν· καὶ ἐγένετο <u>χάλαζα καὶ πῦρ</u> μεμιγμένα ἐν <u>αἵματι</u> καὶ ἐβλήθη εἰς τὴν γῆν, καὶ **τὸ τρίτον τῆς γῆς** κατεκάη καὶ **τὸ τρίτον τῶν δένδρων** κατεκάη καὶ **πᾶς χόρτος χλωρὸς** κατεκάη.

Table 9. Exodus 9:23–25 and Revelation 8:7

When the second angel blows the trumpet, "something like a great mountain, burning with fire" (ὡς ὄρος μέγα πυρὶ καιόμενον) is thrown

---

29. Cf. Charles, *Revelation*, 1:233; Aune, *Revelation 6–16*, 519; Mounce, *Revelation*, 178. Joel 2:30 and *Sib. Or.* 5:377 depict the combination of fire and blood.

30. Beale and McDonough, "Revelation," 1112; cf. Charles, *Revelation*, 1:233.

31. Casey, "Exodus Typology," 161. In Table 9, Exod 9:23–25 (LXX) is quoted from Beale and McDonough, "Revelation," 1112.

into the sea (Rev 8:8). The likeness of a mountain can be a metaphor of a kingdom such as Babylon. This understanding is supported by Rev 18:21 and Jer 51:63–64 (cf. 1 *En.* 18:13; 21:3; *Sib. Or.* 5:512–531).[32] Concerning the burning mass, Beckwith suggested the background of Enoch 18:13 (cf. 21:3) and *Sib. Or.* 5:158.[33] As the result of casting the likeness of a mountain, a third of the sea turns into blood, a third of the living creatures in the sea die, and a third of the ships are destroyed (Rev 8:8b–9). These phenomena recall the first Egyptian plague in Exod 7:20–21, where Moses turned the Nile into blood and the fish in the river died. Therefore, like the first trumpet judgment, an Egyptian plague is a basic component of the second trumpet judgment, and other elements are added.

When the third angel sounds the trumpet, a great star blazing like a torch (ἀστὴρ μέγας καιόμενος ὡς λαμπὰς) falls from heaven on a third of the rivers and on the springs of water (Rev 8:10). In consequence, a third of the waters turn bitter, and many people die from the bitter waters. Although some details are different, in that people could not drink the water that was changed as a result of plague, this scene recalls the first Egyptian plague (Exod 7:14–25).[34] The star, named Wormwood (Ἄψινθος), made the water taste as bitter as wormwood (Rev 8:11). This name evokes Jer 9:15 and 23:15 and "the [name's] familiar use as a symbol of divine punishment."[35] Bitter water also recalls Exod 15:23, where Moses made the bitter waters of Marah drinkable, although the change of water is reversed.

The fourth trumpet judgment (Rev 8:12) recalls the ninth Egyptian plague of darkness. According to Exod 10:21–23, because of dense darkness in all the land of Egypt for three days, people could not see one another and could not move from where they were. Unlike the total darkness of Egypt, the fourth trumpet judgment limits the effect of the plague to one third.[36] Concerning this modification, Beasley-Murray argued as follows: "John gives [the Egyptian plague of darkness] some characteristic modifications, partly in accordance with apocalyptic style and partly to keep to the principle that in the will of God these plagues have a limited

---

32. Beale and McDonough, "Revelation," 1113.

33. Beckwith, *Apocalypse*, 557; cf. Beasley-Murray, *Revelation*, 157–58; Beale, *Revelation*, 476.

34. Beckwith, *Apocalypse*, 557; Beasley-Murray, *Revelation*, 158.

35. Beckwith, *Apocalypse*, 557; cf. Beale and McDonough, "Revelation," 1113.

36. "The fourth angel blew his trumpet, and *a third of the sun* was struck, and *a third of the moon*, and *a third of the stars*, so that *a third of their light* was darkened; *a third of the day* was kept from shining, and likewise the night" (Rev 8:12, italics added).

effect on the world."[37] The divine purpose of limitation to one third in the trumpet plagues is understood as "repentance" or "warning" rather than destruction (cf. Rev 9:20–21) because the trumpet judgments are not the final judgments;[38] but in the last series of judgments (i.e., seven bowls), the plagues are applied universally. Like the prior three judgments that show the basic component in the Exodus plagues as well as the added elements, the fourth trumpet judgment also does so. The added element of the fourth trumpet judgment is the OT tradition that associates darkness with judgment (e.g., Isa 13:10; Joel 2:2, 31; Amos 5:18; 8:9).[39]

This research has addressed the added elements of the first four trumpet judgments only in the OT and Jewish literature. As scholars argued, however, "Regular and unusual events in nature (dust storms, a prolonged sirocco, and volcanic eruption) and their consequences (drought, famine, plagues, and raining fire)" also need to be considered as the primary background of the first four trumpet judgments.[40] Especially, the image of volcanic eruption needs to be considered as the primary background of the first four trumpet judgments.

> The trumpet plagues are based loosely on the Exodus plagues, which allude to the preeminent Old Testament paradigm of God's redemptive action on behalf of his people.... The disasters of the first four trumpets—hail and fire mixed with blood, a huge mountain all ablaze thrown into the sea, natural waters poisoned by gases, and the sun, moon, and stars darkened—are all characteristics of a massive volcanic eruption, as in the AD 79 eruption of Vesuvius that buried for nearly two millennia the cities of Pompeii and Herculaneum on the Gulf of Naples.... Thus, while John is building on the imagery of the Exodus plagues, he also is innovating his language to correspond to natural disasters experienced in his own day. As a result, the Exodus allusions are somewhat loose.[41]

---

37. Beasley-Murray, *Revelation*, 158.

38. See Mounce's argument: "The trumpet judgements are not final. They affect a significant proportion but not all of the earth (one-third occurs twelve times in vv. 7–12). Their purpose is not so much retribution as it is to lead people to repentance. Like the watchman and his trumpet in Ezekiel 33, they warn the people of impending danger." Mounce, *Revelation*, 176–77.

39. Cf. Beckwith, *Apocalypse*, 558; Beale and McDonough, "Revelation," 1113; Mounce, *Revelation*, 181–82.

40. Casey, "Exodus Typology," 158; cf. Court, *Myth and History in the Book of Revelation*, 41–45.

41. Stevens, *Revelation*, 410. For volcanic eruption as the background of the first four

In sum, each episode of the first four trumpet judgments takes Exodus plagues as its basic component and modifies the Exodus tradition, sometimes adding other elements. The author's use of an Exodus theme is "conscious and deliberate, and in the case of the first four trumpet judgments it is spelled out in detail."[42]

The first group of four trumpet judgments more clearly shows the Exodus theme than the second group of three trumpet judgments does.[43] In the fifth trumpet judgment, the shaft of the pit is opened, from the shaft smoke rises, and the sun and air are darkened with smoke from which "locusts" emerge to torment people without the seal of God (Rev 9:1–11). The plague of darkness recalls the ninth Egyptian plague (Exod 10:21–29). The main character of the fifth trumpet judgment (locusts) recalls the eighth Egyptian plague (Exod 10:1–20). However, some scholars suggested Joel 1–2 as the more accurate OT background: "The fifth-trumpet episode clearly offers a parallel to the Egyptian plague of locusts (Exod 10:1–20), but its elaboration owes more to Joel's description of a locust-judgment which heralds the day of the Lord than it does to Exodus 10."[44] Although Beale did not argue for a relationship between the sixth trumpet judgment (Rev 9:13–21) and Egyptian plagues,[45] Beasley-Murray suggested the relation between the sixth trumpet judgment and the tenth Egyptian plague (cf. Rev 9:18, "A third of humankind was killed").[46] However, he also pointed out, "There is no noticeable dependence on the exodus-narrative in John's account" of the sixth trumpet judgment.[47] The seventh trumpet judgment (Rev 11:15–19) recalls the Exodus, in particular, the seventh Egyptian plague (Exod 9:13–35) and Sinai theophany (Exod 19:16–19).[48]

---

trumpet judgments, see also Charles, *Revelation*, 1:233; Beckwith, *Apocalypse*, 557; Aune, *Revelation 6–16*, 519.

42. Beasley-Murray, *Revelation*, 155.

43. Cf. Casey argued, "Caution must be observed . . . to avoid overestimating the influence of the Exodus tradition in the production of the final presentation of the trumpet judgments. John's pictures in these passages are the product of several sources." Casey, "Exodus Typology," 156.

44. Beasley-Murray, *Revelation*, 159; cf. Beale and McDonough, "Revelation," 1114; Mounce, *Revelation*, 186–89. The OT background of the locust as the symbol of destruction is Deut 28:42; 1 Kgs 8:37; Ps 78:46.

45. Beale, *John's Use*, 200.

46. Beasley-Murray, *Revelation*, 159–60.

47. Ibid., 160.

48. Cf. Beale, *John's Use*, 200.

Rev 11 (7th trumpet judgment)	Exod 9 (7th Egyptian plague)	Exod 19 (Sinai theophany)
15 Then the seventh angel blew his trumpet, and there were loud voices in heaven ... 19 Then God's temple in heaven was opened, and the ark of his covenant was seen within his temple; and there were flashes of lightning, rumblings, peals of thunder, an earthquake, and heavy hail.	23 Then Moses stretched out his staff toward heaven, and the LORD sent thunder and hail, and fire (or lightning) came down on the earth. And the LORD rained hail on the land of Egypt.	16 On the morning of the third day there was thunder and lightning, as well as a thick cloud on the mountain, and a blast of a trumpet so loud that all the people who were in the camp trembled. 19 As the blast of the trumpet grew louder and louder, Moses would speak and God would answer him in thunder. 20 When the LORD descended upon Mount Sinai ...

Table 10. Revelation 11:19 Comparing with Exodus 9:23 and 19:16

The results of the seventh trumpet judgment are meteorological phenomena. Especially hail with lightning and thunder recalls the seventh Egyptian plague (Exod 9); lightning and thunder were mentioned also in Sinai theophanic description (Exod 19). In addition, "The ark of [God's] covenant" in Rev 11:19 recalls the Exodus journey in which the ark was made and delivered (from Exod 25 to Joshua). The scenery background of the seventh trumpet judgment ("God's temple in heaven was opened" in Rev 11:19a) is related to the presence of God; and the loud sounds of trumpet and voices from heaven (Rev 11:15) echo Sinai theophany (Exod 19). As other trumpet judgments take the Egyptian plagues as the basic components and added other elements, the seventh trumpet judgment seems to take the seventh Egyptian plague as the basic component and add Sinai theophanic phenomena. However, the Exodus background of the last three trumpet judgments is controversial compared to scholars' consensus regarding the Exodus background of the first four trumpet judgments.

The Bowl Judgments

The bowl judgments show obvious similarities in the objects of the plagues (even in the order) with the trumpet judgments.[49]

49. Table 11 is borrowed from Stevens, *Revelation*, 451, italics added (used by

Use of the Exodus Theme in Revelation 15

Trumpets	Bowls
1. Hail, fire, blood on *earth*	1. Bowl poured on *earth*
2. Blazing mountain into *sea*	2. Bowl poured on seas
3. Star into *rivers, fountains*	3. Bowl poured on rivers, fountains
4. *Sun*, moon, star struck	4. Bowl poured on sun
5. Air *darkened*, torment	5. Kingdom darkened, anguish
6. Angels at the *Euphrates*	6. Bowl poured on Euphrates
7. Voices, lightning, hail, etc.	7. Voices, lightning, hail, etc.

Table 11. Parallel between the Trumpet Judgments and the Bowl Judgments

The differences between the trumpet judgments and the bowl judgments are found in the structure and the content. First, in the structure, the trumpet judgments (like the seal judgments) are broken down into units of four and three, but the bowl judgments are not. Second, in the content, although the first four trumpet judgments are limited to "one third" of the objects in plagues, the bowl judgments are applied generally from the beginning of the judgments; although the first four trumpet judgments are applied only to nature and not directly to human beings, the bowl judgments directly affect human beings from the beginning of the judgments. If the trumpet judgments are tentative chastisements that are meant to induce repentance, the bowl judgments are punitive and final judgments that are meant to punish the followers of the beast and finally to the evil kingdom.

The first bowl of God's wrath is poured upon the earth. As a result, a foul and painful sore (ἕλκος κακὸν καὶ πονηρὸν) breaks out on the people who have the mark of the beast and who worship its image (Rev 16:2). This punishment calls to mind the Egyptian plague of boils that broke out into sores (Exod 9:10–11). Although the boils broke out on human beings and animals in Egypt (Exod 9:10), the sores break out only on human beings in Rev 16. However, as the boils' effects are limited to only the Egyptians (Exod 9:11), the sores affect only people whose allegiance is to the beast in Rev 16. In addition to Exod 9:10–11, Wis 11:15–16 also is considered as the background of the first bowl judgment.[50] This passage is located after the passages concerning the role of wisdom in the Exodus (leading the Israel-

---

permission of Wipf and Stock); cf. Beasley-Murray, *Revelation*, 238–39.

50. Cf. Beasley-Murray, *Revelation*, 240. "In return for their foolish and wicked thoughts, which led them astray to worship irrational serpents and worthless animals, you sent upon them a multitude of irrational creatures to punish them, so that they might learn that one is punished by the very things by which one sins" (Wis 11:15–16).

ites out of Egypt, Wis 10:15–21; leading the Israelites through the desert, 11:1–14) and is located in the passage concerning the Exodus plague (Wis 11:15–20). Therefore, the use of Wis 11:15–16 (as well as Exod 9:10–11) in Rev 16:2 makes the Exodus plague tradition clearer as the background.

The second and third bowl judgments are based on the first Egyptian plague that the Nile turned into blood and the fish in the river died (Exod 7:17–24; cf. Ps 78:44) and eschatologically reinterpret the Nile plague.[51] "The universalization of the Nile plague to affect all the waters of the earth"[52] underlines the characteristic of the catastrophe as the final judgment, and Rev 16:5–7 (the cry of the angel of the waters and the cry of the altar) emphasizes the justice of the judgment.

In Rev 16:5, "the angel of the waters" (τοῦ ἀγγέλου τῶν ὑδάτων) appears. This angel needs to be considered with the angels in control of the winds (Rev 7:1) and the fire (Rev 14:18). As well as the content of Rev 7, the expression of Rev 14:18 (ἄλλος ἄγγελος . . . [ὁ] ἔχων ἐξουσίαν ἐπὶ τοῦ πυρός) clearly mentions that the angel has authority over the element of nature. Under this understanding, the angel in Rev 16:5 is "he who has control over the waters,"[53] and the translation of ESV, NAB, and NIB ("the angel in charge of the waters") is acceptable. The angels in charge of such elements of nature (i.e., wind, fire, water) are influenced by apocalyptic literature (e.g., 1 En. 60:11–16) in which "all the elements of nature have angels assigned to their care."[54] The angel of the waters cries the reason why the second and third bowl judgments are just: "Because they shed the blood of saints and prophets, you have given them blood to drink. It is what they deserve!" (Rev 16:6). This angel's cry echoes Wis 11:5–9. In the passage, the Nile is expressed as "the fountain of an ever-flowing river" that was "stirred up and defiled with blood in rebuke for the decree to kill the infants" (Wis

---

51. Cf. Collins, "The History-of-Religions Approach to Apocalypticism," 367–81. See the following sentences: "Even if the author of Revelation made use of sources, these sources were presumably selected because of their meaningful contribution to his purpose in writing the book. We must also reckon with the author's modification and expansion of his sources. . . . [Revelation 16:4] should probably be assigned to the source as the eschatological reinterpretation of the first Egyptian plague. . . . The two acclamations in Rev 16:5–7 emphasize and explain the event described in v 4. . . . In Revelation 16, therefore, we seem to have traditional Exodus material, probably already an eschatological reinterpretation of the Egyptian plagues, which has been reworked by the author of Revelation for his own purpose. Vv 5–7 were composed by him in that process" (372–73).

52. Casey, "Exodus Typology," 167.

53. Beasley-Murray, *Revelation*, 241.

54. Ibid., 242.

11:6–7). In other words, the Nile plague is expressed as divine punishment for "the Egyptian's murderous treatment of the Hebrew children."[55] Similarly, the second and third bowl judgments (turning the waters into blood) are expressed as divine—and just—punishment for the ungodly's murderous treatment of the saints and prophets: "As the Egyptians killed the Israelite infants and were punished by water 'stirred up and defiled with blood,' so the subjects of the Antichrist throughout his empire are requited for shedding the blood of the saints and prophets of the Church."[56] The divine judgment on the persecutors of God's people echoes Pss 79:3, 10, 12 (cf. Isa 49:26).[57] Especially Ps 79:3 and verse 10 have the same expression of "pouring out/shedding the blood of [God's people]" that Rev 16:6 has.[58]

Like other trumpet or bowl judgments, the Exodus plague tradition is the basic background of the second and third bowl judgments, and other sources (e.g., Wis 11; 1 *En.* 60; Pss 78, 79) seem to be mixed or added. As Casey evaluated, "The use of the Nile plague in this bowl presentation resembles more closely the Exodus tradition than is the case in the related trumpet judgment accounts, where the use of mountain and star elements is strictly apocalyptic imagery."[59]

As the second and third bowl judgments are based on the first Egyptian plague, the fourth and fifth bowl judgments are based on the ninth Egyptian plague (Exod 10:21–29).[60] In the fourth bowl judgment, the sun's power is intensified to scorch people with fire (καυματίσαι τοὺς ἀνθρώπους ἐν πυρί; Rev 16:8). This phenomenon is similar to the fire from heaven in the seventh Egyptian plague (Exod 9:22–24; cf. διέτρεχεν τὸ πῦρ ἐπὶ τῆς γῆς)[61] and part of the curses for covenantal disobedience in Deut 32:24 (MT): disobedient people will be "consumed by burning heat" (וּלְחֻמֵי רֶשֶׁף).[62] *Sibylline Oracles*

---

55. Ibid.

56. Ibid.

57. Beale, *Revelation*, 819.

58. ἐξέχεαν τὸ αἷμα αὐτῶν (Ps 79:3 [LXX 78:3]; αὐτῶν means "Israel's"); τοῦ αἵματος τῶν δούλων σου τοῦ ἐκκεχυμένου (Ps 79:10 [LXX 78:10]; αἷμα ἁγίων καὶ προφητῶν ἐξέχεαν (Rev 16:6).

59. Casey, "Exodus Typology," 167.

60. For example, Mounce, *Revelation*, 297, n. 33; Beasley-Murray, *Revelation*, 242.

61. Aune, *Revelation 6–16*, 903. In that the result of the fourth bowl judgment is not the sun's extinguished power (darkness) but the sun's intensified power (scorching people), the relatedness of the fourth bowl judgment with the seventh Egyptian plague is stronger than with the ninth Egyptian plague.

62. Beale, *Revelation*, 822. "Jewish writings that, like Rev. 16:8–9, understand the

4:162–78 also depicts the plague of fire consuming people as the divine punishment that will be given to people if they do not repent.⁶³

In contrast, the great multitude standing before the throne and before the Lamb, robed in white, with palm branches in their hands, are promised that "the sun will not strike them, nor any scorching heat" (μὴ πέσῃ ἐπ' αὐτοὺς ὁ ἥλιος οὐδὲ πᾶν καῦμα; Rev 7:16b). In the fourth bowl judgment, people who were scorched by the fierce heat "cursed the name of God" and "did not repent and give him glory" (Rev 16:9). Based on the promise that is given to the redeemed in Rev 7:16 and the reactions of "people" who were seared by the intense heat in Rev 16:9, the objects of scorching heat can be limited to "the ungodly"⁶⁴ or "the followers of evil,"⁶⁵ although the text just mentions οἱ ἄνθρωποι (Rev 16:9) without explanation. This limitation on the objects of the fourth bowl judgment is valid also in the fifth bowl judgment (e.g., "the followers of the beast"⁶⁶). Their blasphemy of the name of God recalls the Exodus tradition, especially Sinai tradition (Exod 20:7; Deut 5:11; cf. Lev 24:16).⁶⁷ In addition, their reaction (not repenting, οὐ μετενόησαν) after the fourth and fifth bowl judgments (Rev 16:9, 11) also calls to mind Pharaoh's response to the Egyptian plagues (Exod 7:13, 22; 8:15, 19, 32; 9:7, 12, 34–35; 10:1, 20; 11:9–10; 14:4).⁶⁸

In the fifth bowl judgment, the resulting darkness recalls the ninth Egyptian plague (Exod 10:21–29). As Wis 16:16⁶⁹ is reminiscent of the fourth bowl judgment, Wis 17 in which "the torments of darkness are vividly portrayed"⁷⁰ also is suggested as the background of the fifth bowl judgment. Considering

---

plagues of fire in Exod. 9:23 and Deut. 32:24 as involving a spiritual dimension of punishment include, e.g., *Targ. Onk.* and *Neof. Deut.* 32:24; *Targ. Pal. Deut.* 32:24; and *Midr. Rab. Exod.* 12.4. The Egyptians were also 'scorched' by fire mixed with hail (*Midr. Rab. Exod.* 12.4) and by burning boils (*Pesikta de Rab Kahana* 7.11)" (823).

63. "Then fire shall come upon the whole world.... And he shall burn the whole earth, and consume the whole race of men, and all the cities and rivers and the sea. He shall burn everything out, and there shall be sooty dust" (*Sib. Or.* 4:173–78). Charles, *Pseudepigrapha*, 396.

64. Beale, *Revelation*, 821.

65. Casey, "Exodus Typology," 168.

66. Mounce, *Revelation*, 297.

67. Cf. Aune, *Revelation 6–16*, 889.

68. Cf. Ibid.

69. Cf. Wis 16:16, "the ungodly, refusing to know you, were ... utterly consumed by fire" (πυρὶ καταναλισκόμενοι).

70. Mounce, *Revelation*, 297.

that the background of Wis 16 and 17 is the Exodus tradition,[71] the Exodus theme in the fourth and fifth bowl judgments is clearer.

The sixth bowl is poured on the great river Euphrates. As a result, its water is dried up "in order to prepare the way for the kings from the east" (ἵνα ἑτοιμασθῇ ἡ ὁδὸς τῶν βασιλέων τῶν ἀπὸ ἀνατολῆς ἡλίου; Rev 16:12). Beale explained this phenomenon: "God gathers together ungodly forces in order to punish them decisively at the end of the age."[72] The drying up of the water that provides a way for people is reminiscent of the Red Sea event (Exod 14:21–22) or the Jordan River event (Josh 3:16; cf. 4:23) during the Exodus journey. The OT prophets also use the same motif of the drying up of the Euphrates River (e.g., Isa 11:15; 44:27; Jer 50:38; 51:36; Zech 10:11; cf. 2 Esd 13:47).[73] In these accounts, as well as the Red Sea event and the Jordan River event, the people who are led along the way are God's people, and the result of their walking through the dried path is their redemption. However, in the sixth bowl judgment, the people who are led along the way are the ungodly, and the result of their walking through the dried path is their final destruction. In other words, John "reverses both the Exodus and second exodus themes which the Old Testament records (cf. Isa 43:16–17; 51:9–10)."[74] However, that the basic concept of John's image (drying up of the Euphrates and making a way through the dried river) is based on the OT (especially the Exodus theme or the second Exodus theme) cannot be negated.

The appearance of three foul spirits (πνεύματα τρία ἀκάθαρτα) is described as "like frogs" (ὡς βάτραχοι). The word "frog" (βάτραχος) occurs only here in the NT.[75] Therefore, the use of the word in the OT and other

---

71. For example, the Egyptian plague tradition (Wis 16:15–19; 17) and the manna tradition (Wis 16:20–29). Even the previous and the later contexts include the Exodus tradition. See Winston's summaries of the contents of Wis as follows: "folly of Egyptian idolatry" (Wis 15:14–19); "Egyptians hunger through animal plague, but Israel enjoys exotic quail food" (Wis 16:1–4); "Egyptians slain by locusts and flies, but Israel survives a serpent attach through the bronze serpent, symbol of salvation" (Wis 16:5–14); "Egyptians plagued by thunderstorms, but Israel fed by a rain of manna" (Wis 16:15–29); "Egyptians terrified by darkness, but Israel illuminated with bright light and guided through desert by a pillar of fire" (Wis 17:1—18:4); "Egyptian firstborn destroyed, but Israel protected and glorified" (Wis 18:5–25); "Egyptians drowned in the sea, but Israel passes safely through" (Wis 19:1–9). Winston, *The Wisdom of Solomon*, 289–323.

72. Beale, *Revelation*, 827.

73. Ibid.

74. Casey, "Exodus Typology," 168–69.

75. The word's occurrences in the OT, NT, and Apocrypha were searched through BibleWorks 7.0.

Jewish literature needs to be examined before defining the background of the word. In the OT, the word occurs fourteen times: twelve times in Exod 8:2–13 (Exod 7:27—8:9, LXX) relating to the second Egyptian plague, and two times in the Psalms (77:45; 104:30). In Jewish literature, the word occurs in Wis 19:10; Josephus, *Ant.* 2.296–98; Philo, *Sacr.* 69; *Migr.* 83; *Mos.* 1.103–6, 144.[76] The important point is that "all mentions of frogs refer to the Egyptian plague."[77] Consequently, the unique usage of the word in the NT also needs to be understood against this background. In addition, considering that "the other preceding bowls and trumpets [are] molded in part on the exodus plagues,"[78] the Exodus plague tradition should be considered as the primary background.[79]

The seventh bowl is poured out into the "air" (ἀήρ).[80] A loud voice comes out of the temple from the throne: "It is done!" (γέγονεν).[81] This announcement finds its significance as part of the final seventh bowl judgment that concludes the entire series of seals, trumpets, and bowls. Before the last series of judgments (i.e., the bowl judgments) begins, John mentioned "seven angels with seven plagues, which are the last, for with them

---

76. Beale, *Revelation*, 832.

77. Ford, *Revelation*, 274. Beale also clearly mentioned that these references are all "in descriptions of the exodus plague." Beale, *Revelation*, 832.

78. Beale, *Revelation*, 832.

79. Beckwith argued the reference to frogs is taken from some mythological tradition (e.g., Persian mythology) rather than from the Egyptian plague tradition. He said, "The loathsome appearance of the frog makes the representation appropriate; possibly it is suggested by the Egyptian plague, Ex. 8:6, but this seems remote. It is more likely that the idea is taken from some mythological tradition. The frog figures in Persian mythology (Völter *Offenb.* 114)." Beckwith, *Apocalypse*, 683–84. However, his argument loses persuasion when considering the usages of "frogs" in the OT and in the Jewish literature (as Beale and Ford argued) and considering the whole context of the trumpet and bowl judgments (as Beale argued). Beckwith suggested another allusive source of Rev 16:13. Although the features that came out of the mouth of a beast are different from frogs, "A certain parallel to this passage is found in Hermas *Vis.* IV. 1, 6, where fiery locusts are seen coming out of the mouth of a fabulous beast." Beckwith, *Apocalypse*, 684; cf. Aune, *Revelation 6–16*, 894.

80. "Air" is the one of "four elements, considered basic from the time of the Greek natural philosophers," together with "earth" (the first bowl judgment in Rev 16:2), "water" (the second bowl judgment [sea] in v. 3; the third bowl judgment [rivers and springs] in v. 4; sixth bowl judgment [the Euphrates] in v. 12), and "fire" (the fourth bowl judgment in v. 8). Except the fifth bowl judgment that is poured on the throne of the beast, all bowl judgments "result in the affliction of the four elements." Aune, *Revelation 6–16*, 899.

81. Cf. Rev 21:3–6, "where the same phrase, 'a great voice from the throne' (φωνῆς μεγάλης ἐκ τοῦ θρόνου λεγούσης) is again followed by 'it is done' (γέγοναν)." Beale, *Revelation*, 842.

the wrath of God is ended" (ἐτελέσθη; Rev 15:1). Therefore, the declaration of γέγονεν "refers to the final consummation of judgment."[82]

As the result of the seventh bowl's pouring, "flashes of lightning, rumblings, peals of thunder, and an earthquake" (ἀστραπαὶ καὶ φωναὶ καὶ βρονταὶ καὶ σεισμὸς) are mentioned first (16:18), and "hail" (χάλαζα) is mentioned later (16:21).[83] This scene recalls the seventh plague in Exod 9:13–35, which consisted of thunder, hail, and lightning,[84] and the later OT passages (e.g., Josh 10:11; Ezek 38:18–22; cf. Isa 28:2, 17; Hag 2:17; Job 38:22–23; Ps 78:47),[85] in which "God repeatedly punished the enemies of his people with hail [and] hail was [described as] part of the accepted arsenal of divine retaliation."[86] The Sinai theophany (Exod 19:16–19) can be considered another allusive source of the scene, especially concerning flashes of lightning, rumblings, and peals of thunder.[87] The later theophanic passages using the storm phenomena (e.g., Isa 29:6; Pss 18:6–16; 77:18), in

---

82. Beale, *Revelation*, 842.

83. Similar phenomena are mentioned repeatedly in Revelation (4:5; 8:5; 11:19; 16:18).

    4:5, coming from the throne
        (flashes of lightning, rumblings, and peals of thunder)
    8:5, at the end of seal judgments
        (peals of thunder, rumblings, flashes of lightning, and an earthquake)
    11:19, at the end of trumpet judgments
        (flashes of lightning, rumblings, peals of thunder, an earthquake, and hail)
    16:18, at the end of bowl judgments
        (flashes of lightning, rumblings, peals of thunder, an earthquake, and hail)

Cf. Beasley-Murray, *Revelation*, 246; Mounce, *Revelation*, 302; Aune, *Revelation 6–16*, 899, 902; Aune, *Revelation 1–5*, 294. Revelation 11:19 and 16:18 depict the same lists of "atmospheric and seismic disturbances" especially including hail. Aune, *Revelation 6–16*, 902; cf. Aune, *Revelation 1–5*, 294. Mounce, not limited to the same atmospheric and seismic lists, expanded his observation to the entire scenes of the last trumpet and the final bowl judgment, and argued the similarities between them. See Mounce, *Revelation*, 302–3.

84. Aune, *Revelation 6–16*, 901; cf. Caird, *Revelation*, 209.

85. Cf. *Sib. Or.* 3.691.

86. Mounce, *Revelation*, 304; cf. Beasely-Murray, *Revelation*, 247–48; Aune, *Revelation 6–16*, 900–902.

87. Aune understood the four passages using storm phenomena (Rev 4:5; 8:5; 11:19; 16:18) as the passages "in theophanic contexts in Revelation" and argued, "The theophanic use of storm phenomena, such as lightning, rumblings, and thunder, grew out of the narrative of the Sinai theophany in Exod 19:16–18, where five phenomena are mentioned, thunder, lightning, a thick cloud, a loud trumpet blast, and an earthquake." Aune, *Revelation 1–5*, 294–95. Mounce also suggested Exod 19:16–18 as the OT source of the four passages by using Moffat's term, "storm-theophany." Mounce, *Revelation*, 303; cf. Moffatt, "The Revelation of St. John the Divine," 5:449.

which the Sinai theophany "served as the model,"[88] also can be considered as the allusive source.[89]

Compared with the seventh Egyptian plague (thunder, hail, and lightning), the seventh bowl judgment adds a seismic phenomenon. Considering Isa 13:13, Hag 2:6, and Zech 14:4 (cf. Mark 13:8; Heb 12:26–27), "Earthquake as an accompaniment of the divine appearing at the end of the age is a standing element of eschatological expectation."[90] As the result of the earthquake in the seventh bowl judgment, the destruction of Babylon-Rome is mentioned in Rev 16:19.[91] The similar prophecy that "Babylon-Rome will be flattened by an earthquake" is found in *Sib. Or.* 5.38–39.[92] The severity of the earthquake is depicted as "such as had not occurred since people were upon the earth" (16:18b; οἷος οὐκ ἐγένετο ἀφ'οὗ ἄνθρωπος ἐγένετο ἐπὶ τῆς γῆς). The similar expressions are used also in the seventh Egyptian plague, depicting the severity of the hail: "such as never has been in Egypt from the day it was founded until now" (Exod 9:18, RSV; τοιαύτη οὐ γέγονεν ἐν Αἰγύπτῳ ἀφ'ἧς ἡμέρας ἔκτισται ἕως τῆς ἡμέρας ταύτης) and "such as had never been in all the land of Egypt since it became a nation" (Exod 9:24, RSV; τοιαύτη οὐ γέγονεν ἐν Αἰγύπτῳ ἀφ'οὗ γεγένηται ἐπ'αὐτῆς ἔθνος). Though the similar expressions have been used in the OT and the Jewish literature,[93] one should consider that the expression is used first in the seventh Egyptian plague. The later sources may be indebted to the first usage. In addition, considering that the same atmospheric plagues (thunder, hail, and lightning) are used as "instruments of the divine wrath on rebellious men,"[94] the seventh Egyptian plague (Exod 9) should be considered as the most important source not only of the expression of "such as had not occurred since people were upon the earth" but also of the whole scene of the seventh bowl judgment.

---

88. Aune, *Revelation 1–5*, 294.

89. Cf. *Jub.* 2:2 ("angels of the sounds, thunders, and lightning) and *Apoc. Ab.* 30:8 ("thunder, voices, and destroying earthquake") also depict the similar phenomena.

90. Beasley-Murray, *Revelation*, 247.

91. Cf. "The punishment of Babylon treated in 17:1—19:10 must be included as an aftereffect of the seventh plague." Aune, *Revelation 6–16*, 903.

92. Aune, *Revelation 6–16*, 900.

93. For example, Exod 9:18, 24; 10:6, 14; 11:6; Joel 2:2; Jer 30:7; Dan 12:1; *T. Mos.* 8:1; 1QM 1:2; 4QDb frag. 3 iv 1–2; 1 Macc 9:27; Jos. *J. W.* 1.12; 5.442; 6.429; Herodotus 6.109; Thucydides 1.21; cf. Mark 13:19; Matt 24:21. Cf. Aune, *Revelation 6–16*, 900; Beasley-Murray, *Revelation*, 246–47.

94. Beasley-Murray, *Revelation*, 246.

Like other judgments, the seventh bowl judgment is based on the Egyptian plague but seems to be mixed with other sources to depict the eschatological judgment (especially with earthquake and hail). By employing traditional languages and transforming the Egyptian plagues in particular, John describes

> his impressionist pictures of the last things. Through it he depicts the unspeakable grandeur of the awe-fulness of the revelation of God's judgments and deliverance at the end of history.... The first exodus is the type of the last exodus, but the latter infinitely surpasses the former, and this applies to both the judgments and the deliverance.[95]

The Exodus Theme in Redemption and Inheritance

The Lamb

The Lamb in Revelation indicates a very important connection with the Exodus theme, especially in the "redemption" perspective. The term of ἀρνίον occurs twenty-nine times in the book of Revelation. Except one case (i.e., Rev 13:11[96]), the term is always applied to Jesus.[97] John describes Jesus as the Lamb that was slain for God's people and now is worthy to be worshipped (cf. Rev 5:6, 9, 12, 13; 7:9, 10). Through the sacrifice of the Lamb, God's people not only are delivered but also become a kingdom and priests to serve God (Rev 1:5–6; 5:9–10; cf. Exod 19:5–6). The Lamb is "the judge and warrior against the demonic forces" (cf. Rev 6:1, 16; 14:10; 17:14); the Lamb "shares an intimate relationship of care and provision for the Church" (cf. Rev 7:17; 14:4; 19:7, 9; 21:9, 14); the Lamb is "the ruler at the eschaton" (cf. Rev 14:1); and the Lamb, "in partnership with God, is the sustaining essence of the heavenly city" (cf. Rev 21:22, 23; 22:1).[98] The death of the Lamb is not only

---

95. Ibid., 247–48.

96. In Rev 13:11, the word ἀρνίον is used for "a satanic counterfeit." Hillyer, "'The Lamb' in the Apocalypse," 228.

97. Twenty eight times that ἀρνίον is used for Jesus are as follows: Rev 5:6, 8, 12, 13; 6:1, 16; 7:9, 10, 14, 17; 12:11; 13:8; 14:1, 4 (2), 10; 15:3; 17:14 (2); 19:7, 9; 21:9, 14, 22, 23, 27; 22:1, 3. Hillyer argued, "The frequency with which 'the Lamb' appears in Revelation emphasizes that this is no mere title, but more a description of our Lord's relation to men through His redemptive death on the Cross." Hillyer, "'The Lamb' in the Apocalypse," 229.

98. Casey, "Exodus Typology," 149; cf. Hillyer, "'The Lamb' in the Apocalypse," 232–36. Hillyer argued, "In the Book of Revelation the uses to which the title 'Lamb' is put

the means of the final defeat of evil or the means of the victory of God,⁹⁹ but the death of the Lamb is also the key that can open the eschaton. Because of "the strange victory"¹⁰⁰ that was earned by his death on the cross, only the Lamb is worthy and able to take the scroll and to open its seals (Rev 5:7, 9).

John repeatedly refers to "the slain Lamb" (τὸ ἀρνίον τὸ ἐσφαγμένον; e.g., Rev 5:6, 9, 12; 13:8) or "the blood of the Lamb" (ἐν τῷ αἵματί τοῦ ἀρνίου; e.g., Rev 1:5; 5:9; 7:14). With these expressions, the portrayal of the Lamb in Revelation can be understood in two ways: originating from the daily Temple sacrifice imagery or from the paschal lamb imagery. To define the more proper basic imagery of the Lamb in Revelation, two passages need to be considered in particular, Rev 1:5–6 and 5:9–10. These two passages have received close attention and have been examined as the passages that show "the use of Exodus typology in the presentation of redemption in the book of Revelation"¹⁰¹ by some scholars.¹⁰² These two passages are doxologies.¹⁰³ In both passages, the above-mentioned expressions (i.e., "the slain Lamb" and "the blood of the Lamb") are used to praise God's grace that freed people from sins by the death of Christ. Interestingly, both passages have the same conclusion, and the same conclusion of doxologies gives a clue for the basic imagery of the Lamb. The conclusion of doxologies mentions God's grace (or the result of redemption by the death of Christ) that made people to be a kingdom and priests to serve God.

Rev 1:6, ἐποίησεν ἡμᾶς βασιλείαν, ἱερεῖς τῷ θεῷ καὶ πατρὶ αὐτοῦ

Rev 5:10, ἐποίησας αὐτοὺς τῷ θεῷ ἡμῶν βασιλείαν καὶ ἱερεῖς

These expressions allude to Exod 19:6: "you shall be for me a priestly kingdom and a holy nation" (ὑμεῖς δὲ ἔσεσθέ μοι βασίλειον ἱεράτευμα καὶ ἔθνος ἅγιον).¹⁰⁴ "The conclusion of the doxology with the citation of Exodus 19:6

---

may be grouped around six themes. Christ is seen as Redeemer, as the Supreme Object of Worship, and Ruler, as Judge, as Pastor, and in His relation with His Church" (232) and examined each theme briefly (232–36).

99. See Wright, *Jesus and the Victory of God*, 540–611.

100. The expression is borrowed from Wright, *Jesus and the Victory of God*, 592.

101. Casey, "Exodus Typology," 136.

102. For example, Fiorenza, "Redemption as Liberation," 220–32; Casey, "Exodus Typology," 136–48; Hre Kio, "Exodus as a Symbol of Liberation," 284–303.

103. Cf. Aune, *Revelation 1–5*, 41, 43–45; Mounce, *Revelation*, 44, 48–50.

104. Although the expression is a little different from Exod 19:6, most scholars agree that the alluded text in Rev 1:6 and 5:10 is Exod 19:6. For example, Beale, *Revelation*, 193–95 (cf. 191), 361–62; Aune, *Revelation 1–5*, 45, 47–48, 362; Mounce, *Revelation*, 50, 136;

[in Rev 1:6 and 5:10] confirms that the Passover lamb, rather than the daily Temple sacrifice, is in John's mind" in Rev 1:5–6 and 5:9–10.[105]

Revelation 7 also supports the paschal lamb imagery as the basic concept of the lamb in the book. In Rev 7, a great multitude is depicted wearing white robes and praising God and the Lamb (7:9–10). The great multitude is explained by one of the elders: "These are they who have come out of the great ordeal; they have washed their robes and made them white in the blood of the Lamb" (7:14). The robe symbolism can be observed in the OT.

> The symbolism of dirty clothes for an unclean life is frequent in the Old Testament (e.g., Isa 64:6, Zech 3:3) as also the corresponding idea of clean clothes for a pure life (Zech 3:4), and even of washing one's clothes when approaching God (cf. Exod 19:10ff.). The idea of washing [garments] in blood already occurs in the song of Genesis 49 (it is said of Judah, 'he washes his garments in wine and his vesture in the blood of grapes').[106]

Among these passages, Exod 19:10–15 needs to be considered as the OT background of Rev 7:14 not only because the concept of "washing one's

---

Caird, *Revelation*, 17; Beckwith, *Apocalypse*, 429–30; Beasley-Murray, *Revelation*, 57, 127.

John's citation of Exod 19:6 differs from the Hebrew or Septuagint texts. Aune argued, "The second-century A.D. Greek translations of Symmachus and Theodotion render the phrase as βασιλεία ἱερεῖς, 'a kingdom, priests,' thus reflecting the same understanding of Exod 19:6 found in Rev 1:6; 5:10." Aune, *Revelation 1–5*, 47. Casey also concluded about the basis for John's citation of Exod 19:6 in Rev 5:10 (as well as in Rev 1:6): "The most likely explanation of John's text form is that he (or the tradition he used) relied on the same text of Exodus 19:6 as that used by Symmachus and Theodotion." Casey, "Exodus Typology," 141. See also Charles, *Revelation*, 1:16.

In addition, Beale argued, "Most renderings of Exod 19:6 in early Jewish writings are also in line with John's view of two distinct functions, which also strengthens the idea that the saints have begun to exercise, not only priesthood, but also kingship (e.g., *Targ. Neof.* Exod. 19:6: 'you shall be . . . kings and priests'; *Targ. Pal.* Exod. 19:6: 'you shall be crowned kings, and sanctified priests'; *Targ. Onk.* 19:6: 'And you, before Me, shall be kings, priests, holy people'; *Midr. Rab.* Exod. 30.13 and 51.4 understand Exod. 19:6 as saying that Israel will be called 'kings' . . .)." Beale, *Revelation*, 195.

105. Casey, "Exodus Typology," 145. Cf. "John unambiguously points to Jesus' death as that of the new paschal lamb, whose blood marks the redemption of God's people from slavery, in this case, slavery to sin. This is only confirmed, however, by the citation of Exodus 19:6 in the third predicative statement about Christ's activity—'he made us a kingdom, priests to his God and father. . . . Jesus' sacrifice is that of the new and greater paschal lamb, and the redemption effected by that sacrifice is the new exodus. . . . There is no doubt that by quoting his version of Exodus 19:6, John intends to set the Christian's redemption in terms of the release and promise given the Exodus generation of Israel" (141–42).

106. Beasley-Murray, *Revelation*, 147.

clothes" is shown in the passage but also because Rev 7:14-17 "evokes an escalated Exodus pattern applied to the church's redemptive pilgrimage."[107] Casey also argued that Rev 7:14 alludes to Exod 19 and 24[108] and that "The Exodus typology continues in the following verses [i.e., Rev 7:15-17]."[109] Due to the clear influence of the Exodus theme in the passage, "it is possible to see in Revelation 7:14ff. the influence of the paschal lamb analogy, an analogy which has been extended by allusion to the ratification ceremony attached to the Sinai narrative."[110] Even in Rev 15, "the association of the Lamb with redemption by relating his salvation to the Red Sea deliverance"[111] makes the Exodus theme clearer in the passage, and this combination also supports the paschal lamb imagery rather than the daily Temple sacrifice imagery.

The lamb imagery in the book of Revelation is based on the paschal lamb imagery that is emphasized with the expression "slain/slaughtered" (ἐσφαγμένον).[112] The slain lamb appears in Rev 5:6 for the first time and is described as having "seven horns" and "seven eyes" (κέρατα ἑπτὰ καὶ ὀφθαλμοὺς ἑπτὰ; Rev 5:6).[113] In the OT, the horn is frequently a symbol of

107. Beale, *Revelation*, 438. Cf. Beale explained the evoked Exodus pattern in Rev 7:14-17 with the following five steps: "(1) a great multitude coming out from tribulation (e.g., τὴν θλῖψιν Exod 4:31 LXX), followed by (2) Israel's 'washing (πλύνω) garments' (Exod 19:10, 14) and (3) being sprinkled by blood (Exod 24:8) to (4) prepare for God's tabernacling among them, which (5) provides them with food, water, protection and comfort" (438-39).

108. Casey, "Exodus Typology," 153-54. These allusions correspond to (2) and (3) in Beale's block quotation above.

109. Casey, "Exodus Typology," 154. This point corresponds to (4) and (5) in Beale's block quotation above. Casey explained that in Rev 7:15-17, "it is promised that God will 'dwell with (σκηνώσει) them' and that they will no longer know hunger, thirst or sorrow. These pictures are all elements of the Exodus tradition, but John's source for them is not the pentateuchal Exodus tradition, but Deutero-Isaiah" (154).

110. Casey, "Exodus Typology," 154.

111. Beasley-Murray, *Revelation*, 150.

112. In Rev 5:6, ἀρνίον ἑστηκὸς ὡς ἐσφαγμένον ("a Lamb standing as if it had been slaughtered") "does not mean that the Lamb only appeared to have been slaughtered but rather that the Lamb had been slaughtered and was not alive, thus combining the two theological motifs of death and resurrection." Aune, *Revelation* 1-5, 353. However, the Lamb's death as a victory (rather than the Lamb's resurrection as a victory) is emphasized in the context. See Beale, *Revelation*, 353-54: "While Jesus was being defeated at the cross, he was nevertheless beginning to establish his kingdom.... This does not mean that the Lamb's resurrection is not conceived of as a victory but only that there is an intention to highlight the death as a victory."

113. Daniel 7:7-8 is chiefly mentioned as the OT background of the Lamb's "seven

Use of the Exodus Theme in Revelation 15

power[114] (often royal power[115]); the eye is frequently a symbol of omniscience/omnipresence.[116] Therefore, the lamb having seven horns and seven eyes means the powerful and omniscient lamb, which mismatches with the slain lamb imagery.[117] Apparently, "Both the seven horns and the seven eyes are appropriate symbols for the 'Lion of the tribe of Judah,' i.e., the Davidic Messiah [Rev 5:5]"[118] rather than for the slain lamb. However, John combines the

---

horns." See Casey, "Exodus Typology," 151; Beale, *Revelation*, 354 (cf. 366–69). Beale argued, "The Lamb may in fact mimic the beast with horns in Dan 7:7ff., since the Lamb is a substitute image for the son of man in Dan 7:13 (one could even discern seven remaining horns on the beast in Dan 7:8 after three had been uprooted from the prior ten).... In Rev 5:6 ironic parody is used in the portrayal of the Messiah in his defeat of the enemy by means of the imagery of Daniel 7, where it is used of the beast's defeat of the saints." Beale, *Revelation*, 354.

Zechariah 3:9 and 4:10 can be considered as the OT background of the Lamb's "seven eyes." Beale, *Revelation*, 355. However, due to the association of "eyes" with the seven spirits of God, Zech 4:10 (cf. 4:2) is chiefly considered as the background. See Casey, "Exodus Typology," 151; Beckwith, *Apocalypse*, 510; Beasley-Murray, *Revelation*, 124; Aune, *Revelation* 1–5, 353–54; Charles, *Revelation*, 1:141; Mounce, *Revelation*, 133, n. 23.

As Aune argued, "The number seven itself is important so that the seven horns and seven eyes *both* appear to be interpreted as the seven spirits of God." Aune, *Revelation* 1–5, 354 (italics are Aune's). At the same time, however, one should remember that "'seven' is figurative for fullness elsewhere in the Apocalypse and in biblical literature." Beale, *Revelation*, 351. The following references also depict the meaning of "seven" in the passage as "fullness" or "perfection": Beasely-Murray, *Revelation*, 124; Charles, *Revelation*, 1:141; Beckwith, *Apocalypse*, 510.

114. For example, Jer 48:25; Pss 18:1–3; 75:10; 89:17; 92:10; 132:17; Dan 7:20–21; 8:3–4 (cf. 1 *En.* 90:37). Aune, *Revelation* 1–5, 353. Beale added Deut 33:17; 1 Kgs 22:11; 1 *En.* 90:6–12. Beale, *Revelation*, 351. Charles added Num 23:22; 1 Sam 2:1; Ps 75:4. Charles, *Revelation*, 1:141.

115. For example, Ps 132:17; Dan 7:7–8, 11–12, 24. Aune, *Revelation* 1–5, 353. Charles added Pss 112:9; 148:14; Zech 1:18; Dan 7:20; 8:3ff. Charles, *Revelation*, 1:141. See also Kaiser, *The Messiah in the Old Testament*, 89. Kaiser argued that a horn symbolizes a powerful king (cf. Dan 7:7–8, 24) or the Messiah (cf. Luke 1:68–69). Kaiser argued three symbols for the Messiah: a horn, a lamp, and a crown.

116. For example, 2 Chr 16:9; Job 28:10; Pss 34:15; 139:16; Prov 15:3 (cf. Sir 11:12; 17:15, 19; 23:19; 39:19; 1 Pet 3:12; Heb 4:13; Pol. *Phil.* 6:2). Aune, *Revelation* 1–5, 354.

117. The powerful and omniscient lamb imagery is based on "the warrior lamb" of the intertestamental literature (1 *En.* 90:9, 37; *T. Jos.* 19:8–9; cf. Rev 17:14). In 1 *En.* 90:9, "horned lambs" symbolize the Maccabees. Charles, *Revelation*, 1:141. In 1 *En.* 90:37, "A white bull" representing the Messiah is described as having "large horns." See Aune, *Revelation* 1–5, 354; Beale, *Revelation*, 351; Beckwith, *Apocalypse*, 510. In *T. Jos.* 19:8–9, "One of this family [the Maccabees] is designated ἀμνός, which destroys the enemies of Israel." Charles, *Revelation*, 1:141. See also Casey, "Exodus Typology," 151; Aune, *Revelation* 1–5, 369; Beale, *Revelation*, 351; Hillyer, "'The Lamb' in the Apocalypse," 229.

118. Aune, *Revelation* 1–5, 354.

Lion and the Lamb in Rev 5:5–6, and this juxtaposition solves the mismatch between the slain lamb and the warrior lamb (in other words, the mismatch between the slain lamb imagery and "seven horns and seven eyes"), and consequently solves the paradox of "conquering through suffering."[119] Concerning John's combination of the lamb (as a symbol of the Messiah) and the special attributes of seven horns and seven eyes, Aune strongly argued, "This composite image is the creation of the author, though the elements are drawn from traditional imagery."[120] In sum, as each judgment episode (esp. first four trumpet judgments and seven bowl judgments) takes Exodus plagues as its basic component but modifies the Exodus tradition and adds other elements to express the eschatological judgment, the lamb imagery in Revelation takes the Exodus tradition (i.e., the paschal lamb imagery) as its basic component but modifies the Exodus tradition by adding other elements to express the judge of the eschatological judgment.

Divine Names

The echo of Exodus in Revelation also can be observed in the names applied to God. In Exodus, Moses asked God about his name (Exod 3:13; "and they ask me, 'What is his name?' Then what shall I tell them?"). God described himself in two ways: (1) "I AM WHO I AM" (ἐγώ εἰμι ὁ ὤν; Exod 3:14); (2) "the God of Abraham, the God of Isaac and the God of Jacob" (θεὸς Αβρααμ καὶ θεὸς Ισαακ καὶ θεὸς Ιακωβ; Exod 3:15, 16). In Revelation, God is described with threefold temporal descriptions (ὁ ὢν καὶ ὁ ἦν καὶ ὁ ἐρχόμενος; e.g., Rev 1:4, 8; 4:8) or twofold temporal descriptions (ὁ ὢν καὶ ὁ ἦν; e.g., Rev 11:17; 16:5).[121] These twofold or threefold temporal descriptions of God can be understood as the expanded expressions of the divine name in Exod 3:14 (ἐγώ εἰμι ὁ ὤν).[122] These names for God, including

---

119. Beale, *Revelation*, 353.

120. Aune, *Revelation 1–5*, 353.

121. Threefold temporal description of God is "who is and who was and who is to come" (e.g., Rev 1:4, 8; 4:8) and twofold temporal description of God is "who is and who was" (e.g., Rev 11:17; 16:5).

122. The similar expressions—twofold or threefold temporal descriptions of God—can be observed in Isaiah (e.g., Isa 41:4; 43:10; 44:6; 48:12) and in the later Jewish literature (e.g., "I am he who is and who will be," *Targ. Ps.-J.* Exod 3:14; "I am he who is and who was, and I am he who will be," *Targ. Ps.-J.* Deut 32:39; see likewise the gloss to *Targ. Neof.* Exod. 3:14). These expressions also are "developed reflections on the divine name in Exod 3:14." Beale, *Revelation*, 187.

the divine name in Exod 3:14, show God's eternalness and faithfulness and consequently make God's promise valid forever.[123] Therefore, these names for God can be his people's hope, even if they are suffering: as he did in the past, he does and will do something for his people.

Tabernacle

Another feature of the Exodus theme in Revelation is the tabernacle motif. To the Israelites who were in the wilderness, God gave his laws and let them make his tabernacle to dwell among them (Exod 29:45–46). The Israelites followed what God told them; and wherever they went the tabernacle was set up in the midst of their place, and the tabernacle of witness meant the divine existence among them. The tabernacle as the place of divine dwelling had been changed to the temple since Solomon. In Revelation, the divine dwelling place is depicted with both "tabernacle" (σκηνή) and "temple" (ναός).[124] Especially in Rev 15:5, what John sees opening in heaven is the temple, that is, the tabernacle of witness (τῆς σκηνῆς τοῦ μαρτυρίου). Beale pointed out that τῆς σκηνῆς τοῦ μαρτυρίου occurs approximately 140 times in the Greek OT and 130 times just in Exodus through Deuteronomy (i.e., during the journey of the Exodus in the wilderness).[125] Therefore, the term "tabernacle of witness" (τῆς σκηνῆς τοῦ μαρτυρίου) echoes the Exodus theme. In addition, by linking the tabernacle of witness with the temple, the references of the temple also recall the dwelling of God in the wilderness during the Exodus.

At the end of John's vision, the New Jerusalem comes down out of heaven from God (Rev 21:2), and he heard a loud voice from the throne saying, ἰδοὺ ἡ σκηνὴ τοῦ θεοῦ μετὰ τῶν ἀνθρώπων, καὶ σκηνώσει μετ' αὐτῶν, καὶ

---

123. See also other self-declarations of God and Christ:

God: I am the Alpha and the Omega (1:8)
Christ: I am the first and the last (1:17)
God: I am the Alpha and the Omega, the beginning and the end (21:6)
Christ: I am the Alpha and the Omega, the first and the last, the beginning and the end (22:13)

Cf. Bauckham, *The Theology of the Book of Revelation*, 54–55.

124. Σκηνή ("tent/tabernacle") is mentioned three times in Rev (13:6; 15:5; 21:3). For "the/his temple" (ναός), see Rev 3:12; 7:15; 11:1, 2, 19; 14:15, 17; 15:5, 6, 8; 16:1, 17; 21:22). "The throne of God and the Lamb" is another reference to the tabernacle or divine dwelling place (Rev 22:1–2; cf. 1:4; 4:2–6, 9, 10; 5:1, 6, 7, 11, 13; 6:16; 7:9, 10, 11, 15, 17; 8:3; 12:5; 13:2; 14:3; 16:10, 17; 19:4, 5; 20:11, 12; 21:3, 5; 22:1, 3).

125. Beale, *Revelation*, 801; cf. Stevens, *Revelation*, 450.

αὐτοὶ λαοὶ αὐτοῦ ἔσονται, καὶ αὐτὸς ὁ θεὸς μετ᾽ αὐτῶν ἔσται (Rev 21:3). In the first part, the term tabernacle (σκηνή) is mentioned; in the second part, the meaning of tabernacle is mentioned clearly ("he will dwell with them"); and the third and fourth parts echo the Exodus formula, "I will take you as my own people, and I will be your God" (cf. Exod 6:7). This echo's repetition in Rev 21:7, "I will be their God and they will be my children," confirms the Exodus theme in the passage. Between these two echoes of the Exodus formula, the removal of tears, death, mourning, crying, and pain is mentioned (Rev 21:4). As well as Rev 7:15–17, in which the promise of no hunger, thirst, or sorrow is mentioned with the dwelling of God, "these pictures are all elements of the Exodus tradition, but John's source for them is not the pentateuchal Exodus tradition"[126] but from Isaiah's second Exodus tradition (Isa 25:8; 35:10; 51:11).[127] Therefore, Rev 21:3–7 is colored by the pentateuchal Exodus tradition and Isaiah's second Exodus tradition. At the end of the New Jerusalem vision, John mentioned, "I saw no temple in the city, for its temple is the LORD God the Almighty and the Lamb" (21:22). Ironically, the disappearance of the temple depicts the fulfillment of God's dwelling among his people that began in the journey of Exodus in the wilderness.

In this section, the Exodus theme in Revelation was examined concerning the dimension of judgment (in the first subsection) and the dimension of redemption and inheritance (in the second subsection). In short, as the Egyptian plagues are the basis of the judgments in Revelation (esp. first four trumpet judgments and bowl judgments) and other sources are mixed with them to depict the eschatological judgment, three features of redemption and inheritance in Revelation (i.e., lamb, divine name, and tabernacle motifs) are based also on the Exodus tradition and are mixed with other sources to depict the eschatological vision.

THE EXODUS THEME IN REVELATION 15–16

Revelation 16 depicts seven bowl plagues, and Rev 15 is "the prelude to the Bowl series."[128] As examined in the previous section, seven bowl plagues are based on the Egyptian plagues but are mixed with other sources to depict the eschatological judgment.[129]

126. Casey, "Exodus Typology," 154.

127. Ibid., 201.

128. Stevens, *Revelation*, 448.

129. Table 12 is a summary of the content of "The Bowl Judgments" in the previous section.

Use of the Exodus Theme in Revelation 15

Rev 16	Exodus Tradition	Other Sources
First bowl judgment	The Egyptian plague of boils (Exod 9:10–11)	Wis 11:15–16
Second and third bowl judgments	The Egyptian plague of the Nile (Exod 7:17–24)	1 *En.* 60:11–16 Wis 11:5–9 Ps 78:44 Ps 79:3, 10, 12 (cf. Isa 49:26)
Fourth and fifth bowl judgments	The Egyptian plague of darkness (Exod 10:21–29) The Egyptian plague of hail (with fire) (Exod 9:22–24) Cf. Deut 32:24 Cf. Exod 20:7; Deut 5:11; Lev 24:16	*Sib. Or.* 4:162–78 Wis 16:16; Wis 17 *Targ. Onk.* *Neof.* Deut. 32:24 *Targ. Pal.* Deut. 32:24 *Midr. Rab.* Exod. 12.4 *Pesikta de Rab Kahana* 7.11
Sixth bowl judgment	The Red Sea event (Exod 14:21–22) Jordan River event (Josh 3:16; cf. 4:23) The Egyptian plague of frogs (Exod 7:25—8:9)	Isa 43:16–17; 51:9–10 Isa 11:15; 44:27; Jer 50:38; 51:36; Zech 10:11; cf. 2 Esd 13:47 Wis 19:10; Josephs, *Ant.* 2.296–98; Philo, *Sacr.* 69; *Migr.* 83; *Mos.* 1.103–6, 144
Seventh bowl judgment	The Egyptian plague of hails (Exod 9:13–35) The Sinai theophany (Exod 19:16–19)	*Jub.* 2:2; *Apoc. Ab.* 30:8 Isa 29:6; Pss 18:6–16; 77:18 Isa 13:13; Hag 2:6; Zech 14:4 (cf. Mark 13:8; Heb 12:26–27) *Sib. Or.* 5.38–39 Josh 10:11; Ezek 38:18–22 (cf. Isa 28:2, 17; Hag 2:17; Job 38:22–23; Ps 78:47; *Sib. Or.* 3.691)

Table 12. The Background of the Bowl Judgments

As the bowl judgments (Rev 16) are colored obviously by the Exodus theme (especially in the presentation of judgment),[130] the prelude to the bowl judgments (Rev 15) is colored also by the Exodus theme (especially in the presentation of redemption and heritance). The Exodus theme in Rev 15

---

130. See also Stevens's argument on the Exodus theme in the bowl judgments: "Also as in the Exodus story, God's actions have continual warnings, seeking repentance, but only resulting in a tragic, conclusive finale. John's narrative strategy is clear. He parallels divine intervention in redemptive history. The first redemption brought down God's judgment on Pharaoh. The last redemption brings down God's judgment on the beast." Stevens, *Revelation*, 452.

is examined in the first chapter and thus here will be summarized briefly. In Rev 15, diverse characters appear: John, the gathering of seven angels, one of four living creatures, and the group of saints. The last character, the group of saints, is depicted as "those who had conquered the beast and its image and the number of its name" (Rev 15:2) and can be explained as "the beneficiaries of these [bowl] judgments."[131] They have some common points with the Israelites in Exod 15: (1) they belong to God; (2) they had been suffering on account of the oppressor who stood against God; (3) but they are saved from (or conquer) the oppressor; (4) they sing a song after their redemption; and (5) the songs of both groups exalt God and praise his miraculous deeds with instruments.

In Rev 15 and Exod 15, both songs are sung by the redeemed multitudes beside the sea. The sea is described as "a sea of glass mingled with fire" (ὡς θάλασσαν ὑαλίνην μεμιγμένην πυρί, Rev 15:2a), "the sea of glass" (τὴν θάλασσαν τὴν ὑαλίνην, 15:2b), and "a sea of glass, like crystal" before the throne (ὡς θάλασσα ὑαλίνη ὁμοία κρυστάλλῳ, 4:6). Although diverse background of these expressions or the heavenly sea has been suggested by scholars (e.g., Ezek 1:22; Gen 1:6–7; *T. Levi* 2:7a; *2 En.* 3:3),[132] the Red Sea episode in Exod 14–15 should be considered the most influential background because Exod 15:8, "the deeps congealed in the heart of the sea," gives the strongest clue for the "sea of glass, like crystal" (cf. Rev 4:6 and 15:2) and the later interpretations of the Red Sea event also state that "the sea became congealed and appeared like glass vessels" or "crystallized . . . kind of glass" (e.g., *Mekilta de Rabbi Ismael*, Beshallah 5.15 on Exod 14:16–21; *'Abot de Rabbi Nathan* 30a; *Midrash* Ps 136:7 based on Exod 15:8).[133] In addition,*'Abot de Rabbi Nathan* shows a very similar expression of the "sea of glass mingled with fire" (ὡς θάλασσαν ὑαλίνην μεμιγμένην πυρί, 15:2a) to illustrate the Red Sea event, "fire was present in the midst of the [sea of] glass."[134]

The song, which is sung by the redeemed multitudes beside the sea of glass mingled with fire, is called "the song of Moses, the servant of God, and the song of the Lamb" (τὴν ᾠδὴν Μωϋσέως τοῦ δούλου τοῦ θεοῦ καὶ τὴν

---

131. Stevens, *Revelation*, 448.

132. Cf. Beale, *John's Use*, 64; *Revelation*, 327–28, 789–92; Osborne, *Revelation*, 562; Beale and McDonough, "Revelation," 1133. See also Beasley-Murray's argument: "As this sea was seen in heaven, the fire would be heavenly fire, perhaps associated with the throne vision; cf. Ezek 1:4, 13, 27." Beasley-Murray, *Revelation*, 253.

133. Beale and McDonough, "Revelation," 1133; Beale, *Revelation*, 791–792; cf. McNamara, *New Testament and Palestinian Targum to the Pentateuch*, 203–4.

134. Beale, *Revelation*, 792.

ᾠδὴν τοῦ ἀρνίου, Rev 15:3a). According to the designation, "the song of Moses" (τὴν ᾠδὴν Μωϋσέως), three passages can be considered as the OT source of the song: Exod 15:1–18, Deut 32:1–43, and Ps 90.[135] Considering that this designation of the song is followed by the designation of Moses as the servant of God (τὴν ᾠδὴν Μωϋσέως τοῦ δούλου τοῦ θεοῦ), Exod 15:1–18 can be considered as the clearest source because only here two designations ("the song of Moses" and Moses as "the servant of God") are mentioned together and even in the same order (i.e., the designation of Moses as the servant of God is mentioned and then the content of the song [of Moses] is mentioned).

Scholars, who agree with the influence of Exod 15 as the background of Rev 15 according to the scenery background and the designation, still doubt the relationship between the content of the songs in Rev 15 and Exod 15. Due to no vivid linguistic parallel between the two songs in Rev 15:3–4 and Exod 15:1–18, other OT passages (e.g., Ps 86:8–10) have been suggested as the OT source of the song in Rev 15. However, considering the genre of Revelation and the apocalyptic literary device at that time (alluding to the content of the source text but rereading and paraphrasing the text), the OT source of the song in Rev 15 cannot be limited to or weigh too much on a linguistic parallel. Rather, thematic parallel in the content can have more persuasion. As table 2, "Thematic Parallel in the Contents of the Songs in Rev 15 and Exod 15," shows, the common themes (with the repeated key words/expressions) are mentioned in both songs: (1) God's great and marvelous deeds (Rev 15:3b; Exod 14:31; 15:4–7); (2) human beings' fear (Rev 15:4a; Exod 15:14–16); (3) God's uniqueness in glory and holiness (Rev 15:4b; Exod 15:11). To be more specific, Rev 15:3b just proclaims, "*Great* and *marvelous* are your *deeds*, LORD God Almighty," and Exod 14:31 says, "The *great work* that the LORD *did* against the Egyptians" and then illustrates God's great works in detail in Exod 15:4–7 (e.g., "Pharaoh's chariots and his army he cast into the sea; his picked officers were sunk in the Red Sea"). Rev 15:4a proclaims, "Who will not *fear* you, O LORD," and Exod 15:14–16 illustrates human beings' fear for God with diverse expressions (e.g., "*pangs seized* the inhabitants of Philistia. Then the chiefs of Edom were *dismayed*"). In a short rhetorical question in Rev 15:4b, "Who will not . . . bring *glory* to your name? For you *alone* are *holy*," God's glory, holiness, and uniqueness are emphasized, and these elements are emphasized also in Exod 15:11, "Who among the gods is like you, O LORD? Who is like

---

135. Cf. for Exod 15:1–18, see Exod 15:1a; for Deut 32:1–43, see Deut 31:19, 22, 30; 32:44; for Ps 90, see the superscription.

you—majestic in holiness, awesome in glory, working wonders?" Exodus 15:11a does not use the expression "alone" like Rev 15:4b to emphasize God's uniqueness; but with different expressions, Exod 15:11a emphasizes God's uniqueness: "Who among the gods is like you, O LORD? Who is like you?" As Rev 15:4b emphasizes God's holiness and glory with the terms "glory" and "holy," Exod 15:11b uses the same key expressions to emphasize God's holiness and glory: "majestic in *holiness*, awesome in *glory*, working wonders." Consequently, the two songs in Rev 15 and Exod 15 sing the same things with somewhat different lyrics: short expressions like a proclamation (Revelation) and longer, detailed, and more concrete expressions like an illustration or explanation (Exodus).[136] In other words, the song in Rev 15 summarizes and paraphrases the song in Exod 15 by following "a widely used apocalyptic literary device" at that time (i.e, alluding to, rereading, and paraphrasing the OT source).[137]

The whole context of Rev 15 shows the structural parallel with the whole Exodus journey: the plagues (v. 1; cf. Exod 7–11), the multitude who were redeemed from enemies and sing a song beside the sea (v. 2; cf. Exod 14), the song of Moses (vv. 3–4; cf. Exod 15), the erection of the tabernacle of witness (v. 5; cf. Exod 40), and the smoke of YHWH's presence (v. 8; cf. Exod 40).[138] This structural parallel in the context of Rev 15 with the whole Exodus journey is argued as "a more complete and systematic use of Exodus typology than in any other part of John's book."[139]

In short, the background (the redeemed multitude sing a song to praise God, the Redeemer, beside the sea), the designation ("the song of Moses, the servant of God"), the content (thematic allusions with the song of Exod 15), and the context of the song in Rev 15 (structural allusions with the Exodus journey) show the strong influence of the Exodus theme, especially the Red Sea episode in Exod 14–15. In Rev 16, seven bowl plagues are described on the basis of the Egyptian plagues, but the Exodus plagues are altered and mixed with other sources to depict the eschatological judgments. Therefore, the Exodus theme in Rev 15 and 16 is obvious.

Then, how does the author use the Exodus theme in the book of Revelation (especially in Rev 15)? The answer will be dealt with in the next section as the conclusion of this chapter, with the key expression of "interweaving."

---

136. See Figure 4 ("Same Contents with Different Lyrics of the Songs in Rev 15 and Exod 15").

137. Hre Kio, "Exodus as a Symbol of Liberation," 215–16.

138. See Table 3 ("Structural Parallel in the Context of Rev 15 and Exodus").

139. Caird, *Revelation*, 197.

Use of the Exodus Theme in Revelation 15

JOHN'S INTERWEAVING THE EXODUS THEME WITH HIS ESCHATOLOGICAL VISION

Concerning the high degree of OT influence (the prophetic books' influence in particular) in Revelation, Beale explained the reason: "The author could think of no better way to describe some of his visions that were difficult to explain than with the language already used by the OT prophets to describe similar visions."[140] In the viewpoint of "vision," Beale's argument would be true. But, the influence of the Exodus theme in Rev 15—or in the whole book of Revelation—also can be explained in a similar way with Beale's argument. The Exodus is not a vision, but a historical event. After the event, however, the Exodus became one of three eschatological models and a paradigm for Israel's salvation in their future or at the eschaton. The main features of John's Apocalypse are God's judgment to the oppressor of his people, God's great and marvelous salvific deeds, and his people's victorious singing scene at the eschaton. A better way to describe these elements than the Exodus is hard to find.

John elaborately interweaves the Exodus theme with his eschatological vision. The thematic components of the Exodus (such as judgment, redemption, and inheritance) are well distributed in the whole book of Revelation.[141] The bowl judgment vision (Rev 15–16) also shows both sides of the Exodus theme: "judgment" (Rev 16) and "redemption and inheritance" (Rev 15). In Rev 16, each bowl plague shows the background of the Egyptian plague(s). The Egyptian plagues are mixed with other sources such as the later OT source or intertestamental literature in the bowl judgments to depict the eschatological judgment, as do the trumpet judgments—especially first four.[142] Unlike the trumpet judgments in which the Egyptian plagues are limited (usually to "one third"), the Egyptian plagues in the bowl judgments are expanded (in the objects of the plagues) or become more severe (in the degree of the plagues) to illustrate the final judgments—that is, not to induce repentance but to punish the evil ones finally. In Rev 15, the background of the Red Sea event (in the scenery similarity, designation, content, and context of the

---

140. Beale, *Revelation*, 332–33.

141. For the Exodus theme in judgment, the trumpet judgments and the bowl judgments are examined in the first subsection of the first section in this chapter; for the Exodus theme in redemption and inheritance, three motifs (i.e., lamb, divine name, and tabernacle motifs) are examined in the second subsection of the first section in this chapter.

142. See Table 12 ("The Background of the Bowl Judgments").

song) and the use of "tabernacle" motifs obviously show the influence of the Exodus theme in the presentation of redemption and inheritance.[143]

John wisely holds the Exodus theme (especially the Egyptian plagues) in his eschatological judgment vision and develops the old context by mixing with other sources (e.g., the later OT sources or intertestamental literature) to illustrate his new context. In the same way, John interweaves his old context (the Exodus theme, especially the Red Sea event and the song in Exod 15) with his new context (the Song of Moses and the Lamb in Rev 15) wisely and elaborately by keeping the old context as the background and developing it with the mixture of other sources (e.g., the later OT praises extolling God such as Ps 86:8–10, 98:2, 145:17). Apparently, the added sources show the vivid linguistic parallels with the song in Rev 15:3-4. However, if the song of Moses and the Lamb is understood only based on the linguistic parallels, the background of the song in Rev 16 cannot be found out, and just can be understood as a "collection," an "amalgam," or a "cento of quotations from many parts of the Old Testament" in order to "make them a jubilant anthem of Christian optimism."[144] However, considering the thematic parallels in the contents of the songs in Exod 15 and Rev 15, the song of Moses and the Lamb is not just a collection or amalgam. The same themes with the same key words/expressions are sung by the redeemed multitudes in Exod 15 and Rev 15 but with different lyrics that may be caused the contemporary literary device especially in the apocalyptic genre (alluding to, rereading, and paraphrasing the source text with great freedom). Along with the allusions of Exod 15 in the scenery background, the designation, and the context of the song in Rev 15, Exodus 15:1–18 needs more attention as the background of the song even in the content.

The "tension" between the old and new contexts in John's writing, namely between the Exodus theme and his eschatological vision, can be observed even in the designation of the song (τὴν ᾠδὴν Μωϋσέως τοῦ δούλου τοῦ θεοῦ καὶ τὴν ᾠδὴν τοῦ ἀρνίου; Rev 15:3a).[145] Although two titles of the song(s) are mentioned here, both titles seem to refer to the same song. The designation of "the song of Moses" and "the song of the Lamb"

---

143. Cf. the other two components of the Exodus theme in redemption and inheritance, the lamb motif and the Divine name motif are not obvious, but still mentioned in the bowl judgment vision (cf. Rev 15:3; 16:9).

144. Aune, *Revelation 6–16*, 874; Moyise, "Singing the Song of Moses and the Lamb," 353; Caird, *Revelation*, 198.

145. The term "tension" was borrowed from Moyise, "Singing the Song of Moses and the Lamb," 348 (cf. "dialogical tension," 349, 350).

Use of the Exodus Theme in Revelation 15

can be explained as juxtaposition. Like the Lamb and the Lion (Rev 5)[146] or Balaam and the Nicolaitans (Rev 2:14–15),[147] the repetition with different words accentuates the single meaning. If the song is one, the song probably will be "the song of Lamb" because throughout the book of Revelation, the Lamb was emphasized and kept being praised as well as God (e.g., Rev 5:9–14; 7:9–10; 14:1–5; cf. 1:5–7).

Then why does "the song of the Lamb" have another title, "the song of Moses, the servant of God"? Joel Musvosvi's analysis needs to be regarded:

> John seems to intend that we view the song of the Lamb in its Old Testament thematic background, Exodus 15. This may be the reason why he uses the double title. The first part of the title is the Old Testament contextual key to the New Testament passage. The duality of the title preserves a distinction between the two events while linking them in a typological relationship.[148]

The two events that were typologically related in the titles are the Exodus through Moses and the new Exodus through Jesus.[149] Thus, the first part of the designation ("the song of Moses") represents its old context (cf. Exod 15, the content of the song); the second part ("the servant of God") confirms the old context (cf. Exod 14:31); and the third part ("the song of the Lamb") represents its new context. The juxtaposition of "the song of Moses" and "the song of the Lamb" does not mean only the role of the first song as the background of the second song, but also means the theological, thematic, typological relationships between them. That "the expression τὴν ᾠδὴν Μωϋσέως . . . καὶ τὴν ᾠδὴν τοῦ ἀρνίου creates insuperable difficulties"[150] may be true, but the researcher argues that the expression of the titles of the song creates the clearest clue of John's deliberately interweaving its old and new contexts.

---

146. Cf. Moyise, "Singing the Song of Moses and the Lamb," 354.
147. Cf. Kistemaker, *Revelation*, 429.
148. Musvosvi, "The Song of the Moses and the Song of the Lamb," 45.
149. See also Stevens's argument: "The hymn is styled as both the 'song of Moses' as well as the 'song of the Lamb' because the redemption story of Moses bringing God's people to the other side of the Red Sea safe from Pharaoh's armies is the redemption story of the Lamb bringing the church to the other side of the tribulation safe from the Dragon's beasts." Stevens, *Revelation*, 449. Beasley-Murray titled Rev 15 as "the last Exodus" and argued that Rev 15 and 16 "emphasize the aspect of God's judgment and deliverance as a counterpart to the first exodus." Beasley-Murray, *Revelation*, 233, 235.
150. Charles, *Revelation*, 2:34.

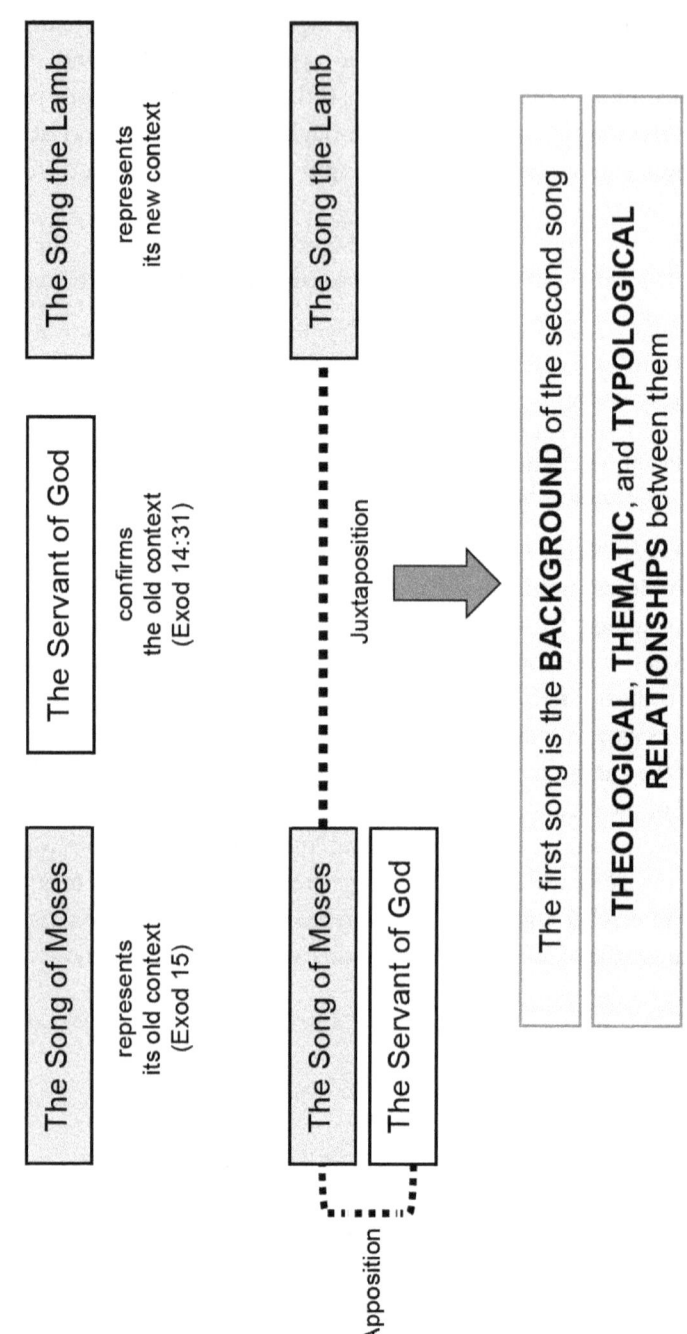

Figure 8. John's Interweaving Skills in the Designation of the Song in Rev 15

4

Conclusion

SUMMARY AND CONCLUSION

THIS RESEARCH FOCUSES ON "the song of Moses, the servant of God, and the song of the Lamb" (τὴν ᾠδὴν Μωϋσέως τοῦ δούλου τοῦ θεοῦ καὶ τὴν ᾠδὴν τοῦ ἀρνίου) in Rev 15:3-4. Despite the explicit designation, "the song of Moses, the servant of God," the OT passages that are considered as the song of Moses (Exod 15:1–18; Deut 32:1–43; Ps 90) have been doubted as the OT sources of Rev 15:3b-4 because no visible linguistic links are apparent between these OT passages and Rev 15:3b-4. Instead, other OT passages that show linguistic parallels with Rev 15:3b-4 have been suggested as the OT sources of Rev 15:3b-4 (e.g., Exod 34:10; Pss 86:8–10; 98:2; 111:2; 139:14; 145:17; Isa 2:2; Jer 10:7; 11:20 LXX; Amos 3:13; 4:13 LXX; 5:8; Mal 1:11). Among these possibilities, Ps 86:8–10 shows the closest linguistic parallels with Rev 15:3-4.

However, considering the contemporary apocalyptic literary device, the source text of a passage in Revelation cannot be limited to or weigh too much on the linguistic parallel. In other words, as other apocalyptic authors at that time did not directly quote the source text but alluded to, reread, and paraphrased the source text with great freedom, the author of Revelation could do so. Therefore, to define the source text of the Song of Moses and the Lamb in Rev 15, diverse approaches are needed. In the first chapter, by examining the scenery background, the designation, the content, and the context of the song in Rev 15 and comparing these elements with Exod

15 or the whole Exodus journey, this research presents an argument that Exod 15 needs more attention as the OT source of the song of Moses and the Lamb in Rev 15. The first task was to analyze the scenery background of the song (i.e., characters, temporal-spatial setting, and plot) and extract the common features between Exod 15 and Rev 15: the redeemed (who belong to God, had been suffering on account of the oppressor who stood against God, and are saved from the oppressor) sing a song (exalting God and his miraculous salvific actions with instruments) after their redemption near the sea. The expressions related to the sea in Rev 15:2, "a sea of glass mingled with fire" (ὡς θάλασσαν ὑαλίνην μεμιγμένην πυρὶ) and "the sea of glass" (τὴν θάλασσαν τὴν ὑαλίνην), especially evoke the Red Sea because Exod 15:8 ("the deeps congealed in the heart of the sea") and other Jewish literature (e.g., *Mekilta de Rabbi Ismael*, Beshallah 5.15 [on Exod 14:16–21]; *'Abot de Rabbi Nathan* 30a; *Midr. Ps.* 136:7) show similar expressions of the Red Sea. Second, although Moses' designation as the servant of God can be easily found in the OT and other literature, Moses' designation as the servant of God and the song of Moses are mentioned together only in Exodus (14:31—15:18). Third, the analysis of the content of the song supported for the thematic parallel between Exod 15:1–18 and Rev 15:3-4. Two songs in Exod 15 and Rev 15 sing about similar motifs (God's salvation and God himself) with somewhat different lyrics: short expressions such as a proclamation (Revelation) and longer, more detailed and more concrete expressions such as an illustration or explanation (Exodus). As other intertestamental apocalyptic literature often summarizes and paraphrases the OT sources, Rev 15:3-4 summarizes and paraphrases Exod 15:1-18.[1] Therefore, despite no vivid linguistic parallels between Exod 15:1-18 and Rev 15:3-4, Exod 15:1-18 can be considered as the source of Rev 15:3-4. Fourth, this research examined the context of the song and argued that the whole context of Rev 15 recalls the Exodus journey: the plagues (Rev 15:1; cf. Exod 7–11), the multitude who were redeemed from enemies and sing a song beside the sea (Rev 15:2; cf. Exod 14), the song of Moses (Rev 15:3-4; cf. Exod 15), the erection of the Tent of Testimony (Rev 15:5; cf. Exod 40), and the smoke of YHWH's presence (Rev 15:8; cf. Exod 40). Furthermore, the plagues in Rev 16 (i.e., the bowl judgments) recall the Egyptian plagues: sores (Rev 16:2; cf. "boils" in Exod 9:8–12), change of the sea and river to blood (Rev 16:3-4; cf. Exod 7:17–19), darkness (Rev 16:10; cf. Exod

---

1. To be more specific, Rev 15:3b summarizes and paraphrases Exod 15:4-7 (including Exod 14:31), Rev 15:4a does the same to Exod 15:14–16, and Rev 15:14b to Exod 15:11.

Conclusion

10:21–23), frogs (Rev 16:13; cf. Exod 8:1–15), flashes of lightning, rumblings, peals of thunder, and a severe earthquake (Rev 16:17–21; cf. Exod 9:23). In sum, according to the analysis of the background, the designation, the content, and the context of the song, Exod 15 shows the strongest influence in Rev 15:3b–4 as well as the Exodus theme in Rev 15 and 16.

The second chapter dealt with the question "Why did John use the Exodus theme in Rev 15?" In other words, what did the author want to express by implementing the Exodus theme, and why did he choose the Exodus theme to express that? An examination of the Exodus theme in the OT (historical books, Psalms, major prophetic books, and minor prophetic books), intertestamental literature (Apocrypha and Pseudepigrapha), and the NT (Gospels and Acts, Pauline Epistles, and Hebrews) provided the background for answering these questions.[2] The research indicated that (1) the Exodus is one of three eschatological models frequently used in the OT, intertestamental literature, and the NT, and (2) the Exodus is a paradigm for salvation that also frequently is used by the OT, intertestamental literature, and the NT. The Exodus is a memorial event that reminded Israel of God's miraculous salvation and became the basis of their expectation of their future salvation from a foreign power (e.g., Nahum, Habakkuk, Jeremiah, Ezekiel, Isaiah) or eschatological salvation (e.g., Isa 40–66). In the OT and intertestamental literature, the Exodus theme was used as a paradigm when the authors expressed their hope for God's salvation. Consequently, for the NT authors who referred to the ultimate eschatological salvation through Jesus Christ, using the Exodus theme seems to be natural. In addition, the first-century Jews thought that they were "still in Exile"[3] and expected the fulfillment of a New Exodus promised in the prophetic books. For them, no better paradigm could explain their eschatological salvation than the Exodus theme.

In the third chapter, the research posed another question: How does the author use the Exodus theme in Rev 15? The Exodus theme in the book of Revelation was examined in the presentation of judgment and redemption. In the section "The Exodus Theme in Judgment," each of the trumpet and bowl judgments was examined. The trumpet and bowl judgments in Revelation were based on Egyptian plagues and were mixed with other

---

2. The examination of the Exodus theme in the book of Revelation was excluded in the second chapter but was focused on in the third chapter.

3. Wright, *Jesus and the Victory of God*, xvii; cf. Wright, *New Testament and the People of God*, 268–69.

sources to depict the eschatological judgment that "infinitely surpasses the former."[4] Concerning the Exodus theme in the presentation of redemption and inheritance in Revelation, three features were noted: the Lamb, divine names, and tabernacle motifs. These features also are based on the Exodus tradition (e.g., paschal lamb imagery; God's name in Exod 3:14; tabernacle in the Exodus journey) and are mixed with other sources to depict the eschatological vision. John's elaborate, deliberate skills interweaving the old context of his source (the Exodus theme plus other sources) with the new context (his eschatological vision) can be observed in the whole book of Revelation, in the vision of the bowl judgments (Rev 15–16), in the song of Moses and the song of the Lamb (Rev 15:3–4), and even in the duality of the song's title. Although two titles of the song are mentioned here, both titles seem to refer to the same song, probably "the song of the Lamb," because throughout the book of Revelation, the Lamb is emphasized and continually is being praised as well as God (e.g., Rev 5:9–14; 7:9–10; 14:1–5; cf. 1:5–7). The dual titles (i.e., the juxtaposition of "the song of Moses, the servant of God" and "the song of the Lamb") show that the first plays a role of background for the second and demonstrate their theological, thematic, and typological relationships. The two events that are typologically related in the dual titles are the Exodus through Moses and the New Exodus through Jesus the Lamb. The expression of the titles of the song creates the clearest clue of John's deliberate interweaving of its old and new contexts.

---

4. Beasley-Murray, *Revelation*, 247.

Conclusion

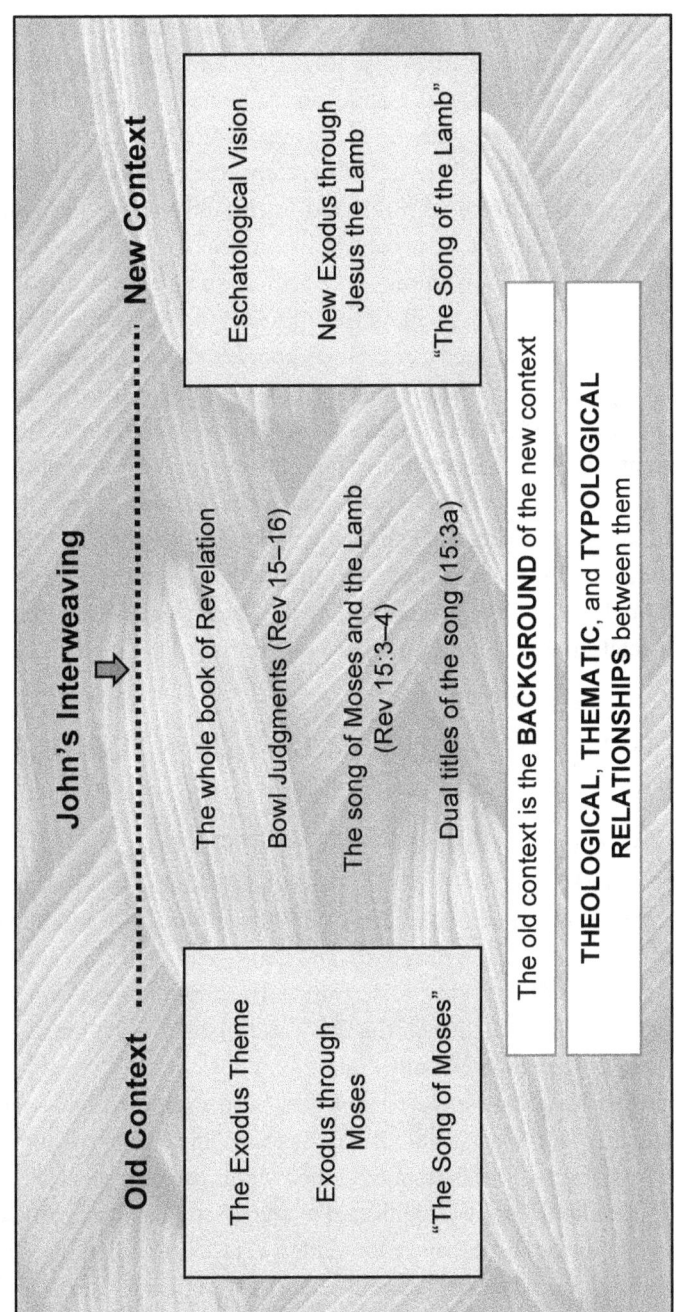

Figure 9.
John's Inverweaving between the Exodus Theme and His Eschatological Vision

In conclusion, the Exodus was a historical event. After the event, however, the Exodus became a paradigm for Israel's (or God's people's) salvation in the future or at the eschaton in the later books of the OT, intertestamental literature, and the NT. The Exodus was also one of three well-known eschatological models. Therefore, the writers of the NT and intertestamental literature who referred to the ultimate or eschatological salvation through Jesus Christ naturally used the Exodus theme. The author of Revelation is no exception. In addition, the main features of John's Apocalypse are God's judgment on the oppressor of his people, God's great and marvelous salvific deeds, and God's people's victorious singing scene. A better way to describe these elements than the Exodus is hard to find. By alluding to the Exodus theme in the scenery background, the designation, the content, and the context of the song in Rev 15:2–4, John reminds the readers of God's miraculous redemption in the Exodus, especially at the Red Sea. By interweaving the Exodus theme with his eschatological vision, John offers a glimpse of the readers' ultimate victory in their present time (even though they are oppressed under the "beast") and at the eschaton. This expectation would have promoted endurance of the readers.

CONTRIBUTION AND SUGGESTIONS FOR FURTHER STUDIES

Research on the use of the OT in the book of Revelation was sparse until the 1980s, as Beale argued that what had been dedicated to the topic (until 1988) were merely three books and six significant articles.[5] More research on this subject was done in the 1990s, and real growth in the field happened at the beginning of the twenty-first century. This monograph belongs to the studies in the field of the use of the OT in Revelation, to be more specific, the Exodus theme in Revelation.

The Exodus theme in Revelation has been examined and argued in some scholarly works: e.g., Pablo Richard's essay "Plagues in the Bible: Exodus and Apocalypse," which examined the Exodus theme (especially plagues motif) in Revelation and was published in 1997; Scott Sanborn's article "The New Exodus in the Risen Lamb: Revelation 1:4–8," published in 1999; David Mathewson's article "New Exodus as a Background for 'The Sea Was No More' in Revelation 21:1C," published in 2003; Steve Moyise's article "Singing the Song of Moses and the Lamb: John's Dialogical Use of Scripture," which

---

5. Beale, "Revelation," 318.

Conclusion

examined the Exodus theme in Rev 15 and was published in 2004; Peter Jung-chu Wu's dissertation, "Worthy Is the Lamb: The New Song in Revelation 5:9–10," which examined the Exodus theme in the new song passage and was published in 2005; Laslo Gallus's article "The Exodus Motif in Revelation 15–16: Its Background and Nature," published in 2008; Benjamin G. Wold's essay "Revelation 16 and the Eschatological Use of Exodus Plagues," published in 2011. This monograph is along the line of these efforts.

This research focuses on the song of Moses and the Lamb (Rev 15:3–4) in the context of the bowl judgment vision (Rev 15–16). Some commentators briefly mentioned the passage's relation with Exodus (or the Exodus theme) because of the similar scenery background (relating to "sea," "the victors," and "singing/song") or the designation ("the song of Moses, the servant of God"). Because of no visible linguistic links between Exod 15 and Rev 15:3–4, however, they suggested other OT passages as the source (e.g., Ps 86:8–10). Brief and insufficient studies on the passage were developed in some scholarly works, especially in two articles: (1) Steve Moyise, "Singing the Song of Moses and the Lamb: John's Dialogical Use of Scripture," published in 2004; and (2) Laslo Gallus, "The Exodus Motif in Revelation 15–16: Its Background and Nature," published in 2008.

In his article, Moyise argued Exod 15 as the background of the song of Moses and the Lamb (Rev 15:3–4) by examining the designation, scenery background, and context (relating to the plagues in Rev 16). Moyise also acknowledged no visible linguistic links between Exod 15 and Rev 15:3–4 as other scholars (such as Ford, Baukham, and Beale) acknowledged.[6] Most scholars hesitated to argue Exod 15 as the OT source of Rev 15:3–4 because of no visible linguistic links even though they acknowledged some influence of Exodus (or Exod 15) in the designation or the similar scenery background. However, Moyise examined the designation, scenery background, and context of the song, synthesized these analyses, and finally argued Exod 15 as the OT background of Rev 15:3–4. In that he overcame strong dependence on the linguistic parallel, which was considered as the essential element to define the OT source in a NT passage, and he approached in a diverse way to define the OT source in Rev 15:3–4, he deserves to be praised. However, his analysis was too brief in the length of one page (if including the conclusion, one and a half pages).

More developed research on Rev 15:3–4 (in the context of Rev 15–16) can be observed in Gallus's article "The Exodus Motif in Revelation 15–16: Its

---

6. Moyise, "Singing the Song of Moses and the Lamb," 360.

Background and Nature," published in 2008. Gallus argued the Exodus theme in Rev 15–16 and especially Exod 15 as the OT background of Rev 15:3–4 by examining the designation ("the song of Moses, the servant of God"), the scenery background (relating to "sea," "the victor," and "singing a song"), and context of the song (mentioning the similar or opposite chronological sequence of the Exodus event in Rev 15–16). Especially, he devoted a large portion of his research to analyze the Exodus plague motif in bowl judgments. His analysis on the general background of bowl imagery in biblical and intertestamental literature and his analysis of each bowl judgment deserve to be mentioned. Gallus's analysis seems to take a step forward from Moyise's analysis by adding his analysis on the thematic components of the Exodus (deliverance, judgment, covenant, presence of the Liberator, inheritance) and by adding his analysis on the Exodus plague motif in Rev 16. Moyise's and Gallus's articles were developed and deepened in this monograph.

To define the OT source in a specific NT passage and the OT source's degree (i.e., quotation, allusion, and echo), one would examine the linguistic parallel between the OT and NT passages first. In the case of examining the OT source of Rev 15:3–4, some passages were argued as the OT source according to the linguistic parallels. However, considering the genre of Revelation and the apocalyptic literary device in that time, the examination of the OT source of a passage of Revelation cannot be limited to or weighing too much on a linguistic parallel. Revelation's indirect quotation (alluding to the content of the source text but rereading the text and paraphrasing it in the apocalyptic writings) is an "apocalyptic literary device" at that time.[7] Therefore, to define the OT source of a passage in Revelation, diverse approaches or analyses are required. One of the possible diverse approaches would be narrative criticism. Although Moyise and Gallus did not use the term "narrative criticism" or (analyzing) "narrative elements," they analyzed some narrative elements of Rev 15 (i.e., characters and spatial setting), compared these elements with the elements of Exod 15, and argued the common points. This monograph developed and deepened their brief analyses. But one scholarly work should be mentioned as the starting point of using "narrative criticism" in this monograph, that is, Peter Jung-chu Wu's dissertation, "Worthy Is the Lamb: The New Song in Revelation 5:9–10 in Revelation to Its Background," published in 2005. In his dissertation, Wu used narrative criticism to define the OT background of Rev 5:9–10 (the new song passage) and argued Exod 15 as the OT background. This

---

7. Hre Kio, "Exodus as a Symbol of Liberation," 215–16.

CONCLUSION

monograph also used narrative criticism to define the OT source of Rev 15:3–4 (ch. 1). Narrative criticism can be one available approach to define the OT source of a NT passage and is recommended as an effective tool to define the OT source, especially for a passage in Revelation.

Wu analyzed narrative elements and further verbal, thematic, and structural parallels between Exod 15 and Rev 5:9–10. His analyses are much deeper than this monograph. Therefore, this monograph still has room for development. Taking his analysis as the starting point of this research, this research compared Exod 15 (including Exod 14:31) with Rev 15:3–4 and found out the thematic parallels between these passages. Some scholars mentioned the relation of contents between Exod 15 and Rev 15:3–4 in the length of one sentence: e.g., Beale thought 15:3b alludes to Exod 15:11, and Mounce thought Rev 15:4 alludes to Exod 15:11.[8] However, their explanations cannot be found. In this research, all elements that were mentioned briefly and partially by scholars to define the OT source of Rev 15:3–4 were examined in some depth and were synthesized. In addition, this research revealed the thematic and structural parallels between Exod 15 and Rev 15:3–4, which were not argued fully by any scholar yet. The two songs in Exod 15 and Rev 15 sing the same things (God's salvation and God himself) with somewhat different lyrics: short expressions like a proclamation (in Revelation) and longer, more detailed and more concrete expressions like an illustration or explanation (in Exodus): e.g., Rev 15:3b (Exod 14:31; Exod 15:4–7); Rev 15:4a (Exod 15:14–16); Rev 15:4b (Exod 15:11). Along with the analysis on narrative elements (to prove the similarity in the scenery background) and examinations of the designation and context of the song, these thematic and structural parallels between Exod 15 and Rev 15:3–4 strengthened the argument that Exod 15 should be considered as the OT source of Rev 15:3–4 with more attention. In the future, if someone can develop the thematic and structural parallels between Exod 15 and Rev 15:3–4 with other approaches or with deeper analysis with abundant knowledge of semiotics or linguistics, the argument that Exod 15 is the OT source of Rev 15:3–4 can be reinforced.

This research can be a starting point for someone who wants to examine the use of the OT in Revelation or who wants to use narrative criticism to define the OT source of an NT passage (especially for Revelation) or who wants to examine the Exodus theme in an NT passage, to be more specific, the Exodus theme (or Exod 15) in Rev 15:3–4. The researcher hopes this monograph will be used as a stepping stone for later studies in these fields.

---

8. Beale, *Revelation*, 794; Mounce, *Revelation*, 285.

Epilogue

IN THE BOOK OF Revelation, Jesus was described as the slain Lamb: e.g., "a Lamb standing as if it had been slaughtered" (Rev 5:6). The death of Jesus is not only the means of the final defeat of evil or the means of the victory of God but is also the key that can open the eschaton.

> You are worthy to take the scroll and to open its seals, for you were slaughtered and by your blood you ransomed for God saints from every tribe and language and people and nation; you have made them to be a kingdom and priests serving our God, and they will reign on earth. (Rev 5:9–10)

In general, death can be understood as the status of a final, perfect defeat that cannot be changed or recovered any more. However, John combines the concept of death and the concept of victory. This combination sounds ironic but works effectively for John's essential message that he wants to deliver through his eschatological vision.

In Rev 15, the saints who were victorious over the beast praise God in front of the throne. Considering the previous context (Rev 13–14), the saints seem to be victorious over the beast via their death, which was caused by their refusal to worship the beast and its image. Outwardly, the beast appeared to be conquering the saints (cf. Rev 13:7). However, the saints conquered the beast (Rev 15:2). The beast and its followers could take physical life from the saints; but the evil ones could not take eternal life and the ultimate victory from the saints that were guaranteed by God the Almighty and Jesus the Lamb. As Jesus gained the victory via his death,

Epilogue

the saints earned the victory via their death—by becoming obedient and faithful to God to the point of death (cf. Phil 2:2).

For the saints who were promised eternal life (i.e., whose names were written in the Lamb's book of life), their physical death could not be their final defeat. Rather, if they chose to follow the beast or to worship the beast's image for longer life on the earth or to receive the mark (the number of the beast's name) on their bodies for better life on the earth, they would have lost their eternal life and their ultimate victory (cf. Rev 14:9–11). Along with this warning, the following exhortations are given to the saints in the midst of tribulations that became more severe after the beasts appeared.

> Let anyone who has an ear listen: If you are to be taken captive, into captivity you go; if you kill with the sword, with the sword you must be killed. *Here is a call for the endurance and faith of the saints.* (Rev 13:9–10)

> *Here is a call for the endurance of the saints, those who keep the commandments of God and hold fast to the faith of Jesus.* . . . Blessed are the dead who from now on die in the Lord. (Rev 14:12–13)

Through the examples of Jesus and the saints in his eschatological vision, John tells his readers about how to live on the earth in the midst of tribulation and what they should choose, expect, and hope in their situations.[1]

To promote the readers' endurance, John offers a glimpse of their ultimate victory by illustrating the saints who were victorious over the beast and now sing the song of Moses and the Lamb beside the sea at the eschaton. He intentionally alludes to the Exodus event, especially the Red Sea event, in the saints' praising scene through the designation, similar scenery background, and thematic and structural parallels in the content and context of the song (Rev 15). Through these literary devices, John recalls the most memorable event concerning God's redemption in the Israelites' history and reminds the readers of who is their God and to whom they belong. The reason the historical event in the past can be their hope in the present and future is that God is the existence "who is and who was and who is to

---

1. At the very beginning of his Apocalypse, John the author describes himself as follows: "I, John, your brother who shares with you in Jesus the *persecution* and the *kingdom* and the *patient endurance*" (1:9). These three keywords (italics) can be extracted from the lives of Jesus and the saints. In John's Apocalypse, the saints were under *persecution* and *endured* tribulations on the earth to be faithful to Jesus/God and finally were victorious over the oppressors and now praise God with victorious songs in front of the throne and become the rulers of the *kingdom* of God. So did Jesus. Jesus and the saints function as the model of the readers.

come" (ὁ ὢν καὶ ὁ ἦν καὶ ὁ ἐρχόμενος; e.g., Rev 1:4, 8; 4:8; cf. Rev 11:17; 16:5). Through the intertextuality between Exod 15 and Rev 15, John encourages the readers to expect their ultimate victory even though they are suffering under the "beast." As God saved the Israelites from the bondages of Pharaoh in history, and as God saves the saints from the persecutions of the beast in an eschatological vision, God will save the readers from their oppressor(s) someday in reality. The readers will praise their sincere Redeemer with victorious songs as the Israelites did beside the Red Sea (Exod 15) and as the saints do beside the sea of glass mingled with fire (Rev 15).

Even now some believers still experience physical persecution because of their faith to Jesus/God. Most believers, even though they are not under physical persecution, face cultural or conceptual persecutions or experience diverse threats or temptations that hinder them from following God in their daily lives. The warnings, exhortations, and encouragements that were given to the saints in John's Apocalypse are valid even for believers in the twenty-first century. After believers finish their limited lives on earth, they will stand in front of their LORD. At that time, their lives on the earth will be evaluated by their LORD and Judge. John encouraged believers not to exchange their eternal life and ultimate victory for finite things. For John, a believer should aspire to praise God forever, his glory and holiness and his great and marvelous deeds that are shown throughout life along with God's holy people.

> "Great and amazing are your deeds, LORD God the Almighty!
> Just and true are your ways, King of the nations!
> LORD, who will not fear and glorify your name?
> For you alone are holy.
> All nations will come and worship before you,
> for your judgments have been revealed."

Bibliography

Allen, Graham. *Intertextuality*. 2d ed. New York: Routledge, 2011.
Allen, Leslie C. *Psalms 101–150*. WBC 21. Rev. ed. Nashville: Thomas Nelson, 2002.
Allison, Dale C. Jr. *The New Moses: A Matthean Typology*. Minneapolis: Fortress, 1993.
Altink, Willem. "Theological Motives for the Use of 1 Chronicles 16:8–36 as Background for Revelation 14:6–7." *AUSS* 24, no. 3 (1986) 211–21.
Anderson, Bernhard W. "Exodus Typology in Second Isaiah." In *Israel's Prophetic Heritage: Essays in Honor of James Muilenburg*, edited by Bernhard W. Anderson and Walter J. Harrelson, 177–95. New York: Harper, 1962.
Anderson, Francis I., and David N. Freedman. *Amos*. AB 24A. New York: Doubleday, 1989.
Aune, David E. "The Apocalypse of John and Palestinian Jewish Apocalyptic." *Neot* 40, no. 1 (2006) 1–33.
———. "Intertextuality and the Genre of the Apocalypse." *SBLSP* 30 (1991) 142–60.
———. "Qumran and the Book of Revelation." In vol. 2 of *The Dead Sea Scrolls after Fifty Years: A Comprehensive Assessment*, edited by P. W. Flint et al., 622–48. Leiden: Brill, 1999.
———. *Revelation 1–5*. WBC 52A. Dallas: Word, 1997.
———. *Revelation 6–16*. WBC 52B. Nashville: Thomas Nelson, 1998.
———. *Revelation 17–22*. WBC 52C. Nashville: Thomas Nelson, 1998.
———. "Revelation 5 as an Ancient Egyptian Enthronement Scene? The Origin and Development of a Scholarly Myth." In *Kropp og Sjel: Festkrift til Olav Hognestad*, edited by Theodor Jørgensen et al., 85–91. Trondheim: Tapir Akademisk Forlag, 2000.
Aus, Roger D. "Relevance of Isaiah 66:7 to Revelation 12 and 2 Thessalonians 1." *ZNW* 67 nos. 3–4 (1976) 252–68.
Bakhtin, Mikhail M. *The Dialogic Imagination: Four Essays*. Edited by Michael Holquist. Translated by Caryl Emerson and Michael Holquist. Austin: University of Texas Press, 1981.
———. *Problems of Dostoevsky's Poetics*. Translated by C. Emerson. Minneapolis: University of Minnesota Press, 1984.

Bibliography

———. *Rabelais and His Word*. Translated by H. Iswolsky. Bloomington: Indiana University Press, 1984.

———. *Speech Genres and Other Late Essays*. Translated by V. W. McGee. Austin: University of Texas Press, 1986.

Bakhtin, Mikhail M., and Valentin N. Volosinov. *Marxism and the Philosophy of Language*. Cambridge, MA: Harvard University Press, 1986.

Bandy, Alan S. "The Layers of the Apocalypse: An Integrative Approach to Revelation's Macrostructure." *JSNT* 31 (2009) 469–99.

Barclay, John M. G. "Manipulating Moses: Exodus 2.10–15 in Egyptian Judaism and the New Testament." In *Text as Pretext: Essays in Honour of Robert Davidson,* edited by Robert P. Carroll, 28–46. Sheffield: JSOT, 1992.

Barnett, Paul. *The Second Epistle to the Corinthians*. NICNT. Grand Rapids: Eerdmans, 1997.

Barr, David L. "The Apocalypse as a Symbolic Transformation of the World: A Literary Analysis." *Int* 38 (1984) 39–50.

———. *Tales of the End: A Narrative Commentary on the Book of Revelation*. Santa Rosa, CA: Polebridge, 1998.

Barrett, Charles K. *The Gospel according to St. John: An Introduction with Commentary and Notes on the Greek Text*. Philadelphia: Westminster, 1978.

Barthes, Roland. *Elements of Semiology*. Translated by Annette Lavers and Colin Smith. New York: Hill & Wang, 1967.

———. *Image, Music, Text*. Translated by Stephen Heath. New York: Hill & Wang, 1977.

———. *S/Z*. Translated by Richard Miller. New York: Hill & Wang, 1974.

———. "Theory of the Text." In *Untying the Text: A Post-Structuralist Reader,* edited by Robert Young, translated by Ian McLeod, 31–47. Boston: Routledge & Kegan Paul, 1981.

Bauckham, Richard. *The Climax of Prophecy: Studies on the Book of Revelation*. Edinburgh: T&T Clark, 1993.

———. "The Eschatological Earthquake in the Apocalypse of John." *NovT* 19 (1977) 224–33.

———. *The Theology of the Book of Revelation*. New Testament Theology. Cambridge: Cambridge University Press, 1993.

Baum, Gregory. "Exodus Politics." In *Exodus—A Lasting Paradigm,* edited by Bas van Iersel and Anton Weiler, 109–17. Edinburgh: T&T Clark, 1987.

Beale, Gregory K. *The Book of Revelation: A Commentary on the Greek Text*. NIGTC. Grand Rapids: Eerdmans, 1999.

———. "The Danielic Background for Revelation 13:18 and 17:9." *TynBul* 31 (1980) 163–70.

———. *Handbook on the New Testament Use of the Old Testament: Exegesis and Interpretation*. Grand Rapids: Baker Academic, 2012.

———. "The Influence of Daniel upon the Structure and Theology of John's Apocalypse." *JETS* 27 (1984) 415–21.

———. The Interpreting Problem of Rev. 1:19." *NovT* 34, no. 4 (1992) 360–87.

———. *John's Use of the Old Testament in Revelation*. JSNTSup 166. Sheffield: Sheffield Academic, 1998.

———. *A New Testament Biblical Theology: The Unfolding of the Old Testament in the New*. Grand Rapids: Baker, 2011.

———. "The Old Testament Background of Rev 3.14." *NTS* 42 (1996) 133–52.

Bibliography

———. "The Origin of the Title 'King of Kings and Lord of Lords' in Revelation 17:4." *NTS* 31 (1985) 618–20.
———. "The Purpose of Symbolism in the Book of Revelation." *CTJ* 41 (2006) 53–66.
———. "Questions of Authorial Intent, Epistemology, and Presuppositions and Their Bearing on the Study of the Old Testament in the New: A Rejoinder to Steve Moyise." *IBS* 21 (1999) 151–80.
———. "A Reconsideration of the Text of Daniel in the Apocalypse." *Bib* 67 (1986) 539–43.
———. "Revelation." In *It Is Written: Scripture Citing Scripture: Essays in Honour of Barnabas Lindars, SSF*, edited by D. A. Carson and H. G. M. Williamson, 318–36. Cambridge: Cambridge University Press, 1988.
———. "Solecisms in the Apocalypse as Signals for the Presence of Old Testament Allusions: A Selective Analysis of Revelation 1–22." In *Early Christian Interpretation of the Scriptures of Israel*, edited by Craig A. Evans and James A. Sanders, 421–66. Sheffield: Sheffield Academic, 1997.
———. *The Use of Daniel in Jewish Apocalyptic Literature and in the Revelation of St. John*. Lanham, MD: University Press of America, 1984.
———. "The Use of the Old Testament in Revelation." In *The Right Doctrine from the Wrong Texts? Essays on the Use of the Old Testament in the New*, edited by Gregory K. Beale, 257–76. Grand Rapids: Baker, 1994.
———, ed. *The Right Doctrine from the Wrong Texts? Essays on the Use of the Old Testament in the New*. Grand Rapids: Baker, 1994.
Beale, Gregory K., and D. A. Carson, eds. *CNTUOT*. Grand Rapids: Baker, 2007.
Beale, Gregory K., and Sean M. McDonough. "Revelation." In *CNTUOT*, edited by G. K. Beale and D. A. Carson, 1081–161. Grand Rapids: Baker, 2007.
Beasley-Murray, George R. *The Book of Revelation*. NCB. Grand Rapids: Eerdmans, 1981.
———. *John*. WBC 36. 2d ed. Nashville: Thomas Nelson, 1999.
Beckwith, Isbon T. *The Apocalypse of John: Studies in Introduction with a Critical and Exegetical Commentary*. Grand Rapids: Baker, 1979.
Beetham, Christopher A. *Echoes of Scripture in the Letter of Paul to the Colossians*. Biblical Interpretation Series. Leiden: Brill, 2008.
Belleville, Linda L. "Tradition or Creation? Paul's Use of the Exodus 34 Tradition in 2 Corinthians 3:7–18." In *Paul and the Scriptures of Israel*, edited by James A. Sanders and Craig A. Evans, 165–86. Sheffield: Sheffield Academic, 1993.
Bentzen, Aage. *King and Messiah*. London: Lutterworth, 1955.
Bergant, Dianne. "Exodus as a Paradigm in Feminist Theology." In *Exodus—A Lasting Paradigm*, edited by Bas van Iersel and Anton Weiler, 100–106. Edinburgh: T&T Clark, 1987.
Bergren, Theodore A. "The Tradition History of the Exodus-Review in 5 Ezra 1." In *Later Versions and Traditions*, Of Scribes and Sages 2, 34–50. New York: T&T Clark, 2004.
Black, Matthew. "The Christological Use of the Old Testament in the New Testament." *NTS* 18, no. 1 (1971) 1–14.
Bock, Darrell L. "Part 1: Evangelicals and the Use of the Old Testament in the New." *BSac* 142, no. 567 (1985) 209–23.
———. "Part 2: Evangelicals and the Use of the Old Testament in the New." *BSac* 142, no. 568 (1985) 306–19.
Boring, M. Eugene. "Narrative Dynamics in First Peter: The Function of Narrative World." In *Reading First Peter with New Eyes: Methodological Reassessments of the Letter of*

First Peter, edited by Robert L. Webb and Betsy Bauman-Martin, 7–40. New York: T&T Clark, 2007.

Bøe, Sverre. *Gog and Magog: Ezekiel 38–39 as Pre-Text for Revelation 19:17–21 and 20:7–10*. Tübingen: Mohr Siebeck, 2001.

Bruce, Frederick F. *The Book of the Acts*. NICNT. Rev. ed. Grand Rapids: Eerdmans, 1988.

———. *The Epistle to the Hebrews*. NICNT. Rev. ed. Grand Rapids: Eerdmans, 1990.

Bultmann, Rudolf. *The Gospel of John: A Commentary*. Translated by G. R. Beasley-Murray. Philadelphia: Westminster, 1971.

Burns, Rita. "The Book of Exodus." In *Exodus—A Lasting Paradigm*, edited by Bas van Iersel and Anton Weiler, 11–21. Edinburgh: T&T Clark, 1987.

Burridge, Richard A. *Four Gospels, One Jesus? A Symbolic Reading*. Grand Rapids: Eerdmans, 1994.

Caird, George B. *A Commentary on the Revelation of St. John the Divine*. New York: Harper & Row, 1966.

Cambier, J. "Les images de l'Ancien Testament dans l'Apocalypse de saint Jean." *NRTh* 77 (1995) 113–22.

Campbell, Antony F. "Psalm 78: A Contribution to the Theology of Tenth Century Israel." *CBQ* 41 (1979) 51–79.

Carson, D. A., and H. G. M. Williamson, eds. *It Is Written: Scripture Citing Scripture: Essays in Honor of Barnabas Lindars*. Cambridge: Cambridge University Press, 1988.

Casey, Jay Smith. "The Exodus Theme in the Book of Revelation against the Background of the New Testament." In *Exodus—A Lasting Paradigm*, edited by Bas van Iersel and Anton Weiler, 34–43. Edinburgh: T&T Clark, 1987.

———. "Exodus Typology in the Book of Revelation." PhD diss., The Southern Baptist Theological Seminary, 1981.

Ceresko, Anthony R. "The Rhetorical Strategy of the Fourth Servant Song (Isaiah 52:13—53:12): Poetry and the Exodus-New Exodus." *CBQ* 56 (1994) 42–55.

Charles, Robert Henry. *A Critical and Exegetical Commentary on the Revelation of St. John with Introduction, Notes, and Indices also the Greek Text and English Translation*. ICC. 2 vols. Edinburgh: T&T Clark, 1966.

Charles, R. H., ed. *Pseudepigrapha*. Vol. 2 of *The Apocrypha and Pseudepigrapha of the Old Testament: In English with Introduction and Critical and Explanatory Notes to the Several Books*. Oxford: Clarendon, 1913.

Charlesworth, James H., ed. *Apocalyptic Literature and Testaments*. Vol. 1 of *The Old Testament Pseudepigrapha*. Garden City, New York: Doubleday, 1983.

Childs, Brevard S. *The Book of Exodus: A Critical, Theological Commentary*. Philadelphia: Westminster, 1974.

———. *Introduction to the Old Testament as Scripture*. Philadelphia: Fortress, 1979.

Clifford, Richard J. "The Exodus in the Christian Bible: The Case for 'Figural' Reading." *TS* 63 (2002) 345–61.

———. "In Zion and David a New Beginning: An Interpretation of Psalm 78." In *Traditions in Transformation: Turning Points in Biblical Faith*, edited by Baruch Halpern and Jon D. Levenson, 121–41. Winona Lake, IN: Eisenbrauns, 1981.

Collins, Adela Yarbro. "The History-of-Religions Approach to Apocalypticism and the 'Angel of the Waters' (Rev 16:4–7)." *CBQ* 39 (1977) 367–81.

Collins, John J. "Introduction: Towards the Morphology of a Genre." *Semeia* 14 (1979) 1–20.

Bibliography

Conzelmann, Hans. 1 *Corinthians*. Hermeneia—A Critical and Historical Commentary on the Bible. Translated by James W. Leitch. Philadelphia: Fortress, 1975.

Court, John M. *Myth and History in the Book of Revelation*. Atlanta: John Knox, 1979.

Craigie, Peter C. et al. *Jeremiah 1–25*. WBC 26. Nashville: Thomas Nelson, 1991.

Cranfield, C. E. B. *The Gospel according to Saint Mark: An Introduction and Commentary*. CGTC. Cambridge: University Press, 1963.

Croatto, José Severino. "The Socio-Historical and Hermeneutical Relevance of the Exodus." In *Exodus—A Lasting Paradigm*, edited by Bas van Iersel and Anton Weiler, 125–33. Edinburgh: T&T Clark, 1987.

Culler, Jonathan. *The Pursuit of Signs: Semiotics, Literature, Deconstruction*. Ithaca, NY: Cornell University Press, 1981.

———. *Structuralist Poetics: Structuralism, Linguistics and the Study of Literature*. Ithaca, NY: Cornell University Press, 1975.

Dallaire, Hélène, and Denise Morris. "Joshua and Israel's Exodus from the Desert Wilderness." In *Reverberations of the Exodus in Scripture*, edited by R. Michael Fox, 18–34. Eugene, OR: Wipf and Stock, 2014.

Davies, W. D. *Paul and Rabbinic Judaism: Some Rabbinic Elements in Pauline Theology*. London: SPCK, 1958.

Davis, Jud. "Acts 2 and the Old Testament: The Pentecost Event in Light of Sinai, Babel, and the Table of Nations." *CTR* 7 (2009) 29–48.

Dean, Rynold D. *Evangelical Hermeneutics and the New Testament Use of the Old Testament*. Iron River, MI: Veritypath, 2009.

DeLapp, Nevada Levi. "Ezekiel as Moses—Israel as Pharaoh: Reverberations of the Exodus Narrative in Ezekiel." In *Reverberations of the Exodus in Scripture*, edited by R. Michael Fox, 51–73. Eugene, OR: Wipf and Stock, 2014.

Dempsey, Carol J. "The Exodus Motif of Liberation: Its Grace and Controversy." *TBT* 47 (2009) 81–86.

Dennison, James T. Jr. "The Exodus: Historical Narrative, Prophetic Hope, Gospel Fulfillment." *Presb* 8, no. 2 (1982) 1–12.

Derrida, Jacques. "Living On: Border Lines." In *Deconstruction and Criticism*, edited by Harold Bloom et al, 75–196. New York: Seabury, 1979.

Deterding, Paul E. "Exodus Motif in First Peter." *Concordia Journal* 7 (1981) 58–65.

Deutsch, Celia. "Transformation of Symbols: The New Jerusalem in Revelation 21:1—22:5." *ZNW* 78 (1987) 106–26.

DeVries, Simon J. *1 Kings*. WBC 12. Waco, TX: Word, 1985.

Dillard, Raymond B. *2 Chronicles*. WBC 15. Waco, TX: Word, 1987.

Dixon, Robert John. "An Examination of the Allusion to Isaiah 52:13—53:12 in the New Testament." PhD diss., State University of New York at Buffalo, 2008.

Dochhorn, Jan. "Und die Erde tat ihren Mund auf: Ein Exodus-motiv in Apc 12,16." *ZNW* 88, nos. 1–2 (1997) 140–42.

Dodd, Charles H. *According to the Scripture: The Sub-Structure of New Testament Theology*. London: Nisbet, 1952.

Dumbrell, William J. *The End of the Beginning: Revelation 21–22 and the Old Testament*. Grand Rapids: Baker, 1985.

———. "Paul's Use of Exod 34 in 2 Corinthians 3." In *God Who Is Rich in Mercy: Essays Presented to Dr. D. B. Knox*, edited by Peter T. O'Brien and David G. Peterson, 179–94. Grand Rapids: Lancer, 1986.

Bibliography

Durham, John I. *Exodus*. WBC 3. Waco, TX: Word, 1987.
Dussel, Enrique. "Exodus as a Paradigm in Liberation Theology." In *Exodus—A Lasting Paradigm*, edited by Bas van Iersel and Anton Weiler, 83-92. Edinburgh: T&T Clark, 1987.
Eller, Vernard. "How the Kings of the Earth in the New Jerusalem: 'The World' in the Book of Revelation." *Katallagete* 5 (1975) 21-27.
Engstrom, Paul L. "Deliverance at the Sea: A Reading of Exodus 15 in Light of Ancient Near Eastern Literature and Its Implications for the Assemblies of God." PhD diss., Luther Northwestern Theological Seminary, 1995.
Estes, Daniel J. "The Psalms, the Exodus, and Israel's Worship." In *Reverberations of the Exodus in Scripture*, edited by R. Michael Fox, 35-50. Eugene, OR: Wipf and Stock, 2014.
Evans, Craig A. *Mark 8:27–16:20*. WBC 34B. Nashville: Thomas Nelson, 2001.
Farrer, Austin. *The Revelation of St. John the Divine*. Oxford: Clarendon, 1964.
Fee, Gordon D. *The First Epistle to the Corinthians*. NICNT. Grand Rapids: Eerdmans, 1987.
Fekkes, Jan, III. "'His Bride Has Prepared Herself': Revelation 19–21 and Isaian Nuptial Imagery." *JBL* 109 (1990) 269-87.
———. *Isaiah and Prophetic Traditions in the Book of Revelation*. JSNTSup 93. Sheffield: Sheffield Academic, 1994.
———. "Isaiah and the Book of Revelation: John the Prophet as a Fourth Isaiah?" In *As Those Who Are Taught*, edited by Claire Mathews McGinnis and Patricia K. Tull, 125-43. Atlanta: SBL, 2006.
Fiorenza, Elisabeth Schüssler. "Redemption as Liberation: Apoc 1:5f. and 5:9f." *CBQ* 36 (1974) 220-32.
Fishbane, Michael. *Text and Texture: Close Reading of Selected Biblical Texts*. New York: Schocken, 1979.
Fisher, Fred L. "New and Greater Exodus: The Exodus Pattern in the New Testament." *SwJT* 20 (1977) 69-79.
Ford, Desmond. *The Abomination of Desolation in Biblical Eschatology*. Washington, D.C.: University Press of America, 1979.
Ford, Josephine M. *Revelation*. AB 38. New York: Doubleday, 1975.
Fox, R. Michael, ed. *Reverberations of the Exodus in Scripture*. Eugene, OR: Wipf and Stock, 2014.
Friedman, Susan Stanford. "Weavings: Intertextuality and the (Re)Birth of the Author." In *Influence and Intertextuality in Literary History*, edited by Jay Clayton and Eric Rothstein, 146-80. Madison: University of Wisconsin Press, 1992.
Frisch, Amos. "The Exodus Motif in 1 Kings 1–14." *JSOT* 87 (2000) 3-21.
Fuller, Michael E. *The Restoration of Israel: Israel's Re-Gathering and the Fate of the Nations in Early Jewish Literature and Luke-Acts*. New York: Walter de Gruyter, 2006.
Gallus, Laslo. "The Exodus Motif in Revelation 15–16: Its Background and Nature." *AUSS* 46 (2008) 21-43.
Gangemi, A. "L'utilizzazione del Deutero-Isaia nell'Apocalisse di Giovanni." *Euntes Docete* 27 (1974) 311-39.
Gheorghita, Radu. "περὶ τῆς ἐξόδου . . . ἐμνημόνευσεν, 'he spoke about the exodus': Echoes of Exodus in Hebrews." In *Reverberations of the Exodus in Scripture*, edited by R. Michael Fox, 160-86. Eugene, OR: Wipf and Stock, 2014.

Bibliography

Gillmayr-Bucher, Susanne. "Between Literary Theory and Text Analysis." In *The Intertextuality of the Epistles: Explorations of Theory and Practice*, edited by Thomas L. Brodie et al., 13–23. Sheffield: Phoenix, 2006.

Gnatkowski, Mel. "The Implied Reader in the Book of Revelation." ThD diss., New Orleans Baptist Theological Seminary, 1988.

Gonzales, Alexander R. "The Point of View of the Book of Revelation: A Literary Study." PhD diss., Dallas Theological Seminary, 2012.

Goulder, M. D. "The Apocalypse as an Annual Cycle of Prophecies." *NTS* 27 (1981) 343–67.

Groenewald, Alphonso. "Exodus, Psalms and Hebrews: A God Abounding in Steadfast Love (Ex 34:6)." *HvTSt* 64, no. 3 (2008) 1365–78.

Guelich, Robert A. *Mark 1–8:26*. WBC 34A. Dallas: Word, 1989.

Gundry, Robert H. "The New Jerusalem: People as Place, not Place for People." *NovT* 29 (1987) 254–64.

Haglund, Erik. *Historical Motifs in the Psalms*. ConBOT 23. Uppsala: CWK Gleerup, 1984.

Hagner, Donald A. *Matthew 1–13*. WBC 33A. Dallas: Word, 1993.

Hanson, Anthony T. "John 1:14–18 and Exodus 34." *NTS* 23 (1976) 90–101.

———. *Studies in Paul's Technique and Theology*. London: SPCK, 1974.

Harman, Allan M. "The Exodus and the Sinai Covenant in the Book of Psalms." *RTR* 73 (2014) 3–27.

Harris, Michael Anthony. "The Literary Function of Hymns in the Apocalypse of John." PhD diss., The Southern Baptist Theological Seminary, 1989.

Harvey, Julien. "La typologie de l'exode dan les Psaumes." *ScEccl* 15 (1963) 383–405.

Hays, Richard B. *Echoes of Scripture in the Letters of Paul*. New Haven, CT: Yale University Press, 1989.

Hays, Richard B. et al., eds. *Reading the Bible Intertextually*. Waco, TX: Baylor University Press, 2009.

Herms, Ronald. *An Apocalypse for the Church and for the World: The Narrative Function of Universal Language in the Book of Revelation*. Berlin: Walter de Gruyter, 2006.

Hillyer, Norman. "'The Lamb' in the Apocalypse." *EvQ* 39 (1967) 228–36.

Howard, James Keir. "Christ Our Passover: A Study of the Passover-Exodus Theme in 1 Corinthians." *EvQ* 41 (1969) 97–108.

Hre Kio, Stephen. "Exodus as a Symbol of Liberation in the Book of the Apocalypse." PhD diss., Emory University, 1985.

———. "The Exodus Symbol of Liberation in the Apocalypse and Its Relevance for Some Aspects of Translation." *BT* 40 (1989) 120–35.

Hunter, Alastair G. "Jonah from the Whale: Exodus Motifs in Jonah 2." In *Elusive Prophet: The Prophet as a Historical Person, Literary Character and Anonymous Artist*, edited by Johannes C. de Moor, 142–58. Boston: Brill, 2001.

Hwang, Jerry. "Turning the Tables on Idol Feasts: Paul's Use of Exodus 32:6 in 1 Corinthians 10:7." *JETS* 54 (2011) 573–87.

Hyde, Clark. "The Remembrance of the Exodus in the Psalms." *Worship* 62 (1988) 404–14.

Hylen, Susan E. "Seeing Jesus John's Way: Manna from Heaven." *WW* 33 (2013) 341–48.

Iersel, Bas van, and Anton Weiler, eds. *Exodus—A Lasting Paradigm*. Edinburgh: T&T Clark, 1987.

Isbell, Charles D. *The Function of the Exodus Motif in Biblical Narratives: Theological Didactic Drama*. Lewiston, NY: Edwin Mellen, 2002.

Bibliography

Janzen, J. Gerald. "Resurrection and Hermeneutics: On Exodus 3:6 in Mark 12:26." *JSNT* 23 (1985) 43–58.

Japhet, Sara. *I & II Chronicles: A Commentary*. OTL. Louisville, KY: John Knox, 1993.

Jauhiainen, Marko. "'Behold, I Am Coming': The Use of Zechariah in Revelation." *TynBul* 56 (2005) 157–60.

Jenkins, Ferrell. *The Old Testament in the Book of Revelation*. Grand Rapids: Baker, 1976.

Johnsson, William G. "The Pilgrimage Motif in the Book of Hebrews." *JBL* 97 (1978) 239–51.

Jones, Peter Rhea. "The Figure of Moses as a Heuristic Device for Understanding the Pastoral Intent of Hebrews." *RevExp* 76 (1979) 95–107.

Kaiser, Otto. *Isaiah 13–39: A Commentary*. OTL. Philadelphia: Westminster, 1974.

Kaiser, Walter C. Jr. *The Messiah in the Old Testament*. Grand Rapids: Zondervan, 1995.

———. *The Uses of the Old Testament in the New*. Eugene, OR: Wipf and Stock, 1985.

Kaiser, Walter C. Jr., et al. *Three Views on the New Testament Use of the Old Testament*. Edited by Kenneth Berding et al. Grand Rapids: Zondervan, 2008.

Keck, Leander E., et al., eds. *The New Interpreter's Bible: General Articles & Introduction, Commentary, and Reflections for Each Book of the Bible, including the Apocrypha/Deuterocanonical Books*. Vol. 4: First and Second Maccabees, Introduction to Hebrew Poetry, Job, and Psalms. Nashville, TN: Abingdon, 1994.

Keesmaat, Sylvia C. "Exodus and the Intertextual Transformation of Tradition in Romans 8:14–30." *JSNT* 54 (1994) 29–56.

Kirby, Diana Jill. "Repetition in the Book of Revelation." PhD diss., Catholic University of America, 2009.

Kistemaker, Simon J. *Exposition of the Book of Revelation*. NTC 20. Grand Rapids: Baker Academic, 2001.

Kline, Meredith G. "Old Testament Origins of the Gospel Genre." *WTJ* 38 (1975) 1–27.

Klund, Robert William. "The Plot of Revelation 4–22." PhD diss., Dallas Theological Seminary, 2002.

Knight, George A. F. *The New Israel: A Commentary on the Book of Isaiah 56–66*. Grand Rapids: Eerdmans, 1985.

Knox, Wilfred L. *St. Paul and the Church of the Gentiles*. Cambridge: Cambridge University Press, 1939.

Kooten, Geurt Hendrik van. "Why Did Paul Include an Exegesis of Moses' Shining Face (Exodus 34) in 2 Corinthians 3? Moses' Strength, Well-Being and (Transitory) Glory, according to Philo, Josephus, Paul, and the Corinthian Scriptures." In *Significance of Sinai: Traditions about Sinai and Divine Revelation in Judaism and Christianity*, edited by George J. Brooke et al., 149–81. Boston: Brill, 2008.

Kowalski, Beate. "Transformation of Ezekiel in John's Revelation." In *Transforming Visions: Transformation of Text, Tradition, and Theology in Ezekiel*, edited by William A. Tooman and Michael A. Lyons, 279–311. Eugene, OR: Pickwick, 2010.

Köstenberger, Andreas J. "The Use of Scripture in the Pastoral and General Epistles and the Book of Revelation." In *Hearing the Old Testament in the New Testament*, edited by Stanley E. Porter, 230–54. Grand Rapids: Eerdmans, 2006.

Kristeva, Julia. *Desire in Language: A Semiotic Approach to Literature and Art*. Edited by L. S. Roudiez. Translated by Thomas Gorz et al. New York: Columbia University Press, 1980.

———. *Semeiotike: Recherches pour une semanalyse*. Paris: Seuil, 1969.

Bibliography

———. "Word, Dialogue, and Novel." In *The Kristeva Reader*, edited by Toril Moi, 34-61. New York: Columbia University Press, 1986.

Lancellottie, Angelo. "L'Antico Testmanto nell'Apocallise." *RivB* 14 (1966) 369-84.

Lane, William L. *The Gospel according to Mark: The English Text with Introduction, Exposition, and Notes*. NICNT. Grand Rapids: Eerdmans, 1974.

———. *Hebrews 1-8*. WBC 47. Dallas: Word, 1991.

Langford, Justin M. *Defending Hope: Semiotics and Intertextuality in 1 Peter*. Eugene, OR: Wipf & Stock, 2013.

Lapide, Pinchas. "Exodus in the Jewish Tradition." In *Exodus—A Lasting Paradigm*. Edited by Bas van Iersel and Anton Weiler, translated by Robert Nowell, 47-55. Edinburgh: T&T Clark, 1987.

Lee, Dal. *The Narrative Asides in the Book of Revelation*. Lanham, MD: University Press of America, 2002.

Lincoln, Andrew T. "The Use of the OT in Ephesians." *JSNT* 14 (1982) 16-57.

Lindars, Barnabas. *The Gospel of John*. NCB. London: Oliphants, 1972.

———. "Place of the Old Testament in the Formation of New Testament Theology." *NTS* 23 (1977) 59-66.

Linton, Gregory Leroy. "Intertextuality in the Revelation of John." PhD diss., Duke University, 1993.

Lohse, E. "Die alttestamentliche Sprache des Sehers Johannes: Textkritische Bemerkungen zur Apokalypse." *ZNW* 52 (1961) 122-26.

Lucas, Roy Edward Jr. "The Use of Narrative Criticism and Discourse Analysis in Studying the Social Backdrop of the Epistle to Titus in Relation to the Challenge to 'Do Good' on the Island of Crete." PhD diss., Southwestern Baptist Theological Seminary, 1993.

Lust, Johan. "The Order of the Final Events in Revelation and in Ezekiel." In *L'Apocalypse johannique et l'apocalyptique dans le Nouveau Testament*, edited by J. Lambrecht, 179-83. Leuven, Belgium: Leuven University Press, 1980.

Malan, Jannie C. "A Complement to the Exodus Motif in Theology." *JTSA* 61 (1987) 3-13.

Mann, Joshua L. "The (New) Exodus in Luke and Acts: An Appeal for Moderation." In *Reverberations of the Exodus in Scripture*, edited by R. Michael Fox, 94-120. Eugene, OR: Wipf and Stock, 2014.

Marconcini, B. "L'utilizzazione del T. M. nelle citazione isaiane dell' Apocalisse." *RivB* 24 (1976) 113-36.

Maronde, Christopher Allan. "Moses in the Gospel of John." *CTQ* 77 (2013) 23-44.

Martin, Lee Roy. "'Where Are All His Wonders?' The Exodus Motif in the Book of Judges." *Journal of Biblical & Pneumatological Research* 2 (2010) 87-109.

Martin, Ralph P. *2 Corinthians*. WBC 40. 2d ed. Grand Rapids: Zondervan, 1986.

Mathewson, David. "Abraham, the Father of Many Nations in the Book of Revelation." In *Perspectives on Our Father Abraham: Essays in Honor of Marvin A. Wilson*, edited by Steven A. Hunt, 169-83. Grand Rapids: Eerdmans, 2010.

———. "Assessing Old Testament Allusions in the Book of Revelation." *EvQ* 75 (2003) 311-26.

———. "Isaiah in Revelation." In *Isaiah in the New Testament*, edited by Steve Moyise and Maarten J. J. Menken, 189-210. New York: T&T Clark, 2005.

———. "New Exodus as a Background for 'The Sea Was No More' in Revelation 21:1C." *TJ* 24 (2003) 243-58.

———. *A New Heaven and a New Earth: The Meaning and Function of the Old Testament in Revelation 21:1—22:5*. JSNTSup 238. Sheffield: Sheffield Academic, 2003.

Bibliography

Mauser, Ulrich. *Christ in the Wilderness: The Wilderness Theme in the Second Gospel and Its Basis in the Biblical Tradition.* Studies in Biblical Theology. London: SCM, 1963.

McKelvey, R. J. *The New Temple: The Church in the New Testament.* Oxford: Oxford University Press, 1969.

McKenzie, Steve. "Exodus Typology in Hosea." *ResQ* 22 (1979) 100–108.

McNamara, M. *New Testament and Palestinian Targum to the Pentateuch.* AnBib 27. Rome: Pontifical Biblical Institute, 1966.

Merrill, Eugene H. "The Meaning and Significance of the Exodus Event." In *Reverberations of the Exodus in Scripture,* edited by R. Michael Fox, 1–17. Eugene, OR: Wipf and Stock, 2014.

Metzger, Bruce M. *An Introduction to the Apocrypha.* New York: Oxford University Press, 1957.

———. "Seventy or Seventy-Two Disciples?" *NTS* 5 (1958–59) 299–306.

Michaels, J. Ramsey. *The Gospel of John.* NICNT. Grand Rapids: Eerdmans, 2010.

Moffatt, James. "The Revelation of St. John the Divine." In *The Expositor's Greek Testament,* edited by W. Robertson Nicoll, 5:279–494. Grand Rapids: Eerdmans, 1951.

Moi, Toril, ed. *The Kristeva Reader.* New York: Columbia University Press, 1986.

Montefiore, Hugh. *A Commentary on the Epistle to the Hebrews.* New York: Harper & Row, 1964.

Morales, Rodrigo J. *The Spirit and the Restoration of Israel: New Exodus and New Creation Motifs in Galatians.* Tübingen: Mohr Siebeck, 2010.

Morris, Leon. *The Gospel according to John.* NICNT. Rev. ed. Grand Rapids: Eerdmans, 1995.

Moskala, Jiří. "Toward the Fulfillment of the Gog and Magog Prophecy of Ezekiel 38–39." *JATS* 18 (2007) 243–73.

Mounce, Robert H. *The Book of Revelation.* NICNT. Rev. ed. Grand Rapids: Eerdmans, 1998.

Mowvley, Henry. "John 1:14–18 in the Light of Exodus 33:7—34:35." *ExpTim* 95 (1984) 135–37.

Moyise, Steve. "Does the Author of Revelation Misappropriate the Scriptures?" *AUSS* 40 (2002) 3–21.

———. "Intertextuality and Biblical Studies: A Review." *Verbum et Ecclesia* 23 (2002) 418–31.

———. "Intertextuality and the Book of Revelation." *ExpTim* 104, no. 10 (1993) 295–98.

———. "Intertextuality and the Study of the Old Testament in the New Testament." In *The Old Testament in the New Testament: Essays in Honour of J. L. North,* edited by S. Moyise, 14–41. JSNTSup 189. Sheffield: Sheffield Academic.

———. "Intertextuality and the Use of Scripture in the Book of Revelation?" *Scriptura* 84 (2003) 391–401.

———. *Jesus and Scripture: Studying the New Testament Use of the Old Testament.* Grand Rapids: Baker Academic, 2010.

———. "The Language of the Old Testament in the Apocalypse." *JSNT* 76 (1999) 97–113.

———. *The Later New Testament Writers and Scripture: The Old Testament in Acts, Hebrews, the Catholic Epistles and Revelation.* London: SPCK, 2012.

———. "The Old Testament in Revelation." In *The Old Testament in the New,* edited by Steve Moyise, 117–27. T&T Clark Approaches to Biblical Studies. New York: T&T Clark, 2001.

Bibliography

———. *The Old Testament in the Book of Revelation*. JSNTSup 115. Sheffield: Sheffield Academic, 1995.

———. *The Old Testament in the New: An Introduction*. New York: T&T Clark, 2001.

———. "The Old Testament in the New: A Reply to Greg Beale." *IBS* 21 (1999) 54–58.

———. *Paul and Scripture: Studying the New Testament Use of the Old Testament*. Grand Rapids: Baker Academic, 2010.

———. "The Psalms in the Book of Revelation." In *The Psalms in the New Testament*, edited by Steve Moyise and Maarten J. J. Menken, 231–46. New York: T&T Clark, 2004.

———. "Singing the Song of Moses and the Lamb: John's Dialogical Use of Scripture." *AUSS* 42, no. 2 (2004) 347–60.

———, ed. *The Old Testament in the New Testament: Essays in Honour of J. L. North*. JSNTSup 189. Sheffield: Sheffield Academic, 2000.

Moyise, Steve, and Maarten J. J. Menken, eds. *Deuteronomy in the New Testament*. London: T&T Clark, 2007.

———, eds. *Genesis in the New Testament*. London: T&T Clark, 2012.

———, eds. *Isaiah in the New Testament*. London: T&T Clark, 2005.

———, eds. *The Minor Prophets in the New Testament*. London: T&T Clark, 2009.

———, eds. *Psalms in the New Testament*. London: T&T Clark, 2004.

Muilenburg, James. "Isaiah 40–66." In *The Interpreter's Bible*, edited by George Buttrick, 5:381–773. Nashville: Abingdon, 1956.

Murphy, Roland. "Scripture and Church History." In *Exodus—A Lasting Paradigm*, edited by Bas van Iersel and Anton Weiler, 3–8. Edinburgh: T&T Clark, 1987.

Musvosvi, Joel N. "The Song of Moses and the Song of the Lamb." *JATS* 9 (1998) 44–47.

Newsom, Carol. "Bakhtin, the Bible, and Dialogic Truth." *JR* 76 (1996) 290–306.

Newton, John. "Analysis of Programmatic Texts of Exodus Movement." In *Exodus—A Lasting Paradigm*, edited by Bas van Iersel and Anton Weiler, 56–62. Edinburgh: T&T Clark, 1987.

Nineham, Dennis E. *The Gospel of St. Mark*. Pelican Gospel Commentaries. Harmondsworth, UK: Penguin, 1963.

Ninow, Friedbert. *Indicators of Typology within the Old Testament: The Exodus Motif*. Frankfurt am Main: Peter Lang, 2001.

Nixon, Robin E. *The Exodus in the New Testament*. London: Tyndale, 1963.

Nolland, John. *Luke 9:21—18:34*. WBC 35B. Dallas: Word, 1993.

Ortlund, Dane. "The Old Testament Background and Eschatological Significance of Jesus Walking on the Sea (Mark 6:45–52)." *Neot* 46 (2012) 319–37.

Osborne, Grant. R. *Revelation*. BECNT. Grand Rapids: Baker, 2002.

Pao, David W. *Acts and the Isaianic New Exodus*. Grand Rapids: Baker, 2002.

Patterson, Richard D., and Michael E. Travers. "Contours of the Exodus Motif in Jesus' Earthly Ministry." *WTJ* 66 (2004) 25–47.

Paulien, Jon. "The Book of Revelation and the Old Testament." *BR* 43 (1998) 61–69.

———. "Criteria and Assessment of Allusions to the Old Testament in the Book of Revelation." In *Studies in the Book of Revelation*, edited by Steve Moyise, 113–29. Edinburgh: T&T Clark, 2001.

———. *Decoding Revelation's Trumpets: Literary Allusions and the Interpretation of Revelation 8:7–12*. Andrews University Seminary Doctoral Dissertation Series 21. Berrien Springs, MI: Andrews University Press, 1988.

———. "Dreading the Whirlwind: Intertextuality and the Use of the Old Testament in Revelation." *AUSS* 39 (2001) 5–22.

Bibliography

———. "Elusive Allusion: The Problematic Use of the Old Testament in Revelation." *BR* 33 (1988) 37–53.

———. "Elusive Allusions in the Apocalypse: Two Decades of Research into John's Use of the Old Testament." In *The Intertextuality of the Epistles: Explorations of Theory and Practice*, edited by Thomas L. Brodie et al., 61–68. Sheffield: Sheffield Phoenix, 2006.

———. "Revisiting the Sabbath in the Book of Revelation." *JATS* 9, nos. 1–2 (1998) 179–86.

Payne, Michael. "Voice, Metaphor, and Narrative in the Book of Revelation." In *Mappings of the Biblical Terrain: The Bible as Text*, edited by Vincent L. Tollers and John Maier, 364–72. London: Associated University Press, 1990.

Petersen, Norman R. *Rediscovering Paul: Philemon and the Sociology of Paul's Narrative World*. Philadelphia: Fortress, 1985.

Piper, John. "Prolegomena to Understanding Romans 9:14–15: An Interpretation of Exodus 33:19." *JETS* 22 (1979) 203–16.

Piper, Otto Alfred. "Unchanging Promises: Exodus in the New Testament." *Int* 11 (1957) 3–22.

Porter, Stanley E. "Allusion and Echoes." In *As It Is Written: Studying Paul's Use of Scripture*, edited by Stanly E. Porter and Christopher D. Stanley, 29–40. SBLSymS 50. Atlanta: SBL, 2008.

———. "Further Comments on the Use of the Old Testament in the New Testament." In *The Intertextuality of the Epistles: Explorations of Theory and Practice*, edited by Thomas L. Brodie et al., 98–110. Sheffield: Sheffield Phoenix, 2006.

———. "The Use of the Old Testament in the New Testament: A Brief Comment on Method and Terminology." In *Early Christian Interpretation of the Scripture of Israel: Investigations and Proposals*, edited by Craig A. Evans and James A. Sanders, 79–96. JSNTSup 148. Sheffield: Sheffield Academic, 1997.

———, ed. *Hearing the Old Testament in the New Testament*. Grand Rapids: Eerdmans, 2006.

Powell, Mark Allan. "Narrative Criticism." In *Hearing the New Testament: Strategies for Interpretation*, 2d ed., edited by Joel B. Green, 240–58. Grand Rapids: Eerdmans, 2010.

———. *What Is Narrative Criticism?* Minneapolis: Fortress, 1990.

Quek, Tze-Ming. "'I Will Give Authority over the Nations': Psalm 2.8–9 in Revelation 2.26–27." In *Early Christian Literature and Intertextuality*, edited by Craig A. Evans and H. Daniel Zacharias, 2:175–87. New York: T&T Clark, 2009.

Rad, Gerhard von. *The Theology of Israel's Historical Traditions*. Vol. 1 of *Old Testament Theology*. Translated by D. M. G. Stalker. New York: Harper & Row, 1962.

Resseguie, James L. *Revelation Unsealed: A Narrative Critical Approach to John's Apocalypse*. Biblical Interpretation Series 32. Leiden: Brill, 1998.

Richard, Pablo. "Plagues in the Bible: Exodus and Apocalypse." In *Return of the Plague*, edited by José Oscar Beozzo and Virgil Elizondo, translated by Paul Burns, 45–54. Maryknoll, NY: Orbis, 1997.

Richardson, Alan. *An Introduction to the Theology of the New Testament*. London: SCM, 1958.

Riffaterre, Michael. "Interpretation and Undeciability." *New Literary History* 12 (1981) 227–42.

———. *Semiotics of Poetry*. Bloomington: Indiana University Press, 1978.

———. "Syllepsis." *Critical Inquiry* 6 (1980) 625–38.

Bibliography

Rist, Martin. "The Use of the Old Testament by the Author of Revelation." *Iliff Review* 17 (1960) 3–10.
Ruiten, J. van. "The Intertextual Relationship between Isaiah 65:17–20 and Revelation 21:1–5b." *EstBib* 51 no. 4 (1993) 473–510.
Ruiz, J. P. *Ezekiel in the Apocalypse: The Transformation of Prophetic Language in Revelation 16:17—19:10.* Frankfurt am Main: Peter Lang, 1989.
Runions, J. Ernest. "Exodus Motifs in First Samuel 7 and 8: A Brief Comment." *EvQ* 52 (1980) 130–31.
Sahlin, Harald. "The New Exodus of Salvation according to St. Paul." In *The Root of the Vine: Essays in Biblical Theology*, edited by Anton Fridrichsen, 81–95. New York: Philosophical Library, 1953.
Sanborn, Scott F. "The New Exodus in the Risen Lamb: Revelation 1:4–8." *Kerux* 14, no. 1 (May 1999) 18–24.
Schellenberg, Ryan S. "Seeing the World Whole: Intertextuality and the New Jerusalem (Revelation 21–22)." *PRSt* 33 (2006) 467–76.
Schiffner, Kerstin. "Lukas Liest Exodus: Kanongrenzen überschreitende Beobachtungen." In *Der Bibelkanon in der Bibelauslegung: Methodenreflexionen und Beispielexegesen*, edited by Egbert Balhorn and Georg Steins, 304–13. Stuttgart: Kohlhammer, 2007.
Schlatter, Adolf. *Das Alte Testament in der johanneischen Apokalypse.* BFCT 6. Gütersloh: Mohn, 1912.
Schreiner, Thomas R. *Paul, Apostle of God's Glory in Christ: A Pauline Theology.* Downers Grove, IL: InterVarsity, 2001.
Schweizer, Eduard. *The Good News according to Mark.* Translated by Donald H. Madvig. Richmond, VA: John Knox, 1970.
Scott, J. Julius Jr. *Jewish Backgrounds of the New Testament.* Grand Rapids: Baker, 1995.
Seitz, Oscar J. F. "Praeparatio Evangelica in the Markan Prologue." *JBL* 82, no. 2 (1963) 201–6.
Shea, William H. "Literary and Theological Parallels between Revelation 14–15 and Exodus 19–24." *JATS* 12, no. 2 (2001) 164–79.
Sloan, David B. "God's Abraham, God of the Living: Jesus' Use of Exodus 3:6 in Mark 12:26–27." *WTJ* 74 (2012) 85–98.
Smart, James D. *History and Theology in Second Isaiah: A Commentary on Isaiah 35, 40–66.* Philadelphia: Westminster, 1965.
Smith, Henry Preserved. *A Critical and Exegetical Commentary on the Book of Samuel.* ICC. Edinburgh: T&T Clark, 1969.
Smith, Robert Houston. "Exodus Typology in the Fourth Gospel." *JBL* 81 (1962) 329–42.
Son, HaYoung. "The Background of Exodus 15 in Revelation 15: Focusing on the Song of Moses and the Song of the Lamb." PhD diss., New Orleans Baptist Theological Seminary, 2015.
Stahlberg, Lesleigh Cushing. *Sustaining Fictions: Intertextuality, Midrash, Translation and the Literary Afterlife of the Bible.* New York: T&T Clark, 2008.
Starling, David I. "Ephesians and the Hermeneutics of the New Exodus." In *Reverberations of the Exodus in Scripture*, edited by R. Michael Fox, 139–59. Eugene, OR: Wipf and Stock, 2014.
Stevens, Gerald L. "The Literary Background and Theological Significance of ΟΡΓΗ ΘΕΟΥ in the Pauline Epistles." ThD diss., New Orleans Baptist Theological Seminary, 1981.
———. *Revelation: The Past and Future of John's Apocalypse.* Eugene, OR: Pickwick, 2014.

Bibliography

Stevenson, Gregory M. "Communal Imagery and the Individual Lament: Exodus Typology in Psalm 77." *ResQ* 39 (1997) 215–29.

Steyn, Gert Jacobus. "'On Earth as It Is in Heaven . . .': The Heavenly Sanctuary Motif in Hebrews 8:5 and Its Textual Connection with the 'Shadowy Copy' [ὑποδείγματι καὶ σκιᾷ] of LXX Exodus 25:40." *HvTSt* 67, no. 1 (2011) 1–6.

Swartley, Willard M. *Israel's Scripture Traditions and the Synoptic Gospels: Story Shaping Story.* Peabody, MA: Hendrickson, 1994.

Swete, Henry B. *Commentary on Revelation.* Grand Rapids: Kregel, 1977.

Talbert, Charles H. *Reading John: A Literary and Theological Commentary on the Fourth Gospel and the Johannine Epistles.* New York: Crossroad, 1944.

Tate, Marvin E. *Psalms 51–100.* WBC 20. Dalls: Word, 1990.

Teeple, Howard M. *The Mosaic Eschatological Prophet.* Journal of Biblical Literature Monograph Series 10. Philadelphia: SBL, 1957.

Thiselton, Anthony C. *The First Epistle to the Corinthians: A Commentary on the Greek Text.* NIGTC. Grand Rapids: Eerdmans, 2000.

Todorov, Tzvetan. *Mikhail Bakhtin: The Dialogical Principle.* Translated by Wlad Godzich. Manchester: Manchester University Press, 1984.

Tracy, David. "Exodus: Theological Reflection." In *Exodus—A Lasting Paradigm*, edited by Bas van Iersel and Anton Weiler, 118–24. Edinburgh: T&T Clark, 1987.

Trudinger, Leonhard Paul. "Some Observations concerning the Text of the Old Testament in the Book of Revelation." *JTS* 17 (1966) 82–88.

Tsan, Tsong-Sheng. "'New Exodus': A Theological Enquiry of the Exodus Motif in Isaiah 19:16–25." *Taiwan Journal of Theology* 32 (2010) 1–22.

Valletta, Thomas R. "The 'Bread of Life' Discourse in the Context of Exodus Typology." *Proceedings* 11 (1991) 129–43.

Vanhoye, Albert. "L'utilisatin du livre d'Ezechiel dans l'Apocalypse." *Bib* 43 (1962) 436–77.

Viviano, Benedict. "Peter as Jesus' Mouth: Matthew 16:13–20 in the Light of Exodus 4:10–17 and Other Models." *SBLSP* 37 (1998) 226–52.

Vlach, Michael J. "New Testament Use of the Old Testament: A Survey of Where the Debate Currently Stands." Paper presented at the annual meeting of the Evangelical Theological Society, San Francisco, November 17, 2011.

Vogelgesang, Jeffrey M. "The Interpretation of Ezekiel in the Book of Revelation." PhD diss., Harvard University, 1985.

Vos, L. A. *The Synoptic Traditions in the Apocalypse.* Kampen: J H Kok, 1965.

Waal, C. van der. *Openbaring van Jezus Christus.* Groningen, Netherlands: De Vuurbaak, 1971.

Watts, John D. W. *Isaiah 34–66.* WBC 25. Waco, TX: Word, 1987.

Watts, Rikki E. *Isaiah's New Exodus and Mark.* Grand Rapids: Baker, 2000.

———. "Mark." In *CNTUOT*, edited by G. K. Beale and D. A. Carson, 111–249. Grand Rapids: Baker, 2007.

Webb, William J. *Returning Home: New Covenant and Second Exodus as the Context for 2 Corinthians 6:14—7:1.* Sheffield: Sheffield Academic, 1993.

Weiler, Anton. "The Experience of Communities of Religious Refugees." In *Exodus—A Lasting Paradigm*, edited by Bas van Iersel and Anton Weiler, 72–80. Edinburgh: T&T Clark, 1987.

Westcott, Brooke Foss. *The Epistle to the Hebrews: The Greek Text with Notes and Essays.* 2d ed. London: Macmillan, 1892.

Westermann, Claus. *Isaiah 40–66: A Commentary.* Philadelphia: Western, 1969.

Bibliography

———. *The Praise of God in the Psalms*. Richmond, Virginia: John Knox, 1965.

Whybray, R. N. *Isaiah 40–66*. NCB. Grand Rapids: Eerdmans, 1981.

Wilcox, Max. "'According to the Pattern (TBNYT) . . . ': Exodus 25:40 in the New Testament and Early Jewish Thought." *RevQ* 13 (1988) 647–56.

Williams, Joshua E. "Promise and Failure: Second Exodus in Ezra-Nehemiah." In *Reverberations of the Exodus in Scripture*, edited by R. Michael Fox, 74–93. Eugene, OR: Wipf and Stock, 2014.

Willis, John T. "An Interpretation of Isaiah 22:15–25 and Its Function in the New Testament." In *Early Christian Interpretation of the Scripture of Israel: Investigations and Proposals*, edited by C. A. Evans and J. A. Sanders, 473–510. JSNTSup 148. Sheffield: Sheffield Academic, 1997.

Willoughby, Thomas N. "'The Word Became Flesh and Tabernacled among Us': A Primer for the Exodus in John's Gospel." In *Reverberations of the Exodus in Scripture*, edited by R. Michael Fox, 121–38. Eugene, OR: Wipf and Stock, 2014.

Winston, David. *The Wisdom of Solomon: A New Translation with Introduction and Commentary*. AB 43. New York: Doubleday, 1979.

Wold, Benjamin G. "Revelation 16 and the Eschatological Use of Exodus Plagues." In *Eschatologie*, edited by Hans-Joachim Eckstein et al., 249–66. Tübingen: Mohr Siebeck, 2011.

Wright, N. T. *Jesus and the Victory of God*. Vol. 2 of Christian Origins and the Question of God. Minneapolis: Fortress, 1996.

———. *The New Testament and the People of God*. Vol. 1 of Christian Origins and the Question of God. Minneapolis: Fortress, 1992.

Wu, Peter Jung-chu. "Worthy Is the Lamb: The New Song in Revelation 5:9–10." PhD diss., Westminster Theological Seminary, 2005.

Young, Josiah. "Exodus as a Paradigm for Black Theology." In *Exodus—A Lasting Paradigm*, edited by Bas van Iersel and Anton Weiler, 93–99. Edinburgh: T&T Clark, 1987.

Zakovitch, Yair. *"And You Shall Tell Your Son . . . ": The Concept of the Exodus in the Bible*. Jerusalem: Magnes, 1991.

Zenger, Erich. "The God of Exodus in the Message of the Prophets as Seen in Isaiah." In *Exodus—A Lasting Paradigm*, edited by Bas van Iersel and Anton Weiler, 22–33. Edinburgh: T&T Clark, 1987.

www.ingramcontent.com/pod-product-compliance
Lightning Source LLC
Chambersburg PA
CBHW072149160426
43197CB00012B/2309